NORWAY TO AMERICA

NORWAY
to
AMERICA
A History
of the Migration

by Ingrid Semmingsen

Translated by Einar Haugen

UNIVERSITY OF MINNESOTA PRESS □ MINNEAPOLIS

Published by the University of Minnesota Press
2037 University Avenue Southeast, Minneapolis, MN 55414
Published simultaneously in Canada
by Fitzhenry & Whiteside Limited, Markham.
Printed in the United States of America.
Fourth printing, 1986.

Translation of *Drøm og dåd* © H. Aschehoug & Co.
(W. Nygaard), Oslo. 1975.

The University of Minnesota Press is grateful to the Norsemen's
Federation, Oslo, Norway, for financial assistance in
publication of the English-language edition of this book.

Library of Congress Cataloging in Publication Data

Semmingsen, Ingrid, 1910–
  Norway to America.

  Translation of Drøm og dåd
  Bibliography: p.
  Includes index.
  1.   Norwegian Americans – History.   I.   Title.
E184.S2S4313   973'.04'3982   78-3201
ISBN 0-8166-0842-3
ISBN 0-8166-1002-2

PREFACE

The Norwegian original of this book was written for the sesqui-
centennial commemoration of the departure in 1825 of the
sloop *Restauration* and the hundreds of thousands of Norwegian emigrants who followed in its wake. They settled in a new
country, lived out their lives there, founded organizations and institutions, and went through a process of adaptation, acculturation,
and assimilation. It is a short narrative account which does not pre-
tend to give a complete survey of the larger themes of Norwegian
migration and the establishment of a "Norway in America." Nor does
it claim to analyze in depth all aspects of the movement and its place
in the field of overseas migrations or the development of ethnic
pluralism in America. My intention was to shed light on some of the
factors that I think are of central importance to an understanding of
the migration.

My research in this field is only a part of the foundation on which
I have based my account. Historical research is essentially collective
work, a dialogue between generations and between contemporary
researchers, colleagues, friends, and students. Only a very few of
these are mentioned in the text. In the notes I have insofar as possible referred only to sources and publications in the English language.
In addition, I wish to acknowledge my debt to colleagues and friends
in the Nordic countries and in the international world of scholarship.

As far as the Norwegian-American part of the text is concerned, I feel especially obligated to the late Dean Theodore C. Blegen and to the Norwegian-American Historical Association he helped organize. During several decades he guided and expanded its activities, which today are being ably continued by his successors.

My special thanks go to Professor Einar Haugen who on his own initiative provided a translation of the Norwegian text. This act of friendship has been of inestimable value.

I also heartily thank Senior Editor Beverly Kaemmer, who with great patience, diligence, and care has corrected my text.

Ingrid Semmingsen

CONTENTS

vii

NORWAY TO AMERICA

MIGRATION

Archaeologists agree that human beings may have lived along the ice-free brim of the Norwegian coast during the last Ice Age. Lapps may have inhabited the Arctic for thousands of years and were perhaps among the earliest settlers of Scandinavia. As the ice pack receded other migrants came. Some were peaceful and brought new tools and techniques. Others, warlike, brought new weapons. The migrants did not settle down immediately, for theirs was a fishing and hunting culture. They moved from site to site as the changing seasons offered possibilities of livelihood in one place and then another — by the sea, in the woods, or in the mountains. Probably early in the third millenium B.C. peoples who had domesticated animals and cultivated grain first came to Scandinavia. Archaeologists maintain that the Indo-Europeans, ancestors of the present population, invaded the country in the centuries before the year 2000, bringing with them the horse. They came from the region around the Black Sea, probably in successive migrations.

Even after the introduction of domestic animals and agriculture, fishing and hunting continued to provide a substantial part of the their sustenance. This was true well into historic times. Yet the people did gradually settle down and became men and women of the soil, farmers (*bønder*), as had the majority of peoples in Europe and Asia before them.

There was no cessation of migrations and great movements of

3

peoples on the Eurasian continent. Indeed the history of this continent can be viewed as a series of migrations, in which peoples and races moved back and forth, on relatively peaceful wanderings and on warlike expeditions marked by burning, plundering, and conquest. Some five centuries before our era the Celts ruled large portions of Central Europe. At about the same time the Hellenes stemmed the Persian advance and continued their own expansion along the shores of the Mediterranean and into Asia Minor. Then Alexander the Great conquered the Hellenes and forced his way to the borders of India with a host of soldiers, merchants, and vagrants. The Romans founded an empire, extending from Spain, France, and England in the west, over the Rhine and the Danube to the Black Sea, including at its peak Asia Minor, present-day Iran and Iraq, the Near East, Egypt, and North Africa.

This empire fell under the rush of the folk migrations, which began with peasants who lived in remote places and were vulnerable to attacks by warlike nomads from the east, above all the Huns. These attacks went on for centuries, forcing farmers to move, driving waves of peoples and tribes across the borders of the Roman empire.

It was the Age of Migrations.

Only the faintest backwash of these migrations reached the shores of Norway. District names like Rogaland and Hordaland on the west coast suggest that tribes named Rygir and Hordir immigrated and took possession of these areas. A few centuries later the Nordic peoples went on forays of trade and plunder. Gradually their goals expanded to conquest and settlement, and they emigrated to populated as well as unpopulated lands. This was the Viking Age, the violent expansion between 800 and 1050 A.D. of the Scandinavians, which carried Norsemen to Russia and Constantinople, to Normandy and the Danelaw, to Shetland, Orkney, and the Hebrides, to Iceland, Greenland, and North America (Vinland).

In about the same period the Arabs were pushing forward into the Mediterranean area, permanently impressing on it their people, their religion, and their secular culture. Continental Europe was on the defensive. In the following centuries Europeans gradually consolidated and made some tentative efforts at expansion. The Crusades were an attempt to establish a beachhead in the Near East. To the north, Germanic peasants were beginning to clear land and colonize the Slavic areas east of the Elbe. But in the east the balance was precarious. The Turks, pressured by the Mongols, pushed forward, conquering Constantinople in 1453, beleaguering Vienna in 1529.

The next four centuries were the great epoch of European expansion. In the east, Poland and later Russia, emerged as powerful states which gave the Slavic peoples possibilities for expansion. But the most important events were in the west, beginning with the great voyages of discovery that carried the western Europeans, at first as traders and later as conquerors, past the southern tip of Africa as far as India and on to unknown continents, westward to America and eastward to Australia.

In some areas the Europeans destroyed existing cultures, as in South and Central America. Elsewhere they conquered land and extracted wealth, not by plundering but by economically exploiting people and resources. In some places they immigrated, settled the land, and pushed back the hunting and gathering peoples. The last was especially characteristic of North America and to some extent of South Africa and later of Australia and New Zealand.

This expansion exceeded all earlier ones. It gave newly discovered continents a European cast, multiplied the European share of the world's population, and led to colonization, rivalry, war, and imperialism. Toward the end of the eighteenth century it caused the first colonial rebellion in European history and the formation of a new, independent state — the United States of America.

The Kingdom of Norway

In the thirteenth century Norway too had been master of an overseas empire, of areas conquered or colonized from the ninth century on, where the inhabitants paid tribute to the Norwegian king. Iceland was an independent republic, and the settlements in Greenland were also considered independent. However, the bishops' sees in Iceland and Greenland were under the jurisdiction of the archbishop of Trondheim, and both acknowledged Norwegian sovereignty.

During Norway's economic and political decline in the fourteenth century, connections with the colonies were weakened, and Norway's political subjection to Denmark in 1537, when it was named a province of Denmark, dissolved ties with the colonies. The islands off

Britain reverted to Scotland and England, Iceland was attached to
Copenhagen, the Norse colony in Greenland died out, and any
memory of Vinland and the voyages there lived on only among the
few learned men who studied the old manuscripts. Norway's foreign
trade was taken over by others, and for two centuries Norwegians
went abroad very little. Their fish and timber were exported in the
bottoms of other nations' ships.[1]

About 1500 the decline had reached its nadir. Following this,
growth began gradually, with a sharp rise in the eighteenth century.
Agriculture progressed as new areas were cultivated, farms were divided, cotters' homes were built — providing space and livelihood for
a growing population. This rural society is often thought of as a series
of almost self-contained, insulated, local societies, stable and
tradition-bound, virtually static. They are seen as small social units,
in which people grew up, worked and died, never leaving the communities where they were born. So it was for many, perhaps most,
but not for all. Young people had to take annual service on farms, and
some had to go outside their home communities to do so. Also, there
were people who wandered about on the badly built roads, peddling
illegally, doing odd jobs, and looking for seasonal work, for example
at harvest time. Their number grew in the eighteenth century, in spite
of "vagrant hunts" organized by the authorities from time to time,
when vagrants were rounded up and brought to prisons and work-
houses.

Also, the population gradually moved from the mountain, fjord,
and valley communities toward the coast into what few small towns
existed there. Even the settled population had to migrate far and wide
in search of income that might supplement the meager earnings of the
farms. The great seasonal fishing expeditions to Lofoten are examples
of work migrations by a settled population. Seafaring provided additional income and involved migrations from Norway, mostly to the
Netherlands. Thousands of Norwegians were registered as members
of Lutheran congregations in Amsterdam and other Dutch cities;
many married and stayed there, especially in the mid-seventeenth
century. They came from coastal districts of Norway — primarily
from Agder — all the way north to Bergen. Most of the men were
sailors who found jobs in the Dutch merchant marine or navy. The

women were servants until they married and became sailor's wives, if they did not return to Norway with a small savings.[2]

Norway and the New Land of America

Norway was not an independent state in the sixteenth century and so did not take part in the colonization of America. For a generation there was a New Sweden on the east coast of North America, and Denmark secured colonies (the Virgin Islands) in the West Indies. Even though there was no New Norway, a few Norwegians did make their way to Nieuw Amsterdam, which in 1663 became New York. American historian J. O. Evjen indicates that some of these immigrants were the ancestors of what would become well-known American families; it is reasonable to suppose that they came by way of the Netherlands. Others immigrated to the Danish colonies in the West Indies as sailors, clerks, or even as officials. In the United States there are scattered reports of Norwegian settlers, for instance a colony of Moravians at the end of the eighteenth century. There were a few notable exploits: the great admiral Curt Sivertsen Adeler spent some time in America, and the name of one Norwegian can be read on a monument from the war of 1812. But there were few immigrants before the tide of emigration that swelled after 1825.[3]

Did Norwegians in the seventeenth and eighteenth centuries know anything about America and the European colonies there? It can be safely assumed that most Norwegians knew nothing about America and that only the learned had some information. For example, the professor and famous author Ludvig Holberg (1678–1748) made passing references to America in his historical writings. He knew there were enterprising merchants in the New England colonies, but he was more fascinated by the gold in Peru and the vast expanses of Mexico.[4]

Toward the end of the eighteenth century Norwegians had more information about America, which awakened greater interest in the country. There were several reasons for this increasing interest. Economic advances in Norway had enhanced the cultural environment and made the country less insular. Even more significant was a growing national pride. Those few Norwegians who, under the united Dano-Norwegian monarchy, worked to create separate

Norwegian institutions and win a freer status for Norway had a particular interest in the rebellion of the American colonies and the war
of independence. They were eager to learn more about the new basis
of popular sovereignty on which the individual states, and eventually
the union, had founded their constitutions. This interest is perceptible in Norwegian cultural life from the 1780s to the writing of a
Norwegian constitution at Eidsvold in 1814. Patriotic Norwegians,
convinced that Norway had not achieved the position it deserved, felt
involuntary sympathy for and even fellowship with this country that
had fought successfully for freedom and independence.

In the late eighteenth century, when European wars created prosperity for Norwegian shipping as long as the country remained neutral, Norwegian skippers and sailors made increasingly longer voyages. Sailors and merchants must have acquired a certain familiarity
with America, though this is difficult to document. During these war
years the United States was by far the most important neutral shipping nation. Neutrality, however, provided no protection against
privateering, and from 1807 when Norway, as an ally of Napoleon,
was forced into war with Great Britain, hundreds of American vessels
were seized as prizes and interned with their crews in Norwegian
harbors, especially in Christiansand. John Quincy Adams met quite a
few compatriots in that town in 1809 on his way to assume the post of
ambassador in St. Petersburg.[5] In this way some personal contact
between Norwegians and Americans was made in the coastal towns.

But in rural communities most people knew nothing of America,
and with few exceptions lived out their lives untouched by the revolutionary ideas and events that were shaking Europe. They felt the
exigencies of war but even more the distress created by the British
blockade.

The first occasion on which we know that America became a topic
of common conversation was in the years 1817–18, in a context relating directly to emigration. At the end of September 1817 a damaged
ship entered the harbor of Bergen. This proved to be a Dutch ship
with about 500 German emigrants from Württemberg on board. A
great many were dissidents who belonged to the society established
by Father George Rapp and were fleeing religious and political repression. In the following months some of these emigrants left for
Danish, North German, or Dutch ports, but most stayed in Bergen for
a year, where they established contact with Norwegian religious dis-

sidents, the followers of Hans Nielsen Hauge. The German emigrants stubbornly insisted they were going to America, and eventually the Norwegian state had to help them find transportation across the Atlantic.[6]

Five hundred strangers, most of them in family groups, must have caused a considerable stir among the 15,000 inhabitants of Bergen and among the skippers and sailors who entered the harbor. But as far as we know none of them wrote down their impressions. We do know that people were concerned about these emigrants and their fate, for it is documented from Christiania (Oslo) that about Christmastime 1817 a rumor circulated that *another* ship had stranded in Norway.

In spring 1818 a fantastic rumor went the rounds in eastern Norway. In the harbor of Christiania lay a ship ready to accommodate emigrants. All who wished to leave were offered free transportation and food on board, free land when they arrived in America, and even a house and some cattle. In its final version the rumor even suggested that anyone who was dissatisfied with conditions in America would be returned without charge.

This rumor probably originated in stories about and by the German emigrants. Some of the emigrants had gone to the capital. A citizen of Christiania born in Hamburg, Consul Andreas Grünning, was active in collecting funds to aid the emigrants and in developing a plan to find transportation for them. Grünning at length managed to interest the Norwegian government in this plan.

The emigration rumors also played a part in domestic Norwegian history, specifically in an outbreak of peasant unrest in late summer 1818. Some officials believed the rumors were circulated by peasants who wished to stir up revolts among the poorer sections of the common people, and the authorities went to some trouble to contradict the rumors. A reward was offered for anyone who would identify those who had spread them.

The rumors died, but not before some working people had made the trip to Christiania to take advantage of this remarkable opportunity. For some weeks and months the words "migration" and "America" must have been bruited about in districts around Christiania. There was no emigration. The rumors proved to be fairy tales. Years passed before people in eastern Norway again began thinking and talking about America and emigration.

THE SLOOP
RESTAURATION,
1825

Norwegian emigration to America began in the nineteenth century with the sloop *Restauration*. It left Stavanger July 4, 1825, with fifty-two persons on board. All, crew as well as passengers, were emigrating, and they had equipped themselves with provisions for three months. In addition they carried a cargo of twenty tons of iron bars and plates. The emigrants had bought the sloop for 1,800 specie dollars, and they hoped to make a profit by selling both vessel and cargo when they arrived in America.[1]

The *Restauration* was a mere nutshell of a vessel for an Atlantic crossing, one-quarter the tonnage of the Puritans' *Mayflower*. It shipped no more than eighteen and one-half commerce lasts, about thirty-eight to thirty-nine tons and was fifty-four feet long, sixteen feet wide. It was built in Hardanger in 1801 and was one of the many sloops that freighted herring to Stavanger or that might venture as far as Gothenburg in Sweden or to Denmark to fetch grain. The sloop had originally shipped only six lasts, but in 1820 it was rebuilt and enlarged in Egersund. It was then named the *Restauration*.

The fifty-two emigrants were not adventurous youths. In this first company that set off for America there were ten married couples, six of whom had nineteen children between them. One child was born on board, a girl who survived the trip to New York. She was baptized Margaret Allen, not a Norwegian name, but that of an English Quaker. The childless husbands were twenty-five to thirty years old, the ones with children, thirty-five to forty-five. The largest family was that of Daniel Rossadal and his wife Bertha from Tysvær, with five children ranging from a few months old to eighteen years. Most of the twelve unmarried men were in their twenties. Jakob Slogvik, who was only fifteen and a member of the crew, was the youngest able-bodied seaman on board. There was one unmarried woman — Sara Larsen, the deaf and dumb sister of the expedition's leader, Lars Larsen Geilane.

Lars Larsen and his wife, one other family, and at least one of the unmarried men came from Stavanger. Most of the others came from communities in the surrounding district of Rogaland, with an especially large contingent from Tysvær, many of whom were related to each other. They must have been relatively well-off economically. They may have invested all they owned in the vessel and its cargo, which represented considerable capital.

Many scholars have discussed why the "sloopers" emigrated from Norway. The considerable research that has been done indicates that one reason relates to the history of the Quakers in Norway.

The Quakers

Den norske Rigstidende printed a notice about the departure of the *Restauration*, stating that the emigrants belonged to a religious society that had attracted many adherents in the Stavanger area in recent years. The Ministry of Church Affairs assumed that this referred to the Quakers and asked Bishop Munch if this was true. The bishop investigated and reported that only one of the party, Lars Larsen Geilane, was a member of the Society of Friends in Stavanger. However, it appears that several emigrants sympathized with the Quakers, even if they were not formally members. At any rate they joined the Quakers after they reached America.

The story of the Quakers in Norway begins with the war against England, which Norway got caught up in about 1807, and the Norwegian vessels that were seized by British warships and conveyed to British ports. The crews were interned in British prisons until peace was declared in 1814. English Quakers visited, comforted, and encouraged the internees. They also proselytized and won over some of the Norwegian prisoners to their religious attitudes and doctrines. When the prisoners returned home, they were scattered in many parts of the country. Only in Christiania and Stavanger were they numerous enough to keep alive a Society of Friends. In Stavanger Elias Tastad was the leader, and ship's carpenter Lars Larsen Geilane was one of his helpers.

Keeping a Society of Friends alive was difficult. Quakers were forbidden to take oaths or enter military service. They could not accept the rituals of the Lutheran State Church at baptism, marriage, and burial. For them the words spoken by a pastor wearing vestments were empty formalities, a distraction from the inner life and light. It was crucial that they be spared such ceremonies. As early as 1816 a Quaker couple in Christiania were married without ritual or minister. They also failed to have their children baptized and thus came into conflict with the authorities.

In the autumn of 1821 Elias Tastad's infant twins died. He asked permission to bury them in the churchyard without the ritual of the state church. When he was refused, he had them buried in unconsecrated ground on the farm Våland. In the spring of 1822 an older Quaker died and was buried at the same place. Charges were brought against Tastad, and in October 1822 the Supreme Court ordered that he dig up the bodies by a certain date. If he did not meet the deadline, he would have to pay a running fine of five specie dollars per day. The judgment was never executed. English Quakers pleaded with Norwegian officials and with King Carl Johan on behalf of their Norwegian brethren. In 1824 the decision was repealed.

As early as 1817 the Norwegian government had become aware of problems caused by the new denomination. At the suggestion of Christian Krohg, Minister of Ecclesiastical Affairs, a commission was appointed to investigate the situation and make proposals for a law concerning the Quakers. The commission proposed that the Quakers be permitted to stay in Norway and follow their own practices, but only in certain cities. Furthermore no one under twenty-five years old could be admitted to the Society, and when a person of appropriate age decided to join, he or she had to explain and justify this decision to the local authorities. Quakers were forbidden to proselytize, on penalty of deportation. This limited reform was presented to the parliament, the *Storting*, in 1824, but it was defeated. Not until 1845 did a law grant religious freedom to people outside the state church.

English Quakers who spoke on behalf of their Norwegian fellows did not encourage them to leave the country. On the contrary they urged them to hold firm and endure the trials to which they were subjected. They praised Elias Tastad for his steadfastness. Even so, some left for England, among them Lars Larsen Geilane, who tried to find work as a carpenter in London. He failed and returned to Stavanger, but others went to England and remained there.

In October 1823 the Quakers of Stavanger again submitted a petition asking permission to live according to their faith and to follow their religious customs. The district governor supported the petition: certainly he believed it would be harmful were the sect to spread further, but he noted that the members in Stavanger were hardworking and diligent. He feared that a refusal "would not change their conviction, but the result would probably be that they would emigrate."[2]

The Norwegian Quakers were members of an international denomination and were in close contact with the English Friends, who sent them well-known preachers and missionaries. One of them was Stephen Grellet, a French émigré who had lived in America twelve years. He and William Allen visited the Norwegian Quakers in 1818, William Allen again later. We do not know whether he told them anything about that country or the position of the Quakers there. But a man like Lars Larsen Geilane probably knew the United States existed and perhaps knew it was a country without a state church.

As indicated earlier, it is certain that not all the emigrants were Quakers. An American newspaper reporting the arrival of the sloopers in New York wrote that they belonged to a religious community which in their homeland was called "the holy ones" and had many traits in common with the Quakers. This description suggests the Haugeans, followers of the great lay leader Hans Nielsen Hauge (1771–1824). The Haugean movement flourished in and around Stavanger, and there may have been some contact between Quakers and Haugeans. Quaker missionaries who visited Norway showed a great interest in the Haugean movement, and they in turn excited interest. In 1818 one of them spoke to about 200 at a meeting in Stavanger, although the Society of Friends officially had only eight members.[3] Probably there were Haugeans on the benches in that room.

No doubt the idea of emigrating was conveyed and kept alive by other factors as well. The year-long stay of the German emigrants in Bergen must have been generally known in Stavanger. It is reasonable to suppose that the religious dissent of these emigrants and their firm intention to leave for America was of special interest to the Quakers, Quaker sympathizers, and others who had been "converted." However the idea of emigrating originated in this group, a strong motivation was their dissatisfaction with the restrictions set by the Norwegian state church. They yearned for a church where laymen could be active, and they looked eagerly to a country with religious freedom. Only a few sloopers remained Lutheran in America; the rest joined other religious denominations.

They prepared themselves thoroughly for emigration over several years. When the district governor of Stavanger was writing that a rejection of the Quakers' petition might lead to their emigration, they (or their sympathizers) had sent off two men to investigate conditions in America. One of them died there, but the other returned in the summer of 1824. This man was Cleng Peerson, and his report provided a strong impetus to their plans for emigration. He stayed in Norway a short time and then returned to America to prepare for the arrival of his countrymen and women. They in turn began taking steps to carry out their plans, as we learn from a letter Cleng Peerson wrote from New York at Christmas 1824. He told of several contacts with friends regarding the purchase of land "as previously mentioned" and of the support the Friends had promised when the others arrived, in connection with the purchase of land and the sale of the vessel they were going to buy.

The Voyage and Arrival in America

The story of the sloopers' Atlantic crossing quickly became a folk tale. It is said that when the *Restauration* had passed through the English channel, it entered a small English port. Here the sloopers sold brandy, though this was a forbidden commodity. Later they fished out of the sea a drifting barrel containing Madeira wine. They drank so much wine that the virtually unattended sloop drifted into the port of Funchal in Madeira, "just like a pest ship." This much we know to be true: they did visit Funchal and they stayed there for a week equipping themselves with provisions. They also visited the

Norwegian-Swedish consul in Funchal to have him stamp their ship's papers. They then continued their voyage and were at sea three months, arriving in New York October 9, 1825. Cleng Peerson and some American Quakers met them there, and the newspapers wrote about them. The *New York Daily Advertiser*, October 12, 1825, noted that the farmers wore coarse, homespun clothing in contrast to the calico, and gingham and the gay shawls, probably imported from England, worn by those who had lived in the city. The journalist also admired the courage of the skipper and the adventurousness of the passengers for crossing in a vessel which in his opinion was not suitable for the Atlantic.[4]

The sloopers soon needed all the help the Quakers could give them. It was discovered that they had unwittingly violated the American federal act of 1819 which permitted only two passengers for every five tons of tonnage of a transatlantic passenger vessel. The *Restauration* had altogether too many people on board in proportion to the tons it shipped. Even if American authorities showed "the best will to mercy," as the Norwegian-Swedish consul wrote home, the law had been violated. They impounded the ship and notified the skipper that he was liable to fines of $150 per extra passenger. This amounted to more than $3,000, for which skipper Lars Olsen Helland and leader Lars Larsen Geilane would primarily be liable.

A well-known New York Quaker came to their assistance, put up bond money for them, and probably also helped to formulate the petition for release of the ship and waiver of the fine which was sent to Washington just a few days after the ship arrived. The petition was granted, and the document so stating was signed on November 5 by President John Quincy Adams.[5]

The sloop was sold, unfortunately for only $400. The sloopers thus had far less money at their disposal than they had expected to have. Again the Quakers stepped in and furnished equipment and travel money so they could move to the northern part of New York. Here Cleng Peerson had arranged for the purchase of land in Kendall Township, once more through the Quakers.

Life in America

So began the daily labor and the strenuous pioneering in the great forests on the shores of Lake Ontario. Circumstances were extremely difficult in the early years, sometimes causing great distress among the settlers.

They earned money doing odd jobs, but to the extent that this did not meet their needs, they were dependent on the charity of others and received gifts from Americans who lived nearby. One of the settlers wrote many years later that in the beginning they were all poor, most of them became ill, and, with the exception of Cleng Peerson, they spoke no English. It took a long while before they were able to raise enough money to live on. "I must admit that when we first came here, we found everything wrong that was not as in Norway." But they *had* to adjust: they could not return. They had no money and were in any case repelled by the idea of going home as paupers. "We soon discovered that those who worshipped God in another way than we were good people, and that the difference was not so great." [6] In a few years they started earning more money and by the early 1830s the period of tribulation was over.

The *New York Daily Advertiser* said they would soon be followed by more Norwegians. This turned out not to be true, perhaps because of the harsh conditions in the settlers' early years. Yet a few did come; one of the sloopers went home to marry and brought his bride back with him. Although the Kendall colony maintained contact with friends and families in Norway, those who knew about it did not find the prospect of moving to America attractive. This would change, owing to the efforts of two men.

In the year the Norwegians settled at Kendall, the Erie Canal was opened. This 375-mile-long canal with a number of locks, ran from Albany on the Hudson — which could be reached by steamer — through a pass in the Appalachian Mountains to Buffalo on Lake Erie. The canal was an important step forward in transportation techniques. It penetrated the mountain barrier that had separated the coast from the interior. Now it became profitable to transport heavy goods such as grain. The canal opened the way to the upper part of the Mississippi Valley, to new areas of the vast region that came to be called the Middle West. Even if travel on the canal was slow, performed by mule-drawn barges, it was a great boon for personal travel. By 1830 the barges were conveying great numbers of people west, Americans and Europeans who were looking for new land. Once in Buffalo, they could take steamers, to Toledo for example, where new canals would carry them farther, or to remote little towns like Chicago or Milwaukee. From there they could go hunting for land, cheap land — $1.25 per acre.

Cleng Peerson, who spoke English, was the settlers' contact with the outside world. He garnered information about the growing hosts of migrants and the vast plains to the west. In 1833 he started off, not by the canal but on foot. He walked from the western part of New York, mile after mile, through Ohio and Indiana to Illinois. At this point we encounter Cleng the storyteller, a man adept at embroidering his narrative with details perhaps less truthful than grand. In a personal memoir written by another Norwegian immigrant a few years later we are told that Cleng reported reaching a hillside in northern Illinois. He was worn and hungry, and he threw himself on the ground to rest. But when he saw the river and the valley that opened before him, he forgot his hunger and his weariness. He got on his knees and thanked God who had brought him to so beautiful and so fruitful a place. He felt like Moses looking into the Promised Land.

But unlike Moses, Cleng was given more than just a glimpse of the land. He actually led the immigrants into it. He brought the news of this land back to Kendall, and during the next two years most of the Norwegians there migrated westward to the Fox River and its valley in Illinois, some sixty miles southwest of Chicago. Meanwhile land values around Kendall had risen sufficiently so that the Norwegians could sell their properties at a profit. In this way they acquired some capital to make a new start in the West.

The other man who influenced Norwegian emigration in this period was a letter writer named Gjert Gregoriussen Hovland. He had come to Kendall in 1831, and at least from as early as the spring of 1835 he was a prolific letter writer, sometimes sending almost identical letters to several addresses. Some of his letters were brought back to Norway in 1835 by an emigrant visiting his homeland. The letters as well as the returnee aroused considerable attention. People came from the surrounding valleys to see this man and hear what he had to tell. The Hovland letters were copied and sent to other communities — to Voss, Telemark, and Valdres. Everywhere they filled people's minds with thoughts of exodus.[7]

Further Migrations

Norwegian agriculture produced some poor yields in the mid-1830s, and the news that Gjert Hovland's letters brought was well calculated to make a deep impression: there was "beautiful and fertile soil," "employment and a livelihood for anyone who is willing to work," laws that secured "the common man's well-being and advantage," freedom of religion and enterprise, social equality. A farmer in Ryfylke wrote his brother in America that it sounded as if one could live in affluence in America, while there were hard times in Norway. Interest in America was growing, and many were preparing to leave.

Indeed interest in leaving for America was so great that the Stavanger shipping firm of Køhler decided to try the emigrant trade. Two brigs were equipped and sailed in the summer of 1836 with 167 emigrants on board. Most were family groups of mother, father, and many children. Almost all were peasants from the Stavanger area and from the southern part of Hordaland.

There was a connection between the Quakers and these groups also.[8] The district governor in Stavanger believed that many of those who emigrated in 1836 were either Quakers or Quaker sympathizers. The skipper on one of the vessels wrote to the leader of the Quaker society in Stavanger, Elias Tastad, telling about the crossing. "You can never imagine how many people have come to see my passengers" in New York. According to the skipper the inspection had left a favorable impression. His passengers were "quiet, well-behaved people, who wore their best clothes and had a good coloring." He wrote further that he had so many greetings for Tastad that he found it impossible to write them all down.[9]

Most of the newcomers headed west to the Fox River and the surrounding area. On the way it was good to have a stopover, and many found one in Rochester, New York, where Lars Larsen Geilane had settled to carry on his trade as a carpenter and shipbuilder. So many came to Lars Larsen that he wrote to Stavanger in 1837 that people should think twice before they started out for America. They should at least have enough money to pay for their trip to the interior. His wife wrote the same to Elias Tastad: "Twelve have arrived here today who are now eating their supper with us. About two weeks ago some ninety or a hundred persons came here. These stayed nearly a week's time in our and my brother's house, and we fed nearly all of them. . . . Most of them have now left for Illinois. . . . Elias, I will now ask you as a friend not to advise anyone to come who cannot get along on their own when they get here, for they nearly all come to us, and we cannot help so many. We do all we can. I have gone around town to find employment for them, and Lars has taken many of them out into the country." [10] The Larsens in Rochester apparently believed that Elias Tastad could influence the emigrant traffic. Perhaps he could. The emigration figures for Rogaland did not rise appreciably over the next few years. But the impulse to emigrate had spread to other parts of Norway.

From then on emigration was an annually recurring phenomenon in Norway. Each year companies of emigrants started off — some on Norwegian barques and brigs, others via Gothenburg on Swedish or American ships that freighted Swedish iron, still others via Le Havre, which was then a center of European emigrant shipping. The base was becoming broader.

PIONEERS

Cleng Peerson

Cleng Peerson was an extraordinary man, a riddle of a person. Even in his lifetime he was a somewhat mythical figure. Fantastic things were told about him, and the storytellers often found it difficult to sift truth from fable. It is not unlikely that Cleng contributed to the legend when telling of his own adventures, which he often did. He was nearly middle-aged when he came into contact with the Stavanger group about 1820 and became its envoy to America.[1] He had led an adventurous life. But he was taciturn about his youth: the oral sources do not say much about it.[2]

Klein Pedersen Hesthammer was his name in the parish register for Tysvær in Rogaland. He was confirmed there in the fall of 1800 when he was seventeen and a half years old. Later reports claim that he had traveled a great deal: he knew English, he understood French, and he could manage among Germans as well. Perhaps he went to sea after his confirmation and some time later left the ship to wander through Europe in the years when Napoleon was the dominant figure and wars and revolutions were the order of the day. In later life we know that he was a wanderer.

In 1818 he was back in Norway, still in Rogaland, this time at Talgje in the Boknfjord, where he had been living for some years. The pastoral visitation protocol for Stavanger Deanery reports that a married man, Kleng Pedersen Hesthammer, had caused offense by encouraging others "to refrain from church attendance and participation in the Lord's supper." Later Cleng is said to have left for Denmark. Cleng, then, was a dissenter. Had he absorbed religious ideas during his travels in Europe, for example in Germany? Had he met the German dissenter emigrants during their involuntary stay in Bergen from 1817 to 1818? Or had he already made contact with the little Quaker group in Stavanger? We do not know.

He was married at this time, but the marriage was not a happy one, according to a much later report by one of the early emigrants. His wife is said to have been a wealthy widow, much older than Cleng. She does not figure in his later life.

He must have been a man of ideas, perhaps with some philosophical tendencies, especially regarding religion. He was not a member of the Society of Friends, even though he had contacts with them. In America he wrote to Father George Rapp's communitarian society in Pennsylvania. And twenty years later he briefly joined another such society, the Bishop Hill Colony in Illinois, which was founded by Swedish dissenters. Historian Mario S. De Pillis has suggested that the land purchases Cleng made in the first Norwegian colony at Kendall and his communication with Rapp indicate that Ole Rynning, another early Norwegian emigrant, may have been right in claiming (in 1838) that Cleng wished to gather all Norwegians in America into a colony where everything would be owned in common.

If Cleng did have such plans, he was scarcely the man to put them into effect. He was an initiator and a pathfinder, but not an organizer or a reliable architect of social order. Ole Rynning phrased it well when he noted that although Cleng was constantly active, hard work was not his forte. He did not seek wealth for himself. "He worked for all and benefited all, but often in so clumsy a way that few or none thanked him for it."[3]

Undoubtedly he provided the final necessary impulse to the departure of the sloopers in 1825, but we do not know if the journey was his idea. He was not the leader of the expedition. He did play a considerable role in the pioneer period at Kendall, not least by securing economic help from the Americans in the neighborhood. He led the emigrants on to the Fox River in Illinois, a decisive step in Norwegian emigration, since it brought the emigrants into the Midwest and placed them on its fruitful soil. This was a center from which they could spread north and west. But Cleng did not become a leader or an architect of the social order at Fox River either. He continued to migrate both geographically and intellectually.

By 1837 he had left Fox River, pushed on west, and founded a settlement in northeastern Missouri. This proved unsuccessful, and two years later he was in Iowa, which he gave as his home state on a visit to Norway in 1843. After this came his adventure in Bishop Hill, which also failed to add to his happiness. Deprived of all his goods — even his new wife, since women were not allowed to leave the colony — "sick in body and soul," he wandered several more years until he settled among the Norwegians who had gone to Texas. He was then well into his sixties, and though he still set off on long trips, he at least had a base to which he could return. He died in Texas when he was eighty-two. He was buried in a Norwegian graveyard in a little settlement far from the place where the mainstream of Norwegian emigration had found its goal.

Cleng Peerson looms as the "father of emigration." But there were a number of other distinctive personalities in the early years. None of them could match Cleng's wanderlust, but they were, in their own ways, deviant or oppositional, at odds with family, society, or authorities. They chose to leave Norway, and they saw the new land as an opportunity to remedy dissatisfactions they had experienced in the homeland.

Hans Barlien

Hans Barlien was from Overhalla. Born in 1772, he successively farmed, owned a home in the city where he carried on the potter's trade, tried to run a glass factory for a time, and finally returned to farming. He was endowed with mechanical talent, a self-taught clockmaker who invented many things, some of which proved useful. But he was a bit of a fantast and did not know enough about the laws of physics. He failed when he tried to construct wings for flying and cork skis for walking on water.[4]

From early youth Barlien had read whatever he could find, especially the rationalist writings of the eighteenth century. He read Voltaire and once distributed to his neighbors a handwritten translation of one of his works. He must have experienced the French Revolution and its ideas in a very personal way.

Barlien was one of those who wanted to open the way to new crafts for the farming population. He saw the sawmill privileges, the laws restricting trade, and the guilds as artificial barriers which should be torn down because they were oppressive.[5] In 1815 he was elected to parliament (the *Storting*). He was an eloquent opponent of the official class, and as early as 1817 he openly agitated for electing only peasants and craftsmen to the national assembly. His aversion to officials was so intense that he was willing to support King Carl Johan's agents, who went about the country trying to create opposition to the *Storting* and the Constitution. The officials returned his hatred and saw to it that from then on he was kept out of political life; he gradually lost the confidence of the farmers as well.

In his personal life he also departed from accepted norms: he was a freeholder's eldest son, but he married a servant girl. He must have been obstinate, almost cantankerous — he initiated many lawsuits, which eventually caused him financial trouble. In 1837, when sixty-five years old, he broke away and emigrated. At this time he was a lonely man, whose children were scattered around the country and whose wife had for many years lived with one of their daughters.

"Here at last I can breathe freely," he wrote in a letter that was in many respects a contribution to the political debates of Norway in the 1830s. It was also a hymn of praise to President Jackson's democracy: "Here no one is persecuted for his religious convictions. Each person can worship God in any way that agrees with his persuasion. Pickpockets and lawyers, unscrupulous debt collectors, morally corrupted officials and idlers are here deprived of all power to harm the people. No barriers stand in the way of free enterprise. Everyone enjoys undisturbed the fruits of his own diligence, and through a sagacious, liberal legislation the American citizen is protected against the tyranny of the authorities. The so-called free Norwegian constitution has so far only served to weigh the people down with taxes, increase the fees of the officials, and promote extravagance and sloth."[6] These are the words of a spokesman for the extreme left in Norwegian politics of the 1830s.

Johan Nordboe

Cleng Peerson was abroad from the days of his youth. Hans Barlien was a rebel on the national political scene. Both were influenced by events in other parts of Europe. Johan Nordboe was a farmer, but he too was not an ordinary man.

When Nordboe was confirmed in Ringebu, Gudbrandsdal, in 1783, barely fifteen years old, the pastor noted that he read well and knew the whole Catechism and the Explanation of the Catechism by heart. Little is known of his adult years in Norway. He sold the farm he inherited in Ringebu and later bought a farm in another valley, which he also sold, probably because he had to. He also sold a small farm that he had turned over to his younger brother. In a letter from Illinois he excused himself for this, putting the responsibility on "the rich man." He expressed the wish that his brother would follow him to America, but added: "I know of no way I can send him money, and he is not in a position to come here."

In Norway his occupation is always listed as "painter"; this probably means that he did interior decorating of farm homes, including *rosemaling* (flower painting, a traditional Norwegian folk art). He was an artist, as we see from the self-portrait which has been preserved by his descendants in America, as well as from other portraits he painted.

He must have known the old folk medicine, including the use of herbs. We know that in Norway he had the reputation of being able to give good medical advice and that in America he vaccinated against smallpox; his much younger wife was a midwife. His letters, containing accurate descriptions of the flora and fauna of the Illinois prairie, reveal great intellectual curiosity, a talent for systematic observation, and rather extensive knowledge. "Perhaps you remember," he wrote in 1837 to a friend in his home parish, "that I told you last time we spoke together that I would not stop my journey before I had reached the western part of Missouri."

In his letters, Nordboe attacked Norwegian conditions as sharply as Barlien did. He deplored what he called "privileges and monopolies," and the laws that required farmers to provide transportation for officials. He contrasted this with the religious and economic freedom of America: "Every man believes what he thinks is right, and neither monks nor priests have any influence." "The farmer can sell his crops wherever he wishes. Anyone can produce whatever he is able to and sell it where he will. One can make wine or distill brandy: no one will come and seal your apparatus." Distilling liquor was unrestricted in

Norway when Nordboe wrote his letter, which suggests that he had tried his hand at the art in his youth while it was still illegal in the countryside (before 1816).

We know that he moved several times within Norway before making the final decision to sail to America, when sixty-four years old, bringing with him his wife and four children. He was a lone swallow in the emigration movement; no flight from Ringebu immediately followed him. But he, in spite of his advanced age, was one of those who broke with the country in which he had lived a long life.[7]

There is an element of flight in Nordboe's and Barlien's emigrations and much bitterness and disappointment. For them America was the last opportunity life would offer.

Bjørn Kvelve

Bjørn Kvelve from Vikedal was another powerful, even rebellious person, ready to break with tradition. He married above his station an officer's daughter, Abel Catherine von Krogh, whose family looked on the marriage as a misalliance. The marriage may also have alienated him from his own class. He bought a sloop and became a trader, probably selling herring. He sold his goods in Stavanger, where he came into contact with the leading Quakers. Throughout his life he was close to them without joining them. His son, the well-known Norwegian-American writer Rasmus B. Anderson, founder of Scandinavian studies at the University of Wisconsin, reports that his father was a born debater and agitator. In Norway he would gather a group around him on the church grounds before the service and criticize Norwegian laws and officials.[8]

Bjørn Kvelve was a more vigorous figure than Barlien and Nordboe. He was a young man, in his middle thirties, when he left Norway in 1836. His son says that he was one of the leaders of an emigrant group which left Stavanger that year and that his persuasiveness caused a great many to join the company.

Ole and Ansten Nattestad

The first emigrants from the valley of Numedal in central Norway were also young people, the brothers Ole and Ansten Nattestad, unmarried younger sons on a farm high up in the valley. They had tried to make their livings in various ways. Ole had been a peddler and a craftsman and had transgressed the trade laws as well as the privileges of the guilds. In 1836 the two brothers took up cattle trading and set out on the ancient mountain road across to Rogaland to buy sheep which they would drive back east and sell. There they learned about emigration and America, and in Tysvær, Cleng Peerson's home community, they had a chance to read letters written by Norwegian emigrants. Like the others we have mentioned, the brothers had experienced hard living conditions and had beaten their heads against social barriers. They had been wanderers in their homeland, what was called in the language of that day "free and unencumbered." Excited by the stories of a new country, they believed them, or at least they wanted to see if they were true. There was an element of curiosity, a need for new experience, one could say adventuresomeness, in their decision to leave. They were well aware that conditions in Norway were restricted, especially for younger sons from the country who had no hope of inheriting a farm.

Ole Rynning

The most extraordinary of the early Norwegian emigrants was Ole Rynning, gifted pastor's son from Snåsa in Trøndelag, democrat and patriot, very much a man of Henrik Wergeland's period.[9] Like Wergeland, Rynning was an outdoor man, a sportsman who wished to steel himself to live "in Norseman's style," for example by ice bathing. Why did Rynning leave? Perhaps because he had abandoned the study of theology against his parents' wishes and thereby fallen out with them? Or did he grieve over a departed sweetheart? Was he turning over in his mind bold, semi-utopian plans to help Norwegian farmers by securing farmland for them? A much later account by his nephew, Norwegian-American pastor B. J. Muus, when added to stories by early emigrants, hints at something of the kind. Pastor Muus reported that in Snåsa Ole Rynning had wanted to buy a marsh from his father for cultivation and that he decided to leave for America when he was unable to raise the money. "A great and good idea was central to all his thinking," said Ansten Nattestad to a journalist in the 1860s. "He hoped to secure a happier home for the oppressed, poverty-stricken Norwegian worker on this side of the ocean. To realize this wish he shunned no sacrifices, endured the most extreme exertions and patiently accepted misunderstandings, disappointments, and privations.''[10] There may have been a connection between Barlien's emigration and that of Ole Rynning; we know that Rynning's father and Barlien knew each other when they were young and that they corresponded later in life.

Ole Rynning was in his late twenties when he left Bergen in 1837 with some eighty other emigrants on the barque *Ægir* under Captain Christian K. Behrens. In spite of his youth he seems to have been accepted from the start as a leader of the group. Not only did he organize on board the celebration of Norway's Constitution Day, May 17, but he also wrote a song for the day. In his song he was the first of many to point out parallels between the ancient voyages of Norwegians to "the distant strands of Vinland the Good" and the modern emigration.[11] He arranged the journey from New York to the interior for the whole group. He negotiated for the purchase of land in Chicago and was the leader of a small group that went out to inspect the area recommended to them. In Chicago he kept his companions' spirits up when they received a frightening report about the alleged misfortunes of countrymen.

In choosing land, however, he was not sufficiently lucky, or competent. The district he helped select proved to be malaria-ridden and marshy, and the settlement at Beaver Creek, Illinois, became one of the unhappiest in the history of Norwegian emigration. Most of the settlers died in a few years, and the small number who survived fled.

Among the dead was Ole Rynning himself. But during his illness he did something that won him a significant place in the story of Norwegian migration. He wrote a book — *True Account about America for the Information and Help of Peasant and Commoner.* The manuscript was brought to Norway and was published as a book of thirty-eight pages, divided into ten chapters. In this way Ole Rynning tried to present as much objective information as possible about this country that people were getting interested in but knew so little about. He found his audience. It is not known how many copies were printed, but a second edition appeared in 1839. There are many contemporary witnesses to its popularity, whether in the valleys of Setesdal, Hallingdal, or in Voss.

There is a special aura to those who die young, whose souls are

relatively unscarred and whose promise is never fulfilled. Ole Rynning was one such. A contemporary letter tells us that he left behind,
with all with whom he had been in contact, the reputation of a sincere
and unselfish man.[12]

Johan Reinert Reiersen

Johan Reinert Reiersen, editor from Christiansand, was of a different
cast. A son of teacher and precentor Reiersen in Holt on the south
coast, he managed to get to the university on his own in 1832, with
two other young men from Holt. All three had been taught by the
elder Reiersen, and two of them got economic support from wealthy
factory owner Jacob Aall. One, Knud Knudsen, was a cotter's son,
later nationally famous as a linguist, and the other a farm boy, Knud
Jørgensen, who became a minister. All three were on their way up,
but young Reiersen got off on the wrong track from the beginning. He
pulled a mean trick on his companion Knud Knudsen, which barred
him from an academic career and eventual positions in Norway. He
left for Copenhagen, married, and started various journalistic enterprises — unprofitable and ultimately ruinous to his father-in-law.
After a time in Hamburg, Reiersen came to Christiansand in 1839.
There he started a newspaper, one of the early attempts to found an
opposition paper in a Norwegian provincial city. He made himself
highly visible in town affairs for some years, trying to found new
industries and win better road connections with the surrounding
trading area. He worked for the cause of temperance and wished to
reform the school system, all to counteract "the influence of the aristocracy" and to create "public spirit."

Most reports we have of Reiersen are marked by ill will toward him,
perhaps because he was cast of lighter metal than people like Barlien
and Rynning. He soon lost interest in Christiansand and wasted his
opportunities there as he had abroad. Yet he clearly had the ability to
win people's confidence. He was sent to America, like a new Cleng
Peerson, to gather information about the country, and he was followed by a group in the Agder district who settled on land he had
chosen in Texas. Perhaps he emigrated to attempt a new start, where
no one knew his past. Those who accompanied him must have
thought that he had overcome his weaknesses and that America
would be the place for them and for him.[13]

Elise Tvede Wærenskjold

One of his companions, a remarkable figure among the early emigrants, was a woman, Elise Tvede, daughter of the pastor in the community where the elder Reiersen was precentor. She was a contemporary of the founder of the Norwegian women's movement — Camilla Collett, also a pastor's daughter — and, like her, a physically strong and independent woman. When she was older she was known for her sharp tongue. She stuck firmly to her opinions and was probably never soft and yielding in the accepted feminine way. She had received the instruction then considered proper for young girls in a cultured environment. She knew German, English, and French, and she did some painting. No doubt her father was her principal teacher, but it is tempting to believe that contacts with the nearby Nes Ironworks and its cultured proprietor, Jacob Aall, also played a part in her general education. A noted writer and historian, Jacob Aall was her father's cousin and good friend, besides being her godfather.

Her father had impressed upon her the importance of popular education, having worked to improve the schools in Holt. When she was twenty-four years old Elise decided to try teaching, first in Tønsberg and then in Lillesand, where she lived after marrying Svend Foyn, the man who later became famous as the inventor of the whaling harpoon. In Lillesand she intended to start a handicraft school for girls, but when she applied to the authorities for rent-free premises, she was turned down: a woman had no business bringing up "proposals of this nature." The marriage was not successful, and in 1842 she and Foyn were divorced. They had no children and decided to separate when they realized they were not compatible — a rare and courageous act for that time.

Elise Tvede must have known Reiersen, who was five years older than she, from childhood. When she became interested in the temperance movement in Lillesand, Reiersen was active in the same cause in the neighboring town of Christiansand. In Lillesand she was the first female member of the society, a circumstance which, she later reported, did not frighten her. She found it challenging to do unusual things. She supported the temperance movement financially and in personal appearances. In 1843 she wrote a brochure *Appeal to All Noble Men and Women to Unite in Temperance Societies in Order to Eradicate the Drinking of Liquor and Drunkenness etc.* She published it anonymously:

the cover read "by a Lady." In 1846 she assumed editorship of the "pamphlet" *Norway and America*, a small periodical with news about emigration and America. People were astonished when they learned that the editor E. Tvede was female.

A year later she left for Texas, married again, and as Elise Wæren-skjold became one of the leading personalities in the little Norwe-gian group there. She defended the state of Texas in Norwegian and Norwegian-American newspapers, and wrote a history of the first settlement as well as organizing a temperance society and a reading circle. She was a diligent letter writer, and her letters are now avail-able in English, published by the Norwegian-American Historical As-sociation.

She maintained her contacts with Norway, not only by her corre-spondence, but also by reading Norwegian literature and periodicals. She read Ibsen but did not enjoy his work; she preferred novelists Jonas Lie and Alexander Kielland. In 1888 she subscribed to Gina Krog's feminist periodical *Nylænde* (*Pioneering*). A year later she wanted to get Halvorsen's *Dictionary of Authors*, which had just be-come available. She was then seventy-three years old.[14]

Common Traits

Is it possible to find any common features that mark these early emigrants and distinguish them from those who came later? All of them, whether for personal reasons or because of circumstances, had fallen out with their surroundings early in life. They were buffeted about in ways that made them more socially aware than most of their contemporaries. They belonged to the generation born before or about 1814, the year of Norway's free constitution, and they tried to maintain their personal, individual rights in a society that was in many ways reducing its options. Although the year 1814 had brought political renewal and a message of freedom and social change, society continued to be tradition-bound. Perhaps some of them had a vision or dream that by emigrating they might create possibilities not only for themselves, but for a great number of Norwegians, possibilities that would bring a richer life with greater freedom and greater fellow-ship.

We do not know whether these figures were typical early emigrants. But because most of them wrote and reported their activities, we know something about them and can consider them pioneers in the history of Norwegian emigration. All of them did not stimulate a movement in their home communities. People like Barlien and Nordboe were too old to do so and perhaps too lonely. Ole Rynning and Elise Wærenskjold did not hold attitudes typical of the Norwegian official class in the 1830s and 40s. But by their pens they won influence in wider circles. Of those portrayed here, the Nattestad brothers and Bjørn Kvelve probably bring us closest to the recruiting base for Norwegian emigration in the years that followed.

There must have been many other emigrants of whom we know little or nothing. By chance we know of a young woman from Bergen who married an American sailor in 1815 and settled in Boston. Her brother Peder Anderson followed in 1830 and became an outstanding industrialist in Lowell, Massachusetts. He drew nephews and nieces after him, so that much of the family was transplanted to American soil.[15] Pascal Paoli, named for the Corsican freedom hero, left Trondheim for America between 1815 and 1820, and his son Dr. Gerhard Paoli, followed in 1846.

When a Norwegian arrived in New York, wrote Nordboe in 1837, he should go down to the dock and cry out, "Svedisker, norveisk mann!" Someone would soon come whom he could talk with. After that he should ask for Swedes like Bekmann, master rigger, and Østerberg, baker, or Norwegians like merchant Fr. Wang, a son of the pastor in Vågå, or Tybring, son of the pastor in Drammen, or Johnsen from Larvik, or Williamsen.[16]

There may have been others, lost to history, who broke from town or farm communities. Most of them, especially those from rural communities, left behind a new unrest, a ferment which helped spur the restlessness and tension that already existed.

EXODUS, 1836–65

T here are no reliable statistics on the number that emigrated from Norway in the decades following 1836. Norwegian authorities did begin quite early to gather information that would give them a perspective on the extent of the new movement. The government ordered district governors to include the number of emigrants in the quinquennial reports they were to prepare on the economic situation. The governors passed the order down through the bureaucracy to the pastors, who had to issue attestations to all who moved out of their parishes, and to the sheriffs and police chiefs who issued passports to all who left the country. A little later they also tried to get annual statements from the port authorities in the emigration cities and from the consulates in the more important immigration ports. But there is no exact registration of all emigrants before the end of the 1860s. Even so it is possible to perceive something of the rhythm of the movement.

For a time after 1836 a few hundred persons left each year. Then in 1843 the number jumped to 1,600. Even though this remained the peak for some time, the number did not again sink below a thousand until after 1930. In the two depression years, 1849 and '50, nearly 8,000 persons left Norway for America. In other words, nearly half of the 17,000 to 18,000 persons who emigrated from Norway up to and including 1850 left in these two years.[1]

In the 1850s the number continued to grow, but it varied greatly from year to year. In one year 1,600 left, in another more than 6,000. In 1861 there was a new high of 8,000 emigrants. In that year the Civil War broke out in the United States, followed by Indian unrest and uprisings, all of which contributed to the cooling of emigration fever. But in 1866 mass emigrations again occurred, and for a number of years figures were high.

America Fever

How did the impulse to emigrate spread in the forty years from the exodus of the sloopers to the end of the Civil War? It might be expected that it would first have struck deep roots in southwestern Norway and then spread to the north and east. But this did not happen. The number of emigrants did increase in Ryfylke and the southern parts of Hordaland, but almost no one left neighboring Jæren. On the other hand, emigration surged to the north in Voss and in the inner valleys of Sogn, and to the east in Telemark, Numedal, and many other interior valleys. In the decade from 1836 to 1845 nearly two-thirds of all emigrants came from Telemark, Numedal, and Hallingdal. After that, Valdres, Land, and Gudbrandsdal became the leading districts.[2]

Much of the information about the phenomenon of emigration reached these valleys through letters and by word of mouth. It is not really surprising that the news leaped across the mountains to the upper valleys of the east. Mountain men were traveling folk, and communications were good across the mountains along century-old paths. It has been said that the mountain folk traveled farthest, that they were the cosmopolitans in this age. The lowland people were more settled, their world more constricted.

This tradition of travel and movement may be a factor in the spread of emigration, a reason why it caught on in some districts, while others were relatively untouched by the "America fever," at least for a time. On the other hand, it is not certain that the lowland people were indeed more settled. People regularly left these communities, although most of the movement was from eastern Norway to the cities along the Oslo fjord, or from lower Telemark and the inner valleys of Agder to the towns on the south coast.

In western Norway there were traditions of migration to the city of

Bergen from the adjoining parishes and from remoter coastal districts such as Sunnfjord and Nordfjord. The idea of emigrating did not catch on well in districts where there was a fixed pattern of internal migration. People had contacts in town, knew its conditions, and could go to live there with an uncle or older brother. In any case it was less costly than a move to America.

The Haugeans

The Quakers played an important role in 1825 and 1836. But they were few and so did not become a major impulse to emigration, even though some did emigrate. Their contact with the Haugeans was more significant. Haugeanism was a national religious movement, which had stirred people and given them a new view of the world. Laymen were, for the first time in the history of Norwegian Lutheranism, mobilized to play an active role in religious leadership — they were the "Puritans" and "Pilgrims" of Norway. There is a strain of Haugeanism among the early emigrants from many communities, and it is noteworthy how strongly Haugeanism and lay activity influenced the Norwegians in America from the first. The Haugeans were no longer persecuted in the second half of the 1830s, when emigration began. The conventicle law that had forbidden religious meetings conducted by laymen was repealed in 1842, and in 1845 Norway adopted a relatively liberal law concerning dissenting religious denominations. If Haugeanism is to be considered a factor in the background of early emigration, it is not because Hauge's followers were in conflict with national authorities.

But they may have had problems in the local communities. Historian Halvdan Koht has emphasized the continuing opposition in Norwegian rural society to officialdom and the state, an opposition which in earlier times had occasionally taken the form of open revolt.[3] Other historians and several anthropologists have stressed the stability, the almost static quality of the old rural communities. They give us a picture of societies in which impulses from without were slowly accepted and integrated and where people followed traditional, generally accepted, but never formally codified rules for how one should behave at home, at work, and on great occasions. Everyone knew that the sower should toss the seed out under a crescent moon to get a good crop. There were many customs to be observed at Christmas-time if one was to keep evil spirits away. Women in Hallingdal wore a special headdress the first time they went to church after bearing a child. There were rules for brewing ale and for sending gifts from the neighborhood àt weddings and funerals. Eilert Sundt, Norway's early sociologist and a keen observer, pointed out in the 1850s that such local customs were a great help to young people. The young boy knew how he should greet people he met on the road and how he should behave toward a girl and her parents if he wished to be well received. But Sundt was also aware that these customs were gradually breaking down.[4]

The popular religious revival associated with Haugeanism actively helped to break down old customs in many aspects of life and in such central areas as the relationship of men and women. For example, the Haugeans resisted such ancient customs as bundling, the "Saturday eve" courtship custom. They were governed by models outside rural society, and the directives of their leaders were a higher law than that of the community. They asserted the right of the individual to obey his or her conscience, and if necessary they challenged even the authority of parents. In this way they created unrest in the local communities. There is a direct connection between Haugeanism and the political opposition of rural representatives in the *Storting* in the 1830s.

Haugeanism also led to geographical mobility, for Hauge sent his men around the country to places where he thought they might be useful. After his death lay preachers and book peddlers continued to travel, introducing new forms of social contact. Haugeans gave supporters books and letters, new instruments for spreading ideas and impulses. A few active Haugeans left for America, because, as Gullik Gravdal reported: "The 'readers' were not exactly persecuted in Numedal, but they were the targets of much slanderous talk, and they had to endure a great deal of scorn and many insults from those who disagreed with them."[5]

Haugeanism was significant as a powerful new influence from without. It prepared the ground psychologically, helped to detach ordinary people from the old society, and enabled them to receive new signals and make radical decisions such as leaving for America. There is no contradiction in the fact that the Haugeans were strongly represented in the agrarian opposition in the *Storting* and that they were a significant influence for emigration.

If one tries to measure the interest of Norwegian peasants in political affairs through their participation in elections during the decades after 1814, the results are meager. This is true of parliamentary elections and of communal elections, which were introduced in 1837. Did things change after 1814? Had the long revolutionary epoch and the year 1814 — when men had sworn in church that they would sacrifice life and blood for their fatherland, when they had spoken of freedom, the sovereignty of the people, and the equal rights of all — made an impression on the common people? We do not know. None wrote down what they thought about these matters. We can follow a Hans Barlien or a Johan Nordboe, and in Asbjørnsen's tales of folk life there is a glimpse of an east Norwegian farm owner who read the opposition paper *Statsborgeren* (*The Citizen*). But little is known of the ordinary people.

Norway in the 1820s and 1830s

It does seem that the generations entering the work force in the 1820s and 30s were hard-working people. "Where do the new livelihoods come from," asked Eilert Sundt at the end of the 1840s, and he answered: "from strenuous efforts by ship's carpenters and sailors, by fishermen and pioneers, by handicraftsmen and clerks, and many others." He spoke also of "the freeborn generation" born in the country from 1815 on, which worked in "quite a different style from former days." This new industriousness, if Eilert Sundt's explanation is accepted, was based on the value of work, the belief that one could gain a better livelihood by greater effort. This belief was not fatalistic; it placed greater confidence in the individual's personal and human value, and emphasized the worthiness of getting along on one's own.[6]

Undoubtedly many did improve their condition in this period. Even the poorest gradually got a little more food, a little better clothing, and they were a little better protected against cold than their ancestors had been. But progress was slow, and there were many reverses — the fishing that failed or the grain that froze or stayed green. The improved standard of living is reflected in the greater number of children who reached maturity. From the 1840s on an especially large number of young people entered the work force. We shall discuss later what these large age groups thought about emigration. Here let us consider what the large families meant for the parents. The fact that fewer children died because of the parents' diligence and greater care could in the end become a cause for concern. Children had to be provided for, fully until they were five or six years old, and partly until they reached confirmation age. At the same time society made greater demands on the parents by ordering them to give the children a certain schooling. In many places the schools were primitive and poor, but the children had to spend some weeks every year under the schoolmaster's rule. During that period they could not work, and the schoolmaster had to be paid. Some schoolmasters may even have gone as far as Rinaldo in Vilhelm Moberg's novel *The Emigrants*: he ventured to teach such wholly useless subjects as history and geography, and even lent a bright boy a book about strange and far-away lands.[7]

Industrious parents also had to think about what would become of their children when they had to leave home and fend for themselves. Such families gladly received the message of a land with endless expanses of soil — fruitful and cheap soil. All Norwegians who have children to bring up "in modest circumstances" ought to come, wrote Gjert Hovland in several letters from America in 1835. A few years later he varied the same theme: "Many who have arrived here . . . are happy over their emigration, especially for their children's sake."[8] This was appealing to some families: Nils Hansen Fjeld in Aurdal had his farm and a good income, but he had many children and worried about their future. In 1847 the whole family left.[9]

Emigration

There were many large families among the early emigrants. Mother and father were probably in the thirty-five to forty age group, and the children followed stepwise from fifteen years and down — four or five, or even six or seven of them. Four-fifths of the emigration from Tinn in Telemark from 1837 to 1843 was family emigration.

Farm families broke away and set out for the unknown. Often they joined in larger groups, companies from one neighborhood or one parish. It gave them a greater sense of security as they set out on the venturesome journey. These people were not really poor. Some of them had considerable means for their times, like Nils Fjeld or Anders Tømmerstigen from Vardal, who had with him a thousand dollars.[10] But they were not equally well off, and people had to be prepared to help one another. There is a record of agreements for mutual aid and support among participants in an emigrant party. Under such conditions an occasional hired man or woman, a bachelor, or a newly married cotter couple might join. But most emigrants were freeholders and their families.

They must have been brave. Again we cite Vilhelm Moberg: "It was the boldest who first set off. The enterprising ones made the decision. The venturesome ones started out first on the journey across the great sea. They were the dissatisfied ones and the initiators who could not endure their lot at home and who became the first emigrants in their community." They were the ones who had sensed the faint breath of the wind of change in 1814, the wind that had again begun to blow in Europe in the 1830s and that blew north as well.

People outside rural society observed the exodus occurring in the valleys. In the papers they referred to narratives that flew like carrier pigeons or wildfire from farm to farm. They used the expression "America fever," indicating that it was contagious: the urge to emigrate, said some, was a contagious disease. It is like demonic possession, said others. The afflicted cannot talk of anything but America, and they are not accessible to reason or argument.[11]

It is not unreasonable to suppose that a hectic, suspense-filled atmosphere arose when letters and reports arrived or, still more, when someone returned from the new land, and that this atmosphere may have led some to make ill-considered decisions to emigrate. The fair number of letters from disappointed and dissatisfied emigrants suggests as much. Those who warned against emigration were right when they said people were taking a great risk. Hard work and drudgery were not the only things that awaited them; many became ill and died young.

Even if one accepts the existence of a mood that deserved the label "America fever," one must still try to explain why it attacked some communities and left others relatively untouched, and why in some places it was the source of a steadily growing stream, while in others it merely caused a brief eruption.

It is not surprising that the report of Ole Rynning's death under miserable conditions at Beaver Creek cooled the enthusiasm of those who wanted to emigrate from Snåsa and that for some years similar accounts concerning numerous well-known, dead countrymen had a like effect in Tinn in Telemark. [12] But other, more general circumstances call for an explanation. The option of emigration must have been familiar in the greater part of the country by the end of the 1840s. People had seen emigrants on their way to the ports in western, southern, and eastern Norway. Nevertheless it was mostly the inner fjord areas and the upper mountain valleys that were infected by the "fever" in this period.

The economic development in various districts and in various occupations, as well as the established migration patterns, provides part of the explanation. In the 1840s, especially the first half, times were good in Norway. Herring and cod fishing offered an alternative to emigration, which many chose. "The spring cod is our America," said a later report from Møre. Northern Norway was also an immigration area because of the opportunities provided by fishing. Farm owners were leaving for America, wrote the district governor of Sogn and Fjordane about Sogn in his report for 1846–50, but cotters, who could not afford the voyage, went to Møre or Nordland. They were fewer than the emigrants to America, but they constituted one-fifth of all migrants from Sogn in this period.

In the lowlands of eastern Norway a growing number of people managed to buy farms, mostly small ones. In the counties of Vestfold and Østfold the number of farm owners grew, but not the number of cotters. The agriculture of the communities became more specialized, and the productivity of the basic industry was growing. The woods were alive with timbering, and the sawmills kept busy. Besides, the towns needed labor for the newly established little factories and workshops, for handicrafts and minor industries of various kinds. In these districts people who had enough to pay for their way across the ocean could invest it in some activity at home and hope for success. For the very poorest the trip was still not possible.

In Agder, especially along the coast, emigration had started early in the 1840s and bloomed hectically in a few communities into the 1850s. Then it suddenly stopped. Sailing ships and shipbuilding offered work, perhaps not such great wages at first but opportunities for economic and social advancement later. Only when the sailing ship crisis arose during the 1880s did Agder again become an emigration district. People were still migrating from valley and fjord down and out to the lowlands, the coast, and northern Norway. But when in America the path to the Midwest opened up, the farm owners from Sogn, Voss, and Hardanger, from Telemark, Hallingdal, and Valdres, from Land and Gudbrandsdal saw a new opportunity for themselves and their children to continue their lives as farmers. They preferred this to the alternative of urbanization. One might say that paradoxically rural conservatism prompted them to make a radical decision. Gradually the number of fellow dalesmen in America became so large that it seemed less strange to join them than to move to other places in Norway. They were perhaps trying to defend and protect an old pattern of life by emigrating. In any case, it was these farmers who determined the direction of Norwegian emigration to America and gave it its character in the first decisive years.

LAND OF FREEDOM
AND OPPORTUNITY,
THE 1850S

From the days of the Puritans, America had been a refuge for religious dissidents from Europe. Quakers, Huguenots, Moravians, and many others followed in their wake, well into the first half of the nineteenth century. The Norwegian Quakers and Haugeans were a part of this movement. Several European dissidents tried to found colonies in America, to which only members of the faith would be admitted. They also tried to practice a kind of Christian socialism or communism involving a community of labor and property. This attempt to set up ideal religious communities was especially characteristic of emigrants from Great Britain and various German states. An outstanding example from Swedish emigrant history is the establishment in 1846 of the great religious community in Bishop Hill, Illinois, by Erik Jansson and his followers.

In the early part of the nineteenth century there were also many social reformers among the emigrants who wished to establish a better secular society than the ones they observed in Europe during the rise of industrialism. They spun theories of how society might be organized to achieve a greater degree of equality and thereby greater solidarity and harmoniousness. Robert Owen, textile manufacturer and philanthropist from Scotland, was one of them; socialists from France and Germany were among the others. They, too, tried to found colonies where they could try out their theories. America offered a proving ground for social utopians, whether they were inspired by the Bible or by the new ideas of their times. The country had liberal laws, and large unpopulated areas. Believers could gather, isolate themselves from unbelievers, and set up their experimental communities. Most of these societies crumbled in a short time, but as late as 1868 there still existed seventy-eight societies or collectives, mostly religious, which in some degree were built on community labor and property. A few of them are still extant.[1]

A third factor in the early emigration was nationalism. Societies and individuals were eager to organize emigration so that countrymen could be gathered into colonies large enough to preserve their national identity and to maintain contacts with the homeland for the benefit of the emigrants as well as the people back home.[2]

If one looks carefully at the story of Norwegian migration, one detects there some minor instances of such plans and ideas. As noted, Cleng Peerson was drawn to the idea of communal religious fellowships; Ole Rynning dreamed, if not of communal property, at least of a union of all Norwegians in America in one colony or society; and a letter from Hans Barlien indicates that he was considering a similar idea. He wanted to buy enough of America's fertile land to accommodate thousands of families, and charter a ship to carry them across. In this way he hoped to help "the upright" in Norway and to found a colony "with such a government as nature has decreed, in which no injustice can thrive."[3]

Imaginative Johan Reinert Reiersen made all-embracing plans. While still in Norway, he wrote that the government should take the initiative in organizing emigration and founding a colony of Norwegians that would be "beneficial both to mankind and the motherland." It is possible that the settlement he founded in Texas was an effort to gather countrymen into one large colony.

Another Norwegian who tried to form a Norwegian religious colony was Nils Otto Tank, son of the landed gentleman Carsten Tank, one of Norway's wealthiest men until he was forced into bankruptcy in 1829. Nils Otto Tank had been converted to the teachings of the Moravians and had served as a missionary for the Brotherhood for many years, part of the time in the Dutch colony of Surinam. Here he had troubles because of his unswerving opposition to slavery and was finally compelled to leave. Through marriage to a Dutch woman he acquired a considerable fortune. On a visit to Norway in 1849 he learned that in Milwaukee, Wisconsin, there was a Norwegian congregation of Moravians who wished to move out into the country to escape the city and its temptations. He decided to become the benefactor of these coreligionists and to use his fortune for their benefit. He bought a large tract near Green Bay in northern Wisconsin and established a Moravian society based on communal labor and ownership. "Ephraim" was the name he gave it. But Tank's plans were star-crossed. Settlers did come and occupy the land he had made available at Green Bay, but in practice they were reluctant to accept his ideas. They mistrusted a man of his social origins and suspected that they might become cotters under the great patron unless they had a full title to their own plots of land. So they moved away after a year or two and founded a new Ephraim a little more to the north, this time on land of their own.[4]

Tank was thus received distrustfully by his countrymen, and his plans caused no stir in Norway. The contrary was true of another Norwegian who tried at about the same time to gather his countrymen in a single colony of their own, namely the master musician Ole Bull (1810–80).

Ole Bull

Bull was a world-renowned violinist, a genius. But beyond that he was a patriot, a democrat, and a lover of freedom. The poet Wergeland had called him "the precious jewel of our poverty" and had written poems in his honor. The national poet Bjørnson (1832–1910) wrote even more lavishly of him: to Norwegian youth Bull had been "the glittering morning sun gilding the mountains of Norway." He was "so marvellously audacious, so shining, so single-minded, so smilingly arrogant — and modest."

Ole Bull had experienced the February Revolution in Paris in 1848. When he returned to Norway that autumn after many years of concert touring in America and Europe, he no doubt hoped that the ideas of the Revolution would bring about a spring thaw in his homeland as well. He did his best in those areas where he could exert his powers. He founded a theater in his home city of Bergen in which everything was to be Norwegian (which had been true of no theater in Norway)

— the plays, the players, the music, and the ballets. After three fruit-ful years he left Norway for an American tour in the fall of 1851.

The years he spent back home were stringent years in Norway. An economic crisis had severely reduced Norwegian exports, with far-reaching consequences for the social structure. In the wake of the economic crisis came political and social unrest, which found its ex-pression in Norway's first political mass movement. The leader of this movement was Marcus Thrane (1817–90), who was also inspired by the February Revolution, especially by the most radical, socialistic ideas that formed part of the background of the revolution.

Ole Bull must have known about Marcus Thrane; in fact, he could scarcely have avoided knowing, but there is no record of what he thought about the man and his movement. One can speculate that democratic Ole Bull would have approved of many of the planks in the program that the movement proposed. For instance the demand for universal suffrage and the proposal that the state should start a land reclamation program and provide land for the landless. He can hardly have been opposed to such a movement. When he left he turned over his theater to the young student Henrik Ibsen, who had had ties to Thrane's movement and had written articles in Thrane's newspaper.

Ole Bull had spent most of his time in Bergen, one of Norway's most significant ports of emigration. He must have seen America-bound emigrants in the streets, flocking to the quay. But he probably did not read Thrane's newspaper and could hardly have known that Thrane encouraged people to leave for America and was even work-ing out plans for organizing emigration parties of poor people.

Yet Bull had lived in Norway those three years, and there must have been a connection between the experiences he had, the im-pressions he received, and the plans he now began to develop. He proposed to buy land for his countrymen in America — a huge tract where Norwegians could build and dwell in happy union. He wanted to found "a new Norway, dedicated to freedom, baptized in inde-pendence, and protected by the mighty flag of the Union." His new Norway would be better than the old.

Anyone who tries to find European models for this project has a difficult task. Ole Bull had traveled far and wide, and had everywhere shown great curiosity about social and political conditions. One late report suggests that he had been interested in utopian colonization experiments. All that can be said with any certainty is that he knew about the collective American intellectuals and artists had founded at Brook Farm in New England.

When he arrived in America early in 1852 he began expounding his plans to personal friends as well as to prominent American politicians, for instance Henry Clay. He inspected properties at various places, including Virginia, but did not give any thought, or so it seems, to the Middle West, where Norwegians so far had been settling. Perhaps he was deterred by reports of unhealthful conditions out there: cholera had accompanied European immigrants to Chicago about 1850 and had spread from there.[5]

At length he chose a tract in the northern part of Pennsylvania, a strange choice indeed for an experiment in pioneering. The landscape was beautiful, to be sure, and the newspapers that wrote about the plan emphasized that the climate was very healthy and the air clean. But the terrain was rugged and hard to clear, and the soil was barren. Perhaps these tree-clad slopes reminded Bull of western Norway. Perhaps someone had hinted that the cliffs contained valuable minerals. At any rate he reserved to himself the mineral rights, if there were any, and he developed magnificent, one could say fantastic, plans. He was going to build factories and sawmills and establish a polytechnic school. He wrote about all this in a letter to his brother, in which he reported "my activities as artist, politician, and governor of my little state in Pennsylvania." He believed he would be able to furnish jobs for several thousand persons in his New Norway.

The first settlers came in early September 1852, and on September 7, just a few days later, came Ole Bull himself. With an engineer he laid out lots for houses for himself and the colonists, and lots for a hotel where new arrivals would lodge. This place was called "Oleana" in honor of the founder. A short distance off there was to be a "New Bergen" and a "Valhalla." Bull selected land that he thought would be suitable for a hothouse and a nursery, and he laid out sites for a sawmill and a carpentry shop, a church and a schoolhouse. In the evening the colony was festively dedicated with singing and the shouting of hurrahs. Bull gave an eloquent address to the colonists and captivated them with the magic of his bow.

Then workaday life began for the nearly 250 Norwegians who were there by the end of 1852. Ole Bull owned the land and the price he asked was relatively high, more than twice as much as they would have paid for government land. In return he made considerable investments in common improvements, and he promised favorable terms of repayment, as well as work for everyone on community enterprises at a dollar a day. But he was not expert at calculating costs, and the great undertaking proved to be more costly than he had imagined. By October he was already in financial trouble and tried to persuade the settlers to accept a daily wage of half a dollar. When they protested, he withdrew the proposal and set off on a concert tour to raise more money.

When he returned to Oleana in May of the following year, some had already left the colony and the rest were grumbling. Once again he managed to mollify his countrymen, who joined him in celebrating Norwegian Constitution Day on May 17 and American Independence Day on July 4, all in grand style. But that was the end of the fairy tale. In September 1853 he withdrew from the enterprise and sold the tract back to the original owners. He had invested and lost considerable sums of money, estimated at from $40,000 to $70,000. In addition he had probably lost money on railway speculations and other projects.

Bull's plans for the New Norway had quickly been made known in the homeland. In Bergen a small book about the project appeared, and the newspapers gave it their attention. With few exceptions they were reserved and skeptical. One of the exceptions was the organ of the Thrane labor movement (*Arbeiderforeningernes Blad*), which was his faithful supporter. The paper extolled Bull as the "man of freedom" who worked for the betterment of his poor countrymen; it even burst into song:

> He knows that here is grief and need:
> He wants to lift your burdens.
> He'll give you freedom and your bread:
> He wants to ease your living.
> . . . .
> You know the man — it's Ole Bull.

As long as it was possible, the paper defended the colony against "the attacks of the aristocrats." As late as the summer of 1853 it was still carrying optimistic accounts of Oleana.

In the countryside the fairy tale had grown even more miraculous. In some places it was reported that Ole Bull offered emigrants free passage, to be sure with the understanding that they would work to repay him after their arrival. One Christiania newspaper complained that people came running up to the editorial offices to register for a berth on the voyage to Oleana and that some young people thought that Bull was about to establish "the millenium on earth."

But it was only a dream — a defeat for Ole Bull who had wanted to perform the magnificent exploit of building a new and better Norway. In the long series of social experiments in America it was only an episode and to sober realists and skeptics another proof that Utopia cannot be realized here on earth. In the end the story of Oleana was smothered in laughter provoked by editor Ditmar Mejdell's lampooning ballad:

> To Oleana 'tis good to fare,
> No more in Norway my chains to bear.
> There roasted piggies run around so grand
> And ask politely if you'd like a slice of ham.[6]

For many years this ballad with its many verses was sung by Norwegians on both sides of the Atlantic (in recent years it has been picked up by American ballad singers like Pete Seeger).

Marcus Thrane

Marcus Thrane, too, had had a dream, a greater one than Ole Bull's: he wanted to establish social equality and justice in his homeland. This, too, proved to be utopian and ended in an even more fateful disaster. The authorities intervened, appointed a commission to conduct hearings around the country, and arrested the leaders. Thrane was imprisoned for several years, and he left for America a few years after his release. Here he was still a man in opposition. He took part in the work of the First (Socialist) International (1864 ff.), edited radical newspapers, and was a declared freethinker who had no love for Norwegian-American Lutheranism or its orthodox clergy. Some of the other leaders of the Thranite movement also emigrated. But it is not known how many ordinary members followed Thrane's appeal to leave Norway and its miserable government.

Like the Haugeans before them, the Thranites had taken a stand in opposition to custom and tradition. Each in his or her community had gone to meetings, had joined in festivities with songs and speechmaking, and in some places had even marched in processions behind banners. They had signed their names — some with the help of others — on petitions to the authorities, and they had chosen delegates to national meetings. Many of them had been blacklisted by the sheriffs, who had been ordered by the government to send in lists of members. Some even had to go before the investigating commission to defend their behavior. The dissatisfaction that had moved them may have been diffuse and the goals unclear, but even in the country districts there must have been some consciously radical persons among the common members. They must have had a firm conviction when they demanded universal suffrage and state aid in the breaking of new land. They must also have learned that the American government had met both these demands; if they did not know it earlier, they would have learned about it in articles and letters in the movement's official organ. When the movement collapsed in Norway, they could try to realize these demands by leaving for the New World. The Thrane newspaper reported that many of the most intelligent members of local societies had left. Detailed research in some local communities confirms that Thranites participated in the emigration of the 1850s. In general one can say that emigration either started or increased in those parts of the country where the movement had had its greatest strength.[7]

The Haugeans had won support in every stratum of rural society. The Thranite movement was also a mass movement. Freeholders' sons who felt the pressure of downward social mobility into the cotters' class joined the Thrane associations as did those who had been upwardly mobile from this class during the good times in the forties and who now felt their progress threatened because it was difficult to obtain credit after the crisis of 1848. But in general it was a movement that revealed and deepened a profound split in rural society by uniting the lower orders, the farm workers, against the large farm owners. There was a new factor in the complex of emigrant motivations — the social unrest of many persons in eastern Norway and Trøndelag who were cotters and did not own land.

Numerically the Thranites were hardly significant in the emigration of the 1850s, but there is reason to think of them as pioneers. They were the first within their social group, the cotters, who managed to make a clean break, who left their homes in disappointment or in protest, and who were able to raise the necessary funds. A decade later they would be followed by many more landless and poor people.

The Discovery of Gold

At about this time fantastic, mind-boggling news came from the farthest parts of America. Gold had been discovered in California, great beds of it, which could be dug out with hoe and spade. A person who was lucky enough to come upon a rich vein could win a fortune in shining gold. As early as 1849 a real "goldman" came home to Norway. He had been working as a ship's carpenter in San Francisco when the news of gold broke in January 1848. He had been one of the first in the gold fields, and he had been lucky, so that on his return he had enough means to start a shipbuilding and shipping firm in Grimstad. There he stayed and was known as "the goldman" all his life.[8] The American "gold fever" caught on in Norway, too. In 1850 Norwegian shipping firms advertised that they could offer passage to California. The most California-minded individuals inserted their own ads; some "cultivated young men" from eastern Norway announced that they planned to work together "under self-made laws" when they arrived in California but that they needed one more member. Two expeditions for California were outfitted in 1850–51. The first was organized in Christiania and sailed just before Christmas with seventy-six passengers, two of them women. In September 1851 the ship anchored in San Francisco harbor, and the passengers started for Sacramento and the gold fields. But the crew members were not about to miss their chance: in a few days most of them had deserted.

The other expedition started from Trondheim, financed by the sale of shares, at that time a new form of doing business in Norway. Some of the shareholders joined the expedition, and others merely risked their capital and hoped for a crop of gold that would give them a generous return on their investment. The initiator and organizer was the mineralogist and editor N. C. Tischendorf. In the newspaper *Nordre Trondhjems Amtstidende*, he wrote "battle hymns" for the expedition and tried to recruit members by giving lyric descriptions of the "glories of California." The expedition started for but never reached California. Their frigate *Sophie* was grounded in Brazil, when it was deemed unseaworthy. A few of the participants reached their destination; more of them returned to Norway after having tried pioneering in Brazil; the investors lost their capital.

The emigrants to California were different from the earlier emigrants. They were men, mostly young and unmarried. Among them were city boys, craftsmen, and clerks from Fredrikshald and Drammen, from Bergen and Trondheim. But most of them were sailors who had seized the opportunity to jump ship. These were people who took chances, gamesmen who gambled on the great prize in the lottery of the gold diggers. Some turned into true vagabonds, going on to new, unknown lands beyond California — to Australia, when gold was found there, or north to a new gold rush by the Fraser River in British Columbia. The first Norwegians in Oregon and Washington came by way of California.[9]

Others stayed in California but left the gold fields for other opportunities, some disappointed and impoverished, some with a little nestegg of gold dust or nuggets of gold that could be used to start a business. As yet they were few: in 1860 there were only some 700 Norwegian-born inhabitants in California. Johan Nordtvedt from Trondheim, educated at the Horten shipyard and recipient of a government fellowship to visit America, saw his opportunity and became the well-known shipbuilder John G. North. Peder Sæter began by making small loans and ended as a wealthy banker. "Sather Gate" at the entrance to the campus of the University of California at Berkeley and the campanile that bears the same name are memorials to his and his wife's generous donations to the university.

The most legendary Norwegian in California, however, was Snowshoe Thompson. When he was ten years old he emigrated with his parents from Tinn in Telemark with the first band of emigrants from that community. He made his contribution as a mail carrier on skis. He had fashioned his own skis in the manner he remembered from his boyhood in Telemark. In the winter when all connections between East and West across the Sierras were broken, he carried the mail and won renown for his endurance and hardiness. American papers wrote about him, noting with amazement that he could travel thirty to forty miles a day, and they tried to explain to their readers how his "Norwegian snowshoes" were made and how they worked.[10]

Evidence of Success

There were many factors in the emigration of the 1850s: gold, social and political unrest, the dreams of a new Norway in America. But the mainstream, which contributed to the increase of emigration even in the prosperous years that lasted until the late 1850s, was the many unobtrusive departures from the inland valleys. Here people had been leaving for several years and already had close contacts with countrymen in the Middle West.

Dean Hauge, a pastor in Sogn, commented in his reports of 1855 and 1860 on the emigration from his pastoral district. He contended that the reasons for increasing emigration were economic and psychological. He mentioned the hopes of the emigrants for "better circumstances," their wish to join kinsmen who had preceded them, but above all "the noble thought" of securing a happier future for their children. He did not believe the motivations were political. His parishioners were "politically quite innocent" and were not interested even in immediate local affairs.

Then there were the accounts from their fellow dalesmen in America. Many had questioned the reliability of these accounts, wrote the Dean. They had claimed that they were grossly exaggerated, owing to the emigrants' wish to have their relatives around them and to their need for labor in "cultivating the newly acquired land." But this suspicion gradually evaporated as accounts came from persons whose reliability he could not question. As a kind of confirmation there was always the money that flowed in every year, to support families at home and to aid those who wished to emigrate. The Dean could provide specific examples. A landless farm worker who had emigrated five years earlier had sent $90 to pay for the passage of his brother's two small children. Two boys, the sons of a cotter, sent their father $15 one year and $25 the next. Both of them had had to work for better-situated emigrants to pay for their passage. "A cotter's son, who was so poor at the time of his emigration that I married him free of charge, sent a draft of 400 specie dollars . . . to his father and his siblings so that they could join him. In this way I could enumerate many specific cases which appear to prove that the returns over there must be very great for those who are willing to work." [11]

Letters from dependable persons, concrete evidence in the form of great and small sums of money, the certainty that one was not heading into the great unknown but could count on a warm reception by friends and family — these were in the 1850s the most important reasons for continued and increasing emigration. Finally, there was a new factor: the fares were falling.

THE LONG JOURNEY

E ven today the right to cross state or national borders, for individuals or groups, is not a matter-of-course. In the Dano-Norwegian monarchy it was forbidden to "remove from the King's realms and dominions" (an injunction that was not always enforced). A corresponding Swedish ban was not removed from the legal code until 1840.

Freedom of movement was included in the French revolutionary declaration of human rights, and in Norway after 1814 the right to emigrate was recognized although it was not listed among the citizen's rights in the constitution. Migrations of considerable size presuppose the freedom to leave one's homeland, just as they presuppose the existence of other countries who are willing to receive foreign citizens. Other necessary preconditions for emigration are a connection — communication and possibilities of transportation — between the sending and the receiving country and costs that are not prohibitive for ordinary people. These are necessary but not sufficient conditions to initiate a movement such as the emigration from Norway in the nineteenth century.

Emigration to America began earlier in Norway than in the other Nordic countries. It is likely that Norway's geographical location and its position as a seafaring nation were important factors.

As indicated in Chapter 2, the influence of the English Quakers on Norwegians imprisoned in Britain, which led to the formation of a

Society of Friends in Stavanger, was a result of Norway's shipping interests and the English blockade in the final phase of the Napoleonic wars. Thus shipping was a factor in early emigration.

If one compares Norwegian with Finnish emigration, which did not begin until the 1860s, it seems that greater geographical distance from America, modestly developed shipping, and high transportation costs combined to create this "delay." A fair number of the early Finnish emigrants came to America by way of northern Norway, where they stayed for some years and earned enough money fishing to pay for the rest of their journey. It seems odd that Iceland, the Nordic country geographically closest to the New World, was also a latecomer in the emigration movement. The reason was simply that Iceland had virtually no shipping of its own. Its connection with the rest of the world was largely provided by other countries — Denmark, Norway, or more often Scotland. In terms of transportation, Iceland was farther from America than was Norway.[1]

Costs of Travel

Today the trip to New York from Norway by air takes six or seven hours from airport to airport and costs about half a month's wages before taxes for the average wage earner. If one wishes to be extravagant and has the time, one can occasionally get a boat that takes as many days as the airliner takes hours and costs a great deal more. About 1840 the passage required from eight to twelve weeks, depending on wind and weather. It cost thirty to thirty-five specie dollars, and passengers had to bring their own food and bedclothes. The shipping firm provided only water and wood.

A hired man on a Norwegian farm earned at most a cash salary of ten specie dollars a year, so that for a trip to America he had to save all the cash he earned for several years, and he would be penniless when he arrived in the New World. It is not surprising that in the early period of emigration government officials repeatedly emphasized that the emigrants were relatively well off financially. One had to own something, either money or goods and property, that one could sell if one wished to set off across the sea.

In the 1830s and '40s emigrants could save some money by going to foreign ports where cargo ships in more or less regular traffic to

America would squeeze in passengers. Gothenburg, where Swedish and American ships loaded iron, was such a harbor. Another was Le Havre in France, the most important emigration port in Europe, where ships came from New Orleans loaded with cotton and shipped emigrants on the return voyage. From southern Norway many ships carried various kinds of cargoes to France, and they, too, could provide cheap passage for a few emigrants. This helps to explain why nearly a third of the Norwegian emigrants, especially those from the Telemark and Agder districts, chose this route in the 1840s.[2]

A small reduction in the fare was about the only advantage they gained. In Le Havre they often had to wait weeks for passage; they were faced with language problems already on board ship; and they risked being put ashore in New Orleans, a longer journey up to Illinois and Wisconsin than from New York. A letter to *Morgenbladet* in July 1846 reports hardships emigrants might encounter in Le Havre if they failed to find passage. Nearly 300 Norwegians spent several weeks in an open field lying like cattle "in tightly closed knots, in an atmosphere tainted by the stench rising from the marshy soil under the influence of the hot sun."[3] Such unforeseen delays sometimes cost money and drained the emigrants' reserves to the extent that they had to be sent home at the expense of the Norwegian state.

Nevertheless, many emigrants chose this route, probably because in the earliest years it was not always easy to get direct passage from Norway. Norwegian shipowners and skippers were not ready to make offers of passage in 1840, at least not in sufficient numbers to meet the demand. They often found it difficult to get suitable return cargoes in New York, even if the skipper was willing to dock in many harbors before he finally got back to Norway. Most shipowners and skippers wanted to have a cargo on their westward passage also. If they sailed from Bergen or Stavanger, they could carry some codliver oil, herring, and other fish products; so it was in these cities that the traffic in emigrants first developed. In the coastal towns to the south there was iron to be shipped. During the 1840s Norwegian iron exports to America doubled, with emigrants and iron riding the same keels.

Gradually more towns joined in and the emigrant traffic grew: only one Norwegian ship carried emigrants and cargo to New York in 1841, but the number had risen to twenty-nine by 1850.

Shipowners and Skippers

From the beginning a question was raised: Did the owners and skippers offer transportation to people who had decided to emigrate, or did they stimulate emigration to fill their ships? They might, for example, advertise that the rapid sailing ship *Richard Cobden* would leave in mid-April, that the ship was copper-sheathed and had a high, airy room between decks, well suited for passenger traffic. So far it was merely information for interested parties; one could only hope that the information was trustworthy. But the skippers sometimes went further, for the newspapers did not always reach their customers. In winter, agents traveled up the valleys and into the fjords to sign up passengers. In the spring of 1843 the newspapers in Bergen accused several captains in the town of regularly carrying on emigrant recruiting — "soul buying" they called it. Captain Bendixen was said to have been in Voss, where he "talked like crazy about America." It was reported that he accepted as payment what people expected to get for the property they intended to sell at auction — money that would not be due until the next summer assizes — as well as promissory notes that would-be emigrants persuaded their debtors to transfer to him. Bendixen replied that he had been invited to Voss by people who *wanted* to emigrate and that there were more of them than he could find room for in his ship. He had not needed to persuade anyone.[4]

The line between giving information and exerting influence is hard to draw. But one can certainly say that in the 1840s the desire to emigrate was primary and that Norwegian shipowners responded to the emigrants' need for transportation. Shipping could in turn exert an influence on emigration, at any rate on where the emigrants were landed. In 1849 the British parliament repealed the Navigation Acts and so opened traffic to the colonies to ships from countries other than Britain. As a result Canada began to play a significant role in Norwegian shipping during the 1850s. If a Norwegian vessel brought emigrants to Quebec, it could now bring timber back to England on the same terms as English ships did. From there it could carry a miscellaneous cargo to Norway or continue into the Baltic. After a long voyage it could return to Norway in late fall or early winter, and then be made ready for the emigrant traffic of the following summer.

Norwegian skippers were quick to seize these new opportunities: as early as 1850 Norway had the largest number of ships' calls in Quebec of any foreign nation. Even if not all the ships carried emigrants, the combination of timber cargoes and emigrant traffic was particularly advantageous because it provided regular employment for a large portion of the year. Some skippers even tried their hand at the Irish emigrant traffic.

The results appear in the statistics on the emigrants' destinations. In the second half of the 1840s most Norwegian emigrants entered via New York, and not until 1850 did the first ones land in Quebec. More came in the following years, and from 1854 to 1865 more than nine-tenths of the 44,000 Norwegian emigrants entered via Quebec on Norwegian sailships. Another result was a reduction in the fares, which made it possible to reach Quebec for $12 to $15.

Traffic through Quebec continued for a few years after 1865, but then a revolution in transportation occurred. Foreign steamship lines with many ships and regular sailings began offering serious competition. They provided quicker crossings; they had specified times of departure and arrival; and they included meals on board in the fare. Norwegian shipowners were not able to meet this competition, and from 1870 to 1910 most Norwegian emigrants sailed on foreign steamers.

Preparing for the Journey

The trip that faced the emigrants in the days of the sailing ship was a long one, and many preparations had to be made before they could leave. A farm owner had to sell his farm with all its stock and tools, with house and chattels, most of it at auction. The emigrants also had to equip themselves with provisions for the entire voyage — nonperishables like dried pork and mutton, salted meat and herring, peas, grain, potatoes and flatbread (an unleavened, brittle bread rolled out flat), flour for porridge, butter, whey cheese, possibly even sour milk and beer. Then they had to have sheepskin coverlets and blankets, since they furnished their own bedding, and they had to have enough cooking utensils with them to prepare food for eight, ten, or twelve long weeks.

In the early years especially they brought a number of objects they thought they might need after they arrived. It might be a spinning wheel or an iron griddle, a good harness or an ax. Jon Ellingbø from Valdres brought all the equipment from his farm smithy, even the bellows. Knut Norsving took a wagon, he later reported, and a great many farm tools. He transported two heavy millstones, which are on view to this day at the Norwegian-American Museum in Decorah, Iowa.

All this baggage containing food and equipment had to be freighted down through the valleys and out through the fjords to the city where the emigrant boat was docked. From Hallingdal and Numedal they went to Drammen, from Telemark and Agder to the Skien Fjord and the south-coast cities. People from Ryfylke and some from Setesdal went to Stavanger, those from Voss and Sogn to Bergen. The men and women of Valdres and some from Gudbrandsdal also came, finding their way across the mountains to the western fjords. Here they had to load their gear on boats that carried them to Bergen. After a time the people of Valdres and Gudbrandsdal chose Christiania as their port of exit.

The coastal towns had an emigrant season, when they were crowded with farm people dressed in homespun and colorful costumes, making their last preparations for the journey. The women from Hallingdal, for instance, usually baked their flatbread in Drammen. "Now it is again that time of year" wrote the poet Aasmund Vinje, "when the emigrants are to be seen in the streets, and ships are being rigged, and water casks are being made for the trip to America." "This is just as regular as the coming of the cuckoo, and the one is as much a part of the order of nature as the other."[5]

Skilling-Magazin carried a story in March 1868 about the emigrant traffic in Christiania. The journalist found a motley collection of boxes and chests down on the quay. They were marked with Norwegian names and American addresses: Milwaukee, North America, Chicago, Madison, or Minnesota. He saw sacks of potatoes, kettles and pans, mattresses and sheepskin coverlets, jugs of brandy and kegs of herring in a profusion that he described as "chaos." Ice still covered the fjord, and two large ferries conveyed one load after the other to the firm edge of the ice. From there the provisions were pushed out to the ship on long sleds, hoisted on board with block and tackle, lowered into the hatches and distributed. What the emigrants needed on the journey went to the room between the decks; the rest was stowed in the hold.

The journalist also inspected the room between the decks, where the emigrants were busy arranging themselves. He noted that two rows of bunks were fastened to the walls on the starboard and port sides of the ship from aft to fore, with space for five persons in each bunk. He saw children's heads projecting from these family bunks, while the adults were busy dragging their belongings around, hammering in nails and pegs for their bags and their legs of mutton, filling the bunks with straw, and putting their blankets and coverlets in place.[6]

Vinje claimed that the emigrants were merry and happy at their departure, and that old folks talked as if they would be rejuvenated once they got to America. Other reports tell of sadness and solemnity, of a last speech, often by a pastor, and the distribution of religious tracts. Undoubtedly excitement and expectation characterized the young more than the adults, who must have believed that their departure was for the good but who knew they would never again see what they were now leaving behind. They sailed through the fjords and the sounds, the coast disappearing into the sea behind them after some hours or days. Many of them were now at sea for the first time in their lives, with ocean as far as the eye could see.

On Board

The emigrants lived on the ship for at least two months. They prepared their food and ate it on the chests that served as tables and chairs. They tried to keep themselves and their children reasonably clean. They rested and slept in the straw between decks, and came up for fresh air and a minimum of exercise on the deck.

They had to organize their existence in a floating, temporary, miniature society, had to adjust to each other and find modes of cooperation and coexistence within the constricted space allotted them, physically as well as socially. No doubt the restrictions on their activities were felt more acutely by the men than by the women, at least the married ones, who might be more troubled by lack of space than by lack of tasks. It was helpful that whole companies were often from the same communities and neighborhoods: they knew each other and had common customs. But their migration had begun; from day to day, almost without their being aware of it, they were gradually changing. They were no longer the same people.

To judge by letters and other accounts the passage was often remarkably easy. Once seasickness had been mastered, and when the winds were not too stiff, spirits were gay and lively. Experienced skippers tried to provide for the passengers by helping them keep clean, sweeping and scrubbing the decks and airing the clothes, as well as providing exercise and entertainment. There were races, wrestling, and dancing on deck. The captain on the *Tegnér* encouraged dancing when the ship was becalmed. If they danced, they would be sure to get wind, he claimed. So the fiddles were brought out, and the passengers danced waltzes, polkas, and schottisches, as well as the old Norwegian country dances, the "spring dance" and the "halling."

May 17, the national holiday, was often celebrated on board. "Out in the Atlantic we had a jolly encounter one time," said an old skipper on a cargo ship. "We had had a couple of rounds of brandy, and the flag was hoisted, and then we see a big frigate ship sailin' handsome on a northwest course. The Norwegian flag was flyin', they was singin' on board, and the skipper swung the wheel around so we come real near. And I'll be jiggered if it wasn't the frigate ship 'Norway' that was a-comin' from home and was carryin' emigrants to Quebec. The skipper's name was even Solberg. There was a big jubilee goin' on aboard, we could see they was walkin' in a procession on the deck, a-wearin' their national costumes. They must a' been from Valdres, every one of them. I'll tell you our signal flags went up in a hurry, we shouted and roared hurrah, while all the emigrants come over to the rail of the 'Norway.'"[7]

But the weather was not always good, and when the wind blew up, the passengers had to stay below decks. The hatches were battened down, and the room became dark and close, the air bad. If this lasted a long time, it could have dire consequences for the passengers' health. There was a doctor on board only if a Norwegian physician happened to be going to America to study or settle there. The skipper usually had a medicine chest and prescribed what he thought would be useful when anyone complained of headache or loose bowels.

The latter symptom could be a danger signal and might mean that a dysenteric fever was about to break out. Another much feared contagious disease was called "ship's fever," probably paratyphus or typhoid fever. Such diseases were hard to control, for the ships were poorly equipped with toilets, and rarely were there sickrooms where the infected could be isolated. Old people and little children had the least resistance to the strains and hardships of the voyage.

And so the deaths began. Caskets were nailed together, the skipper performed the rites, the flag was lowered to half mast, and the corpse was lowered into the sea. The emigrants seem to have taken the deaths, at least when it was not their kin, as something one had to expect. "Everything went well and happily for the passengers aboard," wrote one in 1851, "if we except that we had seven deaths on the trip over."

In 1845 the *Storting* rejected a bill proposing that passengers be guaranteed a minimum amount of space on board the emigrant vessels, as well as a number of other regulations that would have improved the health and well-being of the passengers. The emigrant traffic continued in the spirit of free competition without regulation by Norwegian law. However, legislation was enacted in the United States and Canada to protect passengers from overcrowding. The number of passengers was proportionate to the ship's tonnage. Canadian regulations were less severe, but even these were often violated by Norwegian skippers.

It appears that the number of overcrowded ships actually increased in the 1850s and that conditions on board worsened. The average time of crossing was shorter because bigger and faster ships were built: in 1860, a year when wind conditions were favorable, it was down to thirty-nine days. Even so the death rate in Norwegian ships went up in the late 1850s, contrary to the case with emigrant ships from Liverpool. The death rate was especially high in those years when emigration suddenly increased and the demand for space was great. No doubt the skippers were tempted to crowd in more emigrants than was defensible. In the great emigration year of 1861 about 200 people died in passage.

The Canadian immigration authorities criticized conditions in 1861 and again in 1862. They threatened to impound Norwegian ships that had too many passengers, and they demanded that Norwegian authorities provide a medical examination of emigrants before they were allowed on board. This pressure led the Ministry of the Interior to propose a bill in 1863 to regulate passenger traffic to other continents. This time the law was adopted.[8]

Economic liberalism reached its peak in Norway in the 1860s, with free trade and free enterprise as its slogans. The law concerning passenger traffic to other continents, as well as regulations on liquor and other commodities, may be considered one of the first rejections of the principle of freedom of trade and contracts. Those who represented the shipping interests, especially those from Bergen, spoke against the bill. But this time the majority decided that a group of people as vulnerable as the emigrants were on an Atlantic voyage had the right to protection and that it was the obligation of the state to provide it.

Arriving in America

But the journey was not over when the emigrants landed in New York or Quebec. They still might have a thousand or more miles to go, using the most varied means of transportation. From New York they moved by steamer, by canal boat, and again by steamer. From Quebec they had to take various steamboats up through the Welland Canal and across the Great Lakes. During the 1850s the Canadian railroad network was developed, and when direct connections were established by rail from Quebec to Detroit, most of the emigrants shortened their travel time considerably by using it.

Traveling by railroad, the "steam wagon," was another new experience. Some were even moved to praise it in doggerel verse. But the trip was rarely an unqualified delight, for emigrant traffic was cheap mass transportation. The cars were poor and old-fashioned; some had been used as cattle cars and had not been properly cleaned. Both in New York and Quebec special trains were provided for emigrants: they were slower than others, because they were often sidetracked when the express trains went by. They had no modern luxuries such as dining cars, let alone sleeping cars.

Yet the worst plagues the emigrants were subjected to on their American journey were not the inconvenient cars but the "runners" and other swindlers. The emigrants were poorly equipped to handle such problems. The runners were agents of various travel bureaus, whose job it was to secure passengers for their firms. In the sharp competition the promises of some agents were less scrupulous than those of others. Emigrants who thought they had been lucky to secure very inexpensive tickets might suddenly discover that their tickets did not cover baggage and that they had to pay extra for it each time they changed vehicles.

Some of the swindlers who preyed on emigrants, often the most dangerous, were their own countrymen. "Norwegian rascals" one person called them, writing that in America they had found the "right scene for their criminal talents." A company from Sogn met a Norwegian in 1853 on the canal boat. He told them he was Pastor Ottesen from Manitowoc, and he led prayers for these people both morning and evening. He preached "so beautifully," functioned as their interpreter, gave them milk and helped them in various ways. He also relieved them of most of their money before he disappeared.[9]

Such occurrences were exceptional, and the emigrants did need the agents, if only to arrange the trip to the interior. It was, therefore, advantageous for them that the states of the Middle West were interested in attracting immigrants and had established immigration offices. For some years after 1854 the state of Wisconsin had a Norwegian representative in Quebec to help inexperienced Norwegians and so win them for his state. Minnesota did the same in the 1860s.

When the Norwegians in the 1850s had come as far as Milwaukee or Chicago, they felt that they had virtually reached their goal. Here they might be met by people they knew, who had come to transport them in a cart or wagon hitched to a team of oxen. Or they could hire a driver: "When we got to Chicago," wrote an emigrant in a letter of 1854, "we hired a driver to take us to Tosten Søgaarden's farm, a distance of twenty English miles, and there we arrived at four o'clock on June 16, and so our journey was over."[10]

In this way, after three or four months of strenuous travel, a company of Norwegians would find themselves in a Norwegian pioneer settlement, bearing a strange-sounding name like "Muskego" or "Koshkonong." For most of them the journey had been a great strain. "I'll never do it again," wrote one of them to his family back home.

Others sent useful advice for those who might come later. When the emigrants had conveyed all the greetings from family and friends, when they had reported all the news from the old home community, and when they had had a chance to rest up, they began the workaday life in the new land.

YEARS OF TRIAL
AND TRIUMPH

B y the early 1840s the Norwegian immigrants had advanced into Wisconsin, some from the Fox River settlement and some directly from Norway. Of the many places where they struck camp and began grappling with the oak groves and the prairie sod only two will be mentioned, each of which was to play an important role.

One of these was the Koshkonong settlement, between Madison and Lake Koshkonong, an Indian name twisted by Norwegian tongues into "Kaskeland" and by later jokers into "Kakseland," literally "land of the bigwigs." This was the larger settlement, and it kept growing as new pioneers came into the area. The other was Muskego, close to one of the immigrants' ports of entry, Milwaukee. It never became a large Norwegian center, but the settlement was important in the 1840s, not only because it was a way station for the immigrants but also because it was the seedbed of many developments. The first Norwegian church was erected there; the first Norwegian newspaper was published there.

The leading figure in Muskego was Even Heg, a financially well-off farmer from Lier, southwest of Oslo, who in Norway had been a friend of Hans Nielsen Hauge's. Shortly after his arrival in 1839 Even Heg not only built himself a house to live in but a large barn as well. This barn filled many needs in the years that followed: as meeting room, as church, as sleeping quarters for the newcomers who streamed in. Another of the Muskego leaders, Søren Bache, recorded this influx each year in his diary. In August 1843, the barn was so overcrowded with newcomers that some of them had to sleep on the ground outside, and Bache worried about more crowds in the time ahead. On July 9, 1845, he noted that the first Norwegians had appeared: "During the next two or three months we may hope for weekly contingents of immigrants from Norway." Another time he reported that "three loads of people from Hallingdal" had arrived and passed on, except for two families. In one of these a child had caught smallpox and died the next morning. In the other a child was born some hours later. Both events took place in the barn.[1] Sometimes newcomers stayed because they could not afford to go on, and the families of Muskego had to house them in their little cabins.

When a company of immigrants arrived in Muskego or Koshkonong in the 1840s, weary and worn from many months of traveling, they were not impressed by the housing offered them. If they had had high expectations, they were certainly disappointed. Except for Even Heg few Norwegians had built outbuildings other than an occasional paltry shed, and the homes were small, one-room, timbered houses — log cabins. They were no more than twelve to fourteen feet square, and they were built in haste. No carefully selected, well-dried timber awaited the pioneers. They had had to chop and join without a proper gauge, and if there were cracks between the logs, they were filled with clay, plaster, and pieces of wood. In winter this filling sometimes froze and fell out, leaving holes in the wall "so large that cats could pass freely in and out."[2]

The newcomers also discovered that some of their countrymen had ensconced themselves in dugouts in the hillside; only the front of the "house" was made of wood. Such dugouts were cozy in the winter and cool in the summer; but they were dark and usually even narrower than the log cabins. As late as the end of the 1840s many Norwegians in Koshkonong or Muskego still lived in dugouts; only a few could afford to build houses larger and better than the little cabins.

The furnishings were rough. Beds made of unplaned boards were nailed to the wall, oak stumps served as chairs, and the great emigrant chest was still the table, as it had been on the voyage. Here the newcomers were welcome beneath a hospitable roof: however plain, it was a good place to be.

Disease

The new arrivals were not only weary: some of them carried infections from the journey — from light intestinal infections to more dangerous diseases like dysentery and typhoid fever. It was not easy to keep disease from spreading, for it was impossible to maintain the necessary personal hygiene under crowded conditions. Besides, the settlers usually drew their drinking water from lakes, slow-running creeks, or shallow wells, with great risk for further infection.[3]

Worst of all was cholera, which also came from Europe with the immigrants. About 1850 there were three years of cholera in Wisconsin and Illinois, and in all three the Norwegian settlements were ravaged. "It was a time when one heard the carpenter's hammer blows on the coffins night and day," it was reported from Koshkonong in one of the cholera years, and the tales from Fox River and Muskego were equally somber.

In addition to the diseases that the Norwegians brought with them from the journey or that spread from other immigrants, they were plagued by an indigenous disease that took many lives and disabled many more. Malaria, called "cold fever" in Norwegian because of the chills that characterized the disease, made its victims shake. The usual American name for it was "fever and ague," which the Norwegians adopted and called "ægeren." The malaria mosquito thrived in marshes and brooks, where it remained a threat in states like Wisconsin and Illinois until the late ninteenth century.

Of all the Norwegian settlements in the 1840s Muskego was the most severely ravaged by the disease. According to contemporary accounts seventy persons died there in 1841 and nearly as many two years later, when very many newcomers had to be housed there. Muskego had only 500 or 600 inhabitants, so that 140 deaths meant that nearly a fourth of the population was taken. Søren Bache wrote: "There has been severe illness here this fall since the immigrants from Norway came last summer, with many burials in the churchyard, some days as many as three or four."[4] The suffering suggested by this short notation in his diary is given concrete expression in the story of an American minister who visited Muskego in this fatal fall of 1843. He walked from house to house and found sick people everywhere. In one place he found a father and a daughter, who were shaking with an attack of malaria and were trying to warm themselves over a few bits of coal and taking turns drinking warm water from a copper kettle standing beside the fire. He found the rest of the family "huddled together in bunks filled with prairie hay and with nothing to shelter them from the rigorous cold of a December day save a few sheepskins sewed together." He saw no signs of food in the house, aside from a "wooden bowl, partly filled with what I took to be shorts, kneaded and prepared for baking." In these years the Norwegians were dependent upon aid and support from their American neighbors.[5]

It is easy to understand why some emigrants wrote disconsolate and discouraging letters home under such conditions. One wonders why more of them did not do so: perhaps they felt it was useless to complain. They had made the decision to break with their homeland. They had no money to pay for the trip back, and no one else could help them return.

So there was only one thing to do: keep working and hope for better times. As the years *did* get better and circumstances improved, a lettered person from Drammen named Johansen, who was a store clerk, wrote a reply to "the all-too-hasty reports" that had been sent to Norway "in a time of sorrow." This reply, known as the "Muskego manifesto," was signed by eighty men; it stated that the emigrants had no regrets. "We have no hopes of obtaining riches; but we live under a liberal government in a fruitful land." By diligence and industry they now had achieved the necessary income which gave them the "prospect of a carefree old age." They poked fun at newcomers who complained because they did not have the kind of food they had in Norway: that was "misplaced homesickness." And they cited the Bible: "Be ye fruitful and multiply and replenish the earth."[6]

After the mid-1850s there are no more accounts of distress or catastrophic epidemics. Health control and quarantine regulations in the immigrant ports were enforced with greater effectiveness, and the next great cholera epidemic in the 1860s did not reach the Midwest. Malaria was no longer a serious threat in the drier west of Minnesota and Iowa. As in Norway, measles, scarlet fever, and diphtheria took their toll, especially among the children. "My grandparents lost eight children in a diphtheria epidemic in the 1870s," reported a Norwegian woman from southern Minnesota.

For a long time tuberculosis was widespread in Norwegian areas of America, and the emigrants may have brought this with them, as they brought leprosy. But the leprosy vanished with those who had been infected in Norway, a sign that living conditions and sanitation had improved since leprosy is contagious only for people whose resistance is low.[7] For this early period there are no statistics that provide certain information about births and deaths among the emigrants. Not until the end of the century are there statistics for the various ethnic groups. By that time the mortality rate of Norwegian-Americans was lower than that of the American population as a whole and about the same as for Norwegians in the homeland.[8]

Settlements in the Wilderness

From the close of the 1840s Norwegian settlement consisted of leap-frogging inhabited areas into new wilderness. A thin stream flowed northward in Wisconsin, but the main current was northwest toward the tributaries of the Mississippi River. Soon the first Norwegians crossed the river into the state of Iowa and the territory of Minnesota, which in 1858 was organized as a state and accepted into the Union.

All these leaps were made from the older settlements. They were often preceded by reconnoitering expeditions of pioneers who had lived some years in America, and had experience and could judge the quality of the soil and other factors. These pioneers became the leaders when the expedition got underway. Some were groups of considerable size, often with a majority of people from the same community or district in Norway.

Pastor C. L. Clausen planned and organized one such expedition. It started from Rock Prairie, one of the very earliest Wisconsin settlements, and proceeded far into Iowa, to the Cedar River. Forty families, adults and youngsters with a hundred head of cattle, started off in thirty covered wagons. The journey lasted three weeks, with most of the people walking all the way and driving the cattle. The smallest children could ride but had to be carried over brooks and creeks. Arriving at their destination, they were alone on the prairie, except when a friendly Indian occasionally came by, stopped and looked at them, and thanked them for gifts of bread. Soon the Norwegians discovered that other white people had been there before them. Some distance away in what later became Osage County, these people had driven down stakes with their names on to show that they had made a claim on the land. Nevertheless there was plenty of land left for the Norwegians, and they founded a flourishing settlement, known as the St. Ansgar settlement, Mitchell County.[9]

When a new colony, large or small, was founded, it attracted people from the older Norwegian areas in Wisconsin and even more newcomers from Norway, from the family, the neighborhood, or the valley. In this way relatively compact new areas of Norwegian settlement arose in western Wisconsin, northern Iowa, and southern Minnesota. Names of congregations testified to the origins of the settlers. In Minnesota Vang Prairie was settled by people from Valdres with its Vang parish, Holden by people from Telemark with a parish of the same name. There are still places here called by Norwegian names like Eidsvold, Gol, Toten; Dovre and Oslo are close together in Goodhue County, Minnesota.

In the 1850s Norwegians had begun to settle in cities. Even in the 1830s a few had begun to make their homes in the little cluster of houses known as Chicago, mostly because they did not have the money to go on and needed to find work wherever they could. Others had handicraft skills that were useful in the rapid economic growth which began about this time. In 1860 about 1,100 of Chicago's inhabitants had been born in Norway; most of them were families. Nowhere else in Illinois outside the Fox River settlement were there more Norwegian families than in Chicago. Norwegians and their families were also living in many other small towns: Stoughton and Westby in Wisconsin and Decorah in Iowa were developing into small Norwegian centers. But for the time being the urban influx was modest: the great land-taking on the prairie characterized Norwegian settlement before the Civil War.

In the beginning the Norwegians did not like the open prairie and instead chose sites near brooks and creeks that provided water and near woods that provided timber and wood. Thus they often missed the most fertile soil and it took longer to produce cash crops. It also made the task of clearing more arduous. But the wooded riverbanks and water more nearly resembled the valleys they had left. They reminded them of native hills and heaths, thus providing nonmaterial values that cannot be reckoned.

A few early Norwegian immigrants had enough means to pay for their land as well as to buy two or three cows, a pair of oxen, and the equipment that would enable them to start breaking soil. But most of them had to be satisfied with putting down their stakes on an unoccupied spot, registering their claim, and then looking around for work that would bring in cash and the necessary capital. Some found work digging canals, a strenuous and unhealthy occupation; others earned money cutting timber or working at lumber mills or in the mines. Even when they had settled down and managed to break the sod in their first little field, the husband often had to look for work in the winter.

> We split rails till the forest re-echoed.
> And the chips looked like sparks as they flew;
> You should see how the trees came a-crashing;
> We cut hundreds before we were through.

So says the Wisconsin Ballad, a Norwegian-American song from the 1870s.[10]

Additional cash was necessary, but as much as possible the settlers tried to manage by producing their own food and other goods. They usually bought pigs as soon as they could, for pigs were easy to keep: they fed themselves on acorns and hazel nuts. It is said that pork became "the firm foundation" of their diet in the early period; many of the letters home mention the rich diet, which included pork several times a day.

Otherwise they maintained their native cuisine: making porridge, baking flatbread, churning butter and making cheese, salting and drying their meat. When the Norwegian jurist Munch Ræder came to Muskego in 1847, he met people from Tinn who gave him a friendly reception. "Honest and simple folk," they wore the costume of their valley and spoke its dialect. They offered their guest "excellent milk" and whatever else the household could produce. But only when they were quite sure they were dealing with a real Norwegian, did they bring out their flatbread. They had held it back because the "yankees" always "made fun of it."[11]

Hunting and fishing supplied additional fresh food in the household as long as most of the land was still uncultivated: many praised the delicious taste of the prairie hen. On the prairie one could also pick wild strawberries and plums. Another American novelty was the sugar maple; the sap could be boiled down to make syrup, thus providing sweets.

Norwegian settlers made candles from tallow, boiled their own soap, and in many places they spun and wove the wool of their own sheep. They made many of their own tools, even carts and wagons, including the "kubberulle," an all-wooden wagon, except for the iron mountings that held the wooden wheels together. One well-to-do settler with foresight wrote home that he had secured the "wagon box" of a wagon for "the wheels I brought with me from Norway."[12]

This self-sufficiency was forced upon them by the wilderness; it was something all settlers without capital in isolated settlements had to endure for a certain time, and the Norwegians were prepared for it, since they knew it from home. But on the first day they could drive their ox teams to the nearest town and sell their first loads of wheat, they were happy indeed. This might be a trip that would take several days each way, and they usually drove in large groups.

They welcomed the railroad as it spread out over the prairie. When it reached the nearest village, the settlers had a closer contact with the growing markets in the eastern states and in Europe, which brought in more shining dollars. A new age was dawning, with new problems of prices and marketing, and the time would come when the farmers would look on the railroad companies as greedy profiteers.

In 1863 a Norwegian physician, Dr. I. A. Holmboe, made a study tour among the Norwegians in America. Knowing how poor his countrymen had been in the 1840s in Muskego and Koshkonong, he was impressed by their progress. "It is now a pleasure," he wrote, "to travel around in the somewhat older settlements and see what a reward their labors have given them. They have fine, large farms, many of them several hundred acres in size, which give them wheat and corn in abundance and with an ease that we in Norway have never known. They have put up large, splendid houses, and having now the means to satisfy the demands of a more civilized life, they are quick to respond. One can travel through such settlements, where the men came without a penny some fifteen or twenty years ago, where they have had nothing but the labor of their hands to rely on and have never sought a shortcut to fortune by speculations, but where they now have farms that are worth, with house and furnishings, from four to six or even ten to twelve thousand dollars. Americans say about the Norwegians that they are hard workers."[13] The doctor's conclusions were that most emigrants led a simple, unrefined, but abundant and civilized middle-class life.

There are other such optimistic accounts from the 1860s about prosperity and the transformation of the "desert into fruitful meadows and glorious fields." But the cost had been heavy, and many had fallen by the wayside. Yet new hosts kept going out into the wilderness west and north to struggle with it and take on the trials of pioneer life. From northern Iowa and southern Minnesota the trail led on to the western and especially the northwestern part of Minnesota. Some Norwegians had reached the Dakota Territory before 1860. In the 1870s and '80s this territory, which in 1888 was divided into the two new states of North and South Dakota, became the goal for most of those who were looking for land. The Red River Valley was especially favored by Norwegians, and here they had to reconcile themselves to a treeless, wind-whipped prairie. Now a sod hut or a shed covered with tarpaper and a few laths became the first house, and they had to rely on buffalo chips and prairie grass for fuel.

Here, too, the pioneers had difficult and laborious early years, but the development was more rapid in the 1870s and '80s than it had been in Wisconsin a generation earlier. The railroad came at the same time and sometimes even before the settler. Implements were better and more effective; in a few years they had a reasonably good wheat crop to sell, and so their most pressing material needs were met.

In this way the Norwegians, and Americans, Swedes, Germans, and many other peoples, took part in the tremendous migration west which is so crucial a part of American history in the nineteenth century. It concerned them very little that they forced the Indians back and deprived them of their hunting grounds. They saw themselves as representatives of a higher civilization which was bringing the earth — God's gift — under cultivation.

A PIONEER SOCIETY

In the winter of 1853–54 a Norwegian pastor's wife, Elisabeth Koren, sat in a log house in northern Iowa writing her diary. Her husband had received a letter of call from a Norwegian congregation on Washington Prairie, and just before Christmas 1853 the young couple arrived amid snow and icy blasts at the Norwegian settlement which was no more than four years old. No parsonage had been built yet, and the Korens lived temporarily with a family of mother, father, and two small children. For some three months the two families shared the single-room cottage.

Elisabeth Koren never tried to give a systematic description of life and work on Washington Prairie. She was more concerned with her husband, Wilhelm, and his long, toilsome journeys than with the rural society around her. But she was interested in people, and for months at a time Norwegian peasants were the only company the city girl from Larvik had. The diary therefore provides many glimpses of daily life in a Norwegian settlement near the frontier.[1]

She related that the cabin was about fifteen by sixteen feet and consisted of one room with a loft. One-third of the room was divided from the rest by a chintz curtain. Behind this curtain stood two beds, which in turn were separated by a curtain, so that each family had its own "bedroom," with half a window for each. The rest of the room was a living and dining room at one end and a kitchen at the other. It was simply but quite well equipped, with two regular tables, a chair, three stools, and a walnut cabinet. The windows had white curtains, and on the wall hung a clock, a mirror, and a big pair of sheep shears. Above one window the man of the house, Erik, had put up a shelf, on which lay some books, candlesticks, an oil lamp, and the bolt of a flatiron. The pastor nailed up a shelf over the other window for his books and writing materials.

In the kitchen nook the focal point was the stove and all that went with it. On the walls hung several frying pans and a coffee burner, and "from the ceiling a series of kettles, coffee pots, a flatiron, a tin funnel with matches, our candle snuffer, and besides there is a crossbar on which hang all their 'things' as well as washrags and I don't know what more," Mrs. Koren relates.[2] There was also a kitchen counter with two cupboards and a cellar trapdoor. The whole room was papered with newspapers from the ceiling down. The lowest log was still bare, but Helene, the woman of the house, was diligently covering this with newspapers after they were read.

In the loft the remaining possessions of the family were stored with the food supply. There was a big bin for wheat, pork barrels and flour sacks, besides large and small chests, clothing, and a great many tools. Erik worked as a carpenter when he had the time.

Helene was in command of the domestic activities. She fried pork for practically every meal, baked bread and biscuits, cooked milk gruel, and made pancakes. She treated her family and the pastoral guests to traditional Norwegian spareribs on Christmas Eve. Now and then she pacified the children by giving them syrup, and Mrs. Koren noted their syrup moustaches with a certain distaste.

There was a good deal of traffic in the house at this time, because it was Christmas and because people wanted to see and talk with the pastor. Helene treated the guests: she put on a tablecloth, fetched beer from the basement, cookies and *fattigmann* (a deep-fried delicacy) from the loft. The guests were often asked to dinner or supper as well, and occasionally they got cream porridge (*rømmegrøt*).

Helene washed clothes every Monday and used lye in the water to get them clean; then she handscoured the floor with "the good lye water." She helped care for the animals: Mrs. Koren repeatedly mentions that Helene had gone out to "water the critters." She sewed and mended hose, churned butter, and made whey cheese. This was a well-equipped house and a well-ordered household, which presumably was the reason that the pastor and his wife were quartered there.

Mrs. Koren gradually learned that things were not as good elsewhere. She visited houses in which spaces between the logs were so large that it was hard to keep warm in winter, even when old and young huddled around the stove. She stepped on loose planks that teetered under her, and she slept in lofts where the sky peeked in through the roofboards. She discovered that twelve to fifteen people lived in houses that were smaller than the one in which she had found shelter.

It appears from the diary that cows and pigs usually went about in the open during the winter. One had to guard both the washing and the windows from inquisitive cows, and the pigs "galloped" after Elisabeth and Helene when they were out walking. Many had chickens and some must have had sheep, for the pastor's wife was given wool and sat on sheepskins when she visited other settlements with her husband. In addition they tucked hay around her legs to protect her from the cold.

The pastor obtained a horse, and some others also had horses, but as yet it was mostly oxen that were hitched up when the settlers went anywhere on their sleds. These had sides on which planks were laid to sit on. In the same way they laid planks on chunks of log when services were held in a home, providing seats for as many as possible. Even so some had to go up in the loft and listen to the pastor from there. The women brought their children with them, even the smallest ones, since they could not leave them. If the children got too restless or whimpered too loudly, the mothers would go outside with them.

Time and again Elisabeth Koren noted in her diary that she was met with kindness wherever she went. She was welcomed with a cup of coffee, a glass of milk, or a mug of beer when she arrived, or she might be invited to dinner. Sometimes she was invited to stay overnight if it was getting dark. Now and then Helene also took her children with her and went to visit neighbors. When a young boy died, the whole neighborhood gathered for the funeral: the pastor's wife was invited but excused herself. Afterward she wondered if she had offended the family by rejecting the invitation, but she learned that they had not taken it to heart. For her own part she was glad she had not been present, since it appeared that the funeral had been large and lively. People had enjoyed getting together and talking with one another. Mrs. Koren wondered about the psychology of Norwegian peasants: she could not understand how they could speak of a death in their family so quietly and soberly.

When Elisabeth Koren was home alone with Erik and Helene, she read aloud to them. But they could also read. They read the newspaper, Helene following each line with her finger, Erik reading somewhat more easily. Sometimes he read a sermon aloud to his wife. When several men gathered in the living room, they talked about buying land or trading horses, while they puffed on their pipes and spat on Helene's hand-scoured floor. But above all they now discussed problems that concerned the congregation and the pastor. They held meetings and chose a committee, and they sent around subscription lists to secure money for the pastor's land. They planned the work needed to produce timber for a parsonage and a church.

The diary also provides a few glimpses of the men's daily work. Erik was often in the woods in winter, chopping wood and cutting timber. He winnowed his wheat with a machine and went to Decorah to get some of it ground at the mill there. In April he dragged the field and sowed the grain, and at haying time he swung his scythe. A little later, when the hay was being stacked, Mrs. Koren saw a pioneer wife working with her husband, helping to stamp down the hay into a firm and solid mass. Another summer job was to break more soil. Several pairs of oxen were hitched to the plow, and they were urged to "go 'long." If this did not help, the whip was used, the oxen were driven on, and the prairie sod was cut and turned.

The diary gives us a picture of life in a little society characterized by simplicity and contentment, where there is no longer any want, far less any distress, and where health conditions are generally good. Now and then someone still suffered an attack of malaria, and the young boy who died may have been tubercular. Cholera did not reach Washington Prairie in 1854; but the report of its ravages farther east was enough to alarm anxious souls.

The diary also gives us a picture of a close-knit little community where the family was the smallest and the strongest social unit. This must have been true not only on Washington Prairie but elsewhere also in the Norwegian settlements in America. It is even possible that at this time the family in America was a more important working entity than it was in Norway, since it was so difficult and expensive to secure hired help. Newcomers could work for a time, but they gave little enduring assistance. The most stable worker was the newcomer who was a member of the family, since kin and kinship was a powerful bond, as many reports tell us. But even relatives had eventually to find land or other employment of their own.

The Neighborhood

The second unit in importance was the neighborhood — the people who lived within easy reach. In America the neighborhood had to be created, but through common effort and daily practice it grew into a fellowship that gave protection and security in a strange world. Neighbors helped each other set up houses and harvest crops; they sometimes bought breaking plows together and lent each other oxen for the plowing. When prairie fires threatened, they went out together to take measures that would bring them under control. We may say that they transported their Norwegian custom of collective help (*dugnad*) from their old to their new neighborhoods and this easily because it was also a custom of American pioneering.

In many settlements Norwegians also made an effort to preserve as many as possible of the old rural customs associated with the great holidays of the year and of life. Christmas started on Christmas Eve, as in Norway, and as soon as they could afford it, they ate both spareribs and rice pudding. They celebrated Christmas together down to the Twelfth Day, and in some places young people practiced "Christmas fooling" (*julebukk*). The old fiddle and the old dances had come with them across the sea to the new homes of people from fjord and dale.

The neighborhood evidently functioned as an "invitation group" (*bedarlag*), as Mrs. Koren experienced it in Iowa. At funerals a special "inviter" (*bedarmann*) went around the community, and the guests came loaded with food — *lefse*, butter, cheese, cream, cream porridge, and baked goods. They were treated to food and a drink both before and after the ceremony at the church. These customs were opposed by the Haugeans, but in some of the compact settlements of Norwegians in Wisconsin they lasted to the end of the nineteenth century and were taken along even farther west. A probate record from North Dakota beginning in 1878 was kept in Norwegian. The first case concerned the estate of a deceased Norwegian. His funeral cost only $14; $2 went to Sven Heskin and Erik Moen "for the grave," and $9 paid for a gallon and a half of whiskey and great quantities of sugar and syrup, which presumably were used for making beer. The guests who were going to drink all this must have brought their own food to the funeral.[3]

The neighborhoods of the immigrants could never become as close-knit and intimate as an old neighborhood in Norway. They were not born into them as they were at home, and even if people from the same community tended to settle together, a settlement of people from Hardanger or Voss was never "pure." There were always people from other communities or even from other countries among them. The Norwegian-American neighborhood was determined more by situation than the old had been, and it did not in the same way encompass the lives of its inhabitants. In addition, people were more mobile: newcomers moved in, stayed awhile, and moved on; settlers sold their small property and used the money to start again on larger property farther west.

In both countries the neighborhood community broke up and was replaced by other, more specialized forms of social organization. In America this change coincided with the gradual adaptation to the larger American society which changed the emigrants into Norwegian-Americans. As late as the 1930s elderly farmers in North Dakota recalled with some sadness the solidarity and fellowship of the old days, though they did not deny that pioneer life even in their time had been harsh. Solidarity had given them support in their task of conquering nature, of bringing the earth under cultivation, and in their encounter with the greater American society.

Religious Leaders

The neighborhood could not supply all the social needs of the settlers, which first became evident in their religious life. The emigrants needed a minister. They came from a land with a state church, which most of them had taken for granted in the homeland. They were accustomed to having the pastor baptize their children, confirm the young, and consecrate marriages. They wanted a religious ritual at their entrance into as well as at their departure from life. Now they

had come to a land without a state church, a land swarming with
religious bodies. All these were private, voluntary associations in
which the members themselves defrayed the expenses of church and
pastor and the other tasks of the congregation and the church. All the
religious bodies carried on missionary activities, or, if you will, propaganda, to win converts. The Norwegians had already encountered
this influence in Fox River, and quite a few had joined the Baptists,
the Methodists, or the Mormons. But most Norwegians stayed with
the Lutheran religion they knew from their childhood, which laymen
helped to keep alive in the early, pastorless period. They conducted
prayer meetings, performed home baptisms and other religious rituals. Yet the need for an ordained pastor and a church organization
was soon recognized.

The first company that we know tried to obtain a pastor from Norway was the group that sailed from Drammen in 1839 with Ansten
Nattestad as a leader. Before departure they addressed the Ministry
of Ecclesiastical Affairs and asked for the ordination of a theological
candidate, Peter Valeur, who was willing to come to them. But a few
months later Ansten Nattestad wrote from America that although his
group still wished to have a pastor, they were so few and lived so far
apart that they would not be able to support a pastor of their own.
This incident reveals that the emigrants in America faced a task requiring cooperation and organization beyond the neighborhood and
perhaps even beyond the individual settlement.[4]

Most religious leaders of the emigrants around 1840 were
influenced by Haugeanism. Foremost among these was Elling Eielsen
Sundve from Voss. In Norway he had traveled from one end of the
country to the other as a lay preacher, and people had bowed down
acknowledging their sins under his vigorous sermons. Elling Eielsen
was more sharply opposed to the state church of Norway and its
ministers than most of the Haugeans of his time. He did not become
gentler as the years passed and as he met more and more Norwegian
university-trained pastors in America. The sight of a ministerial cas-
sock and ruff was enough to inflame him. In his eyes the religion of
Norwegian theologians consisted in masses, gowns, and dead ceremonies, while they allowed "the miserable people to tumble about in
their unresurrected lives" and winked at their "drunkenness, curs-
ing, swearing, dancing and fiddling, and other noisy pleasures."[5]

Elling wished to counteract all such sinful delights, and he went to work as soon as he had oriented himself among the emigrants. He had Luther's Minor Catechism translated into English and Erik Pontoppidan's "Explanation" to the Catechism (*Truth unto Godliness,* 1737) printed in Norwegian. In the fall of 1843 he took the decisive step of having himself ordained as a minister, at the request of his supporters. A German Lutheran pastor performed the ordination. Now Eielsen could try to lead his emigrated countrymen on the narrow path through conversion and penitence to his pietistic form of Christianity. During the next few years he was constantly on the move, conducting prayer meetings, performing religious services, and encouraging his followers to organize congregations.

It was not long before he encountered competition. In the same month he was ordained, a young Danish-born student of theology, C. L. Clausen, arrived in the Muskego settlement. He had lived in Norway for a time and had there encountered Søren Bache's father, the Haugean merchant Tollef Bache. He had actually intended to work as a teacher of religion among the emigrants, but the settlers in Muskego insisted that they needed a pastor more than a teacher. At their urging he got himself ordained and was formally called as their pastor.

Six months later the first "state church pastor" arrived. This was Johannes W. C. Dietrichson, a man who firmly supported the dignity and authority of the pastoral office, and who was greatly concerned to transport as much as possible of the forms and rituals of the Norwegian church to the emigrants. From the beginning he looked askance at Elling Eielsen's preaching and openly expressed his antagonism. To him Elling was a "zealot," a dangerous man who on many points deviated from the teachings of Luther.

In the homeland the decisions of Clausen and Dietrichson to make America their field of activity were viewed as an expression of a growing interest in missionary work. Both had considered joining the Reverend Hans Schreuder in his African mission among the Zulus, but chose America because of reports concerning the difficult religious situation among the emigrants. This was probably why several Norwegian theologians responded to calls from America in the next ten or fifteen years. Dietrichson tried to win various kinds of support in Norway for his clerical activities in Wisconsin. A request to the

Ministry of Ecclesiastical Affairs for economic help was rejected. But he did receive a grant to cover travel expenses. His detailed report on the congregational activity at Koshkonong indicates that he also received some private gifts, and that bookdealer Dybwad in Christiania and merchant Helland in Bergen sent him hymnals, catechisms, testaments, and other religious books. The Norwegians in Muskego also got economic support from Norway, primarily from Tollef Bache and his relatives in Drammen.[6]

Establishing a Church

For the emigrants the formation of congregations, which occurred rapidly from the middle of the 1840s, meant that they united, each group in its own locality, around larger enterprises to bring their church life into order. They founded congregations; they gathered money to build churches, often hewing the timber and building them with their own hands. They issued a call to a pastor and made agreements with him concerning a parsonage, salary, and the number of services he was to conduct. In frontier settlements there were few congregations that had a minister to themselves. The pastor had to care for several congregations and spent much of his time on horseback, in a buggy, or on a sled traveling miserable roads between the congregations. The days were usually long for him in the settlements, which he visited only a few days each year. Communion for sixty persons, churching after childbirth for twenty-one women, twenty-one baptisms, catechizing and confirming six young people, besides high mass and service — all in one day after two wakeful nights, as the Reverend Johan Storm Munch reported in 1857 to his brother in Norway.[7]

The church became a focus in the life of the local society: always filled at services and a meeting place after services. Even if all of them did not come to hear the minister, they could meet people and discuss other matters, "such as possible horse trades, the assignment of road work, hiring thrashers or arranging for mutual help, or just hearing the day's news."[8]

Thus a church organization was established on the religious heritage from Norway, whether low church and stemming from Haugeanism or high church and originating in the state church. But the organization was adapted to conditions in America and was based on the active participation of its members.

The clash of high and low church views had been marked in Norway, and it was, unavoidably, even greater in America, where the framework of the state church and its traditions were shattered. In addition, the early leaders on both sides were uncompromising men who would not yield an inch in their convictions. Within both wings congregations united in "synods," which had constitutions and bylaws. Leaders attacked one another and conducted incessant feuds about dogma and doctrine by mouth and pen. For many years compromise was difficult, and one church after another split.

Whether low church or high church, the Norwegian Lutheran synods made their appeals to Norwegians throughout the Midwest, and the founding of the synods became the first enterprise that can be called Norwegian-American. In time it proved to be the greatest organizational work of the emigrants.

The Norwegian-Language Press

One other bond helped unite the local Norwegian communities in the period before the Civil War, the Norwegian-language press.[9] As early as 1844–45 "some of the enlightened" among "the Norwegian farmers" in America had been discussing the possibility of establishing a Norwegian newspaper "in America, this land of newspapers." The model was American, and "enlightened farmer" Even Heg in Muskego was the man who directed the establishment of the first small paper, *Nordlyset* ("The Northern Light"), in 1847. He and Søren Bache provided money for a printing press and James Denoon Reymert became the editor. Reymert had grown up in Farsund, Norway, but had a Scotch mother and had come to America after living several years in Scotland. His knowledge of English and Norwegian, and his interest in American politics made him ideally suited for the position of editor. *Nordlyset* quickly got a few hundred subscribers; but this was not enough, and the paper survived only a year or two. The next several attempts to establish newspapers met the same fate. After a few years the editors had to give up because there was not enough money.

At the end of 1851 a group in which the university-educated pastors played a large role organized a press society and a stock company with a working capital of $2,000, divided into 200 shares, to publish a newspaper. The paper was called *Emigranten* ("The Emigrant") and bore a demanding motto, "Unity, Courage, Persistence." There was not much unity in the Norwegian-American press during the next few years; religious and other differences filled the columns. But the supporters of *Emigranten* persisted and made the paper a focal point among the Norwegian immigrants of the 1850s. Competitors emerged and vanished, while the subscription list of *Emigranten* grew and by 1860 reached nearly 4,000.

Emigranten carried news from many settlements. In its columns contributors discussed the advantages and deficiencies of various areas of the United States. They were granted space when they called attention to new areas suitable for settlement and when they reported advances in the older settlements. The paper also kept its readers informed of significant events in Norway, and from time to time it carried articles about Norwegian history and culture. Historian P. A. Munch, poet Henrik Wergeland, and folklorist Peder Christen Asbjørnsen were presented to the readers. From 1859 on the paper printed the classic rural tales of Bjørnstjerne Bjørnson, *Synnøve Solbakken*, *A Happy Boy*, and *Arne*, shortly after their first publication in Norway.

News from the settlements as well as from Norway helped strengthen the sense of unity among the Norwegians beyond the individual settlement. They could see and read that they were Norwegians in America — after a time quite numerous — and that they had a common cultural heritage.

At the same time *Emigranten* and other Norwegian newspapers worked at another task, that of making their readers familiar with American society, its history and political structure. All the papers were political papers, taking stands in the political debates; slavery and free soil became burning issues in the 1850s. Before the elections, the papers agitated for candidates from various parties, and they did so with such zeal that at times one suspects that some of them, especially the short-lived ones, were subsidized by the respective parties.

Emigranten steered a cautious course in its first years, but after the Republican Party was founded in 1854, with Abraham Lincoln as the leading figure in the Midwest and a program that called for the granting of soil to settlers and the abolition of slavery, the newspaper wholeheartedly supported this party. No Gallup polls were taken that can tell us how concerned the readers of *Emigranten* were with the issues of soil and slavery or what stands they took. But it is obvious that in the 1850s the Norwegians in America were already numerous enough so that the political parties were interested in their votes. In 1859 there were Norwegian-born candidates on the electoral lists in Wisconsin, Iowa, and Minnesota. In Wisconsin both the Democratic and the Republican parties ran Norwegian candidates for the state office of prison director. The Republican candidate won by a great majority: his name was Hans Christian Heg. He was a son of Even Heg in Muskego, where he had arrived at the age of ten. He had been active in the local government of Muskego from youth, and he would win fame among his countrymen during the Civil War. His election in 1859 suggests that the Norwegians had begun to interest themselves in the great political questions of their new country and that they took a stand on them in elections. Some of them, at any rate, had taken the first step in the difficult process of adaptation. They had begun to strike roots.

ENCOUNTERING
AMERICANS

E mphasizing the significance of the Norwegian aspect of American settlement and the small units of social life may have given the false impression that Norwegians were isolated from the American society around them. It is true that the Norwegianness of the locality helped them maintain a sense of their identity and keep alive the bond between what Rølvaag would later call the "old Adam" and the "new Adam." But American society forced itself upon them — it was there and the settlers had to take it into account. Indeed there is no reason to think that most of them desired total isolation.

Norwegians were not like the Hutterites or the Mennonites, people who for centuries had accustomed themselves to being different, to enforcing absolute conformity to their own life-style, and to rejecting consistently all impulses from the outside. Most Norwegians had gone to America hoping for better circumstances, a richer human existence. Most were disposed to accept the conditions they faced, prepared to receive new impressions, and inclined to take a positive view of the new life offered them.

They encountered Americans when they registered their claims at the land office and when they paid for their land. When they went to the nearest town to sell their wheat, they had to deal with Americans, who alone could furnish what they needed — from salt, sugar, and coffee to oxen, plows, and other implements. Most of those who had no means of their own had to seek out American employers to earn what they needed for their livelihood, especially before the passage of the Homestead Act in 1862.

Even Heg and Søren Bache started a store for their countrymen in Muskego, and a few other Norwegians did the same in other villages. In time they dominated the trade in small towns where the Norwegian community was large enough to provide them with customers. Here and there some started sawmills or grain mills. But the main rule was that trade and processing raw materials were the business of Americans, to which "foreigners" were not admitted.[1]

It is also evident that the Norwegians, like all other immigrants who knew no English and were ignorant of conditions, had a sense of their own inferiority. Even in the Midwest — where society was simple and class lines were elastic, where authorities welcomed immigrants because the country needed manpower for its development — they were not accepted on an equal footing. They had to take the heaviest jobs, which the natives refused to do. As the Wisconsin ballad put it:

> But whenever we needed some money
> We would work for the Yankees a time;
> We would labor and slave to our utmost;
> Were so willing 'twas almost a crime.

They were stung by the realization that ignorance of the language exposed them to laughter or at best to kindly condescension. As the ballad goes on:

> 'Twas a long pull learning the language,
> And our spirits were often downcast;
> When a Yankee would ask what our names were
> We would most often answer him, "Yas!"[2]

The English Language

The foreign, meaningless language was a formidable barrier for many, especially the elderly. In the first months it was sound without sense, and only gradually could they pick out words that told them something. Yet it was not long before the first American words were adopted and entered the Norwegian language. This was inevitable, for the words expressed realities they had not known in Norway. The landscape was different: "prairie" was quickly adopted, and for rivers, which were not like the Norwegian *elver*, they used the English word, lightly adapted in Norwegian as *røver*. When a Norwegian went to the land office to register his title to a piece of untilled soil, he was performing an act he had never performed in Norway and so it came to be called *å kleime land* (" to claim land") or *å faile en kleim* ("to file a claim").[3]

In early letters from America a number of such American loanwords appear. Academically trained Norwegians who lived in the settlements for a time complained loudly about the mangling of the Norwegian language. "We never hear words like *hvetemel*," wrote Reverend Olaus Duus in a letter of the 1850s, "but instead 'flour'; never *gjerde*, but 'fence'; never *lade*, but 'barn'; never *stall*, but 'stable'; if a horse is *gardsprungen*, they say that it 'jomper fence'." But it was not easy to keep the language "pure": even academics, including the pastor himself, gradually adopted loanwords to express new realities.[4]

Some observers predicted that the Norwegian language would disappear in a short while because the Norwegians adopted American words into their language so hastily. This might have happened had emigration stopped at mid-century. But the mass emigration that followed provided the Norwegian group with continual infusions of living Norwegian speech. In this way a special Norwegian-American language developed, or rather an American Norwegian, in which many American loanwords were pronounced and inflected in Norwegian, with forms varying slightly according to the dialect. This was a language that could baffle the newcomer, as O. E. Rølvaag portrays in his first novel, *Amerikabreve* ("America Letters," translated as *The Heritage of Per Smevik*). "And then they have such very peculiar names for the meals; even uncle, who should talk exactly like me, calls the evening meal 'søpper', the noonday meal 'dinner', and the morning meal 'brækfæst'. . . . When uncle asks me to do something, I stand there like a fool — a regular dunce who understands nothing."[5]

Norwegian-American linguist Einar Haugen has made this American Norwegian the subject of a thorough sociolinguistic study, *The Norwegian Language in America* (1953). He shows, among other things, how the frequency of loanwords in various areas of meaning indicates the degree and the nature of contacts with and impulses from Ameri-

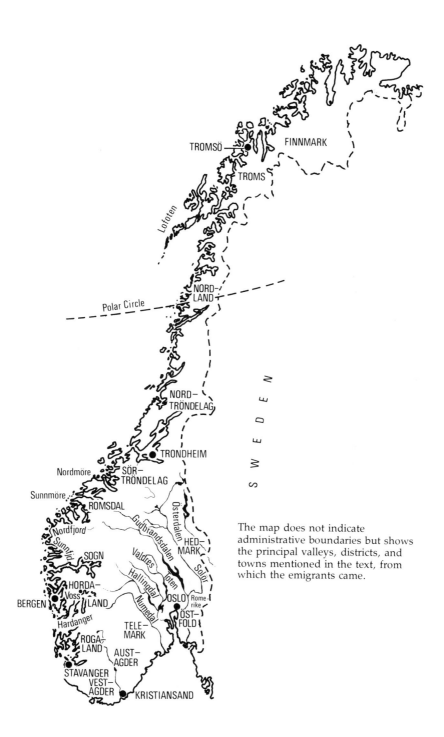

The map does not indicate
administrative boundaries but shows
the principal valleys, districts, and
towns mentioned in the text, from
which the emigrants came.

Number of persons who in 1960 stated that Norwegian was
their mother tongue. Courtesy of H. Aschehoug & Co.

The last preparations. A family that left a mountain farm in Seljestad
in the mid-1880s are loading a cart that will bring their belongings
down to the fjord. Courtesy of H. Aschehoug & Co.

On board the emigrant ship from
Copenhagen, *Hellig Olaf*,
Norwegians met people of many
nationalities, saw unfamiliar faces
and clothes, and heard the
bewildering sound of foreign
tongues. Steamship lines competed
for passengers. One of the early
ones was the Anchor Line that here
announces weekly departures "To
and from America" and the "lowest
prices." Photo 2, courtesy of the
Norsk Folkemuseum; photo 3,
courtesy of H. Aschehoug & Co.

Winter in the forests of northern Minnesota. Courtesy of the Norsk Folkemuseum.

The landscape in Oleana, Pennsylvania, was picturesque, but the land was hard to clear and the soil barren. Today it is part of a park.
Courtesy of the Norsk Folkemuseum.

The railroads advertised in Norwegian newspapers. The Union Pacific here recommends beautiful, level land, plenty of water, and good market connections: "Greater advantages have never in any country been offered to the emigrant and settler." Technology transformed agriculture. Even before the tractor came, a combine could harvest 1,000 acres a day. Courtesy of H. Aschehoug & Co.

"The school bound subtly and inseparably together the few souls who lived out there in the wilderness." O. E. Rølvaag. Lade Farm schoolhouse, Fosston, Minnesota. Reprinted with permission of the Minnesota Historical Society.

Grieg Ladies Singing Society of Chicago, Illinois (founded in 1915), taking part in the Norwegian Constitution Day Parade, *Syttende Mai*, in their Hardanger costumes, 1924. Photograph by M. M. Flanders. Courtesy of the Dr. Alf H. Altern Collection.

Did they remember skating from the "old country"? Skating party on Silver Lake, Scandinavia, Wisconsin, 1908. Courtesy of the Peter H. Peterson Collection.

Barnraising was often a collective undertaking. The whole neighborhood took part. Reprinted with permission of the Minnesota Historical Society.

The manager of the grain elevator (far right) and the stationmaster
(center, with derby) with Indian friends, Kathryn, North Dakota, 1909.
Courtesy of the Hedmarksmuseet og Domkirkeodden, Hamar.

Many Norwegians settled in the wooded areas of the Midwest.
Courtesy of the Norsk Folkemuseum.

can society. Loanwords are especially well represented in all fields related to city life, to economics and business, to public administration and politics. There are many, but fewer, describing peoples' homes, furniture and equipment, cooking and homemaking. There are very few relating to the church and its affairs, to the family, and to human beings, their bodies, thoughts, and feelings.

As a general rule, words that were most closely tied to the personality and to the heritage that the immigrants brought with them had the greatest resistance. There are no American loanwords in what was preserved of Norwegian fairy tales and folklore. But they dominate in areas where the immigrants faced entirely new phenomena, whether farm machines, unfamiliar foods, or forms of social intercourse. A "riper" was the obvious name for a reaper. And what else could one call a "surprise party" or a "picnic?" An elected judge was of course a "justice of the peace" (*jøstis åv de pis*), in no way related to any of the judges back home. Kristofer Janson heard a countryman report that "he was both *nomineta* and *elekta*, even though he was not *eduketa.*" [6]

Local Politics

The high frequency of Americanisms that describe politics is due not just to their novelty but also to the active participation of Norwegian immigrants in local American politics. The American political system presupposed extensive local autonomy, based on the township as its smallest unit. In the Midwest townships were usually rectangular and often cut through a settlement or a neighborhood, only occasionally leaving it with a purely Norwegian population. In the township Norwegians encountered native Americans ("Yankees") as well as other nationalities — Germans or Swedes, Irish or Poles.

In 1850 the township faced tasks not markedly different from those of its Norwegian counterpart, the *herred*. A township was in charge of the public school and a square mile of land inside its borders as the school's property. Sale of this land could provide a fund to cover the expenses of the school. The township also had the task of building and maintaining roads and bridges, as well as caring for the poor.

There were important differences as well. First, the American township had a broader electoral base than the *herred*: all American-born men over twenty-one could vote, and the immigrants were on a

par with them as soon as they had signed a declaration of their intention to become American citizens, what was known as "taking out
their first papers." Even this restriction was not always maintained.

Second, the local government in the Midwest was based on direct
democracy: voters gathered in a town meeting each year. This meeting voted on the budget for the coming year proposed by the outgo-
ing officers, elected a town board, and selected officials to take care of
communal business. The meeting thus chose a town treasurer and a
town assessor. It was the assessor's business to determine the value
of each person's farm and other property, and on the basis of this
determination to assess the taxes needed to meet the budget established by the town meeting.

It is not possible to adequately answer the question of how early
and to what extent Norwegians began to take part in local government and run for office in the townships. A few interested persons
took an active part in political life within the first years after their
arrival and tried to arouse political interest among the immigrants.
James Denoon Reymert, editor of *Nordlyset*, was such a man; as early
as 1848 he wrote: "We must run our town governments ourselves;
there is no one else who can do it for us. The time has come for us to
assume the duties and enjoy the privileges of every American citizen.
It is our privilege to rule ourselves, our own township, and make our
voices heard in the affairs of the county, even in the state as a whole.
Let us undertake this affair with all our zeal."[7]

It was not difficult for a man with Reymert's background to make
himself heard, but the situation was different for an adult farmer
arriving in America without a knowledge of English. Yet there was
much truth in Reymert's appeal to his countrymen, for in those towns
where they constituted a great majority of the population, they had to
participate in the task of securing schools and roads if they wished to
have these benefits. Political activity began at the township level, and
anyone who proved to have leadership qualities there could continue
to the county level and possibly even into the political life of the
state. This applied especially to those who came as children with their
parents or as very young men. We have already mentioned Hans
Christian Heg in Muskego, and there were others. Before the Civil
War there were Norwegian-born county officials in the states of Wisconsin, Iowa, and Minnesota. In 1864 *Emigranten* reported that in a

newly formed county in northern Wisconsin Martin B. Johnson had been elected sheriff and Peter Anderson register of deeds. Magnus Nelson was elected clerk of the county board of supervisors, Knud Anderson district clerk, Jacob Larsen district attorney, Adam Seed coroner, Michael Jensen county surveyor, and Ole Aslakson superintendent of the county school system.[8]

The Scandinavian, and we may safely say Norwegian, cast of the majority of these names shows that Reymert was right in saying that they had to run their own government — there was no one else to do it. On the other hand, it is clear that the Norwegians were underrepresented in proportion to their number in this period and probably for some decades after the Civil War, and even longer with respect to state and federal offices.

A single thorough study by Merle Curti, based on extensive data, shows this for Trempealeau County in western Wisconsin for the period 1860 to 1880. A few Norwegian settlers had arrived in the 1850s, but in the second half of the 1860s they poured in so fast that by 1870 Norwegians of the first and second generations constituted about 40 percent of the population. In this year Norwegians were elected to county offices for the first time, and their numbers grew slowly in the years to 1875. From then on a marked change occurred: in the years 1875 to 1885 a fourth of the county officials, 43 of 172, were born in Norway. This corresponded rather closely to the Norwegian-born share of the total population. Of the 82 America-born officials, one-half were born in Wisconsin; the study does not tell us how many of these were born of Norwegian parents.

The study also contains a detailed analysis of one township with a very high proportion of Norwegians, where the development can be observed even more clearly. Pigeon Township was separated out in 1875, followed by the election of a small but politically conscious and politically trained American minority as officials. The small town of Coral City became a kind of Yankee enclave in a basically Norwegian area. Participation in the elections was high both before and after the separation, but the American minority was strongly overrepresented in the town government of Pigeon during the first two years, even though Norwegian Peter Ekern was elected chairman each year. In 1877 the Americans nominated candidates opposing Ekern and the other Norwegians for all the offices. The election resulted in a

Norwegian victory for most offices, and at the next election the Norwegians made a clean sweep. No Americans were elected except James D. Olds, who was allowed to continue as judge. Olds had discovered that it was good business and good politics to speak fluent Norwegian: he was a "Norwegian Yankee." Such contests are reported from many places; they were a part of the Norwegians' education in the American system and of their entry into local government.[9]

The Trempealeau County study shows that as late as 1870 the Norwegians were poorly represented among the children in the American public schools. The explanation is that many were newcomers who had not yet managed to orient themselves and who were at the bottom of the scale in owning cultivated land, domestic animals, and other property. There is no evidence to suggest that Norwegians in the early period were more zealous than other national groups in providing education for their children. But we do hear of places where even adults sought out English instruction, and as the common school in Norway was improved from 1860 onward, Norwegian immigrants arrived who were more interested in schooling and higher education.

Eventually the school problem became a burning issue for the Norwegians when a disagreement arose within their own ranks. The conflict was initiated by the University-educated pastors and lasted from the end of the 1850s to the end of the 1870s, with a break during the Civil War.[10]

The Norwegian Pastors and Americanization

Around 1860 twelve pastors with a Norwegian theological education were active in America, and names such as Preus, Stub, Koren, and Munch indicated that a bit of Norwegian officialdom had been transplanted to the new land. The pastors constituted a homogeneous group, conscious of representing culture and education in a primitive and immature society. They were emissaries of a church system built on the authority of the pastoral office, and they represented a Norwegian cohesiveness based on the Lutheran faith. They were not prepared to accept everything American as good and were critical in their letters and other documents of many American phenomena. They complained of their countrymen's readiness to ape the Americans: girls found it more prestigious to take service in American homes than in theirs. The pastors held that their parishioners were too easily impressed by "the much-lauded American freedom" of speech and conduct. Episodes might indicate they were sometimes right. An intoxicated Norwegian settled down in the pastor's parlor and refused to leave. He maintained that it was *his* parlor just as much as the pastor's — after all, he had helped pay for it.[11]

Their cultural background in Norway and the task they faced in America combined to stimulate the pastors' interest in the upbringing and education of children and young people, especially in their religious instruction. One of the early undertakings of energetic pastor J. W. C. Dietrichson in the Koshkonong settlement was to start a Norwegian religious school which met several months of the year, with precentor Ole Trovatten from Telemark as the teacher. Other pastors followed his example or tried to carry on instruction themselves. In Koshkonong as elsewhere the children also went to the American school, which at this time lasted only a few months each year. With this arrangement each language seemed to be getting a fair share.

But in a few years the pastors became very skeptical of the American public school. They had three major objections. First, they thought it was ineffectual because of the poorly trained and constantly changing teaching staff and the loose discipline. One cited as an example of lax discipline a young woman teacher's habit of addressing her pupils as "ladies and gentlemen." The pastors in general had a low opinion of female teachers, who were common in America at this time but rare in the Norwegian countryside. Second, they were increasingly concerned that the American school was nonreligious: in the heat of battle they sometimes called it "heathen." Third, they stoutly maintained as a pedagogical principle that primary education ought to be given in the mother tongue, the "language of the heart." Education in English should not start until the age of thirteen or fourteen. They had found the model for this, in principle progressive, view among the German Lutherans, especially the so-called Missouri Synod. In 1858 the Norwegian pastors had made an agreement with this severely orthodox church for training American pastors. The German Lutherans had built congregational schools that provided a complete education, and in 1858 the Norwegian pastors introduced a similar plan for Norwegian schools at a conference of teachers and pastors. Their goal was not merely to supplement the nondenominational American public school but to supplant it.

With that the conflict broke out. The theologians were opposed from two quarters, both characterized by antipathies to the official class nurtured in the homeland. One of these was politically radical, "red republican" in the language of the times. There are traces in it of the French Revolution of 1848 and of the Thrane movement, with touches of rationalism and freethinking skepticism. Among its representatives were two physicians, J. C. Dundas and Gerhard Paoli, besides Marcus Thrane himself.

The other opposition was Christian antiauthoritarianism, with strong elements of Haugeanism. But this was Haugeanism on a broader scale than that of Elling Eielsen and his followers. Its leader in the second half of the 1860s was Knud Langeland, a schoolteacher from Norway and editor of the newly founded and eventually very influential newspaper *Skandinaven*. The pastors were not successful in winning the schoolteachers to their side: in the debate on the public school the teacher replaced the pastor as a leader of the people, a development similar to what happened in Norway at the same time.

So the university-educated pastors lost the battle. Purely economic factors may have been sufficient to cause their defeat: it would have been a great economic sacrifice to build a common Norwegian school in a period when the American school was rapidly developing and constantly demanding greater sums from taxpayers. But the opposition also advanced arguments that reflected a more favorable attitude to the new land and its institutions than that which the pastors represented. Children should learn English from childhood, declared Knud Langeland, and should learn in the schools to become good citizens of their new homeland. They should not be forced into the hierarchical German straitjacket that the Missouri Synod was peddling.

There were no Gallup polls to reveal how concerned the average Norwegian-American newspaper readers were with the school issue, but it seems likely that the lengthy discussion must at any rate have made them aware of the problem and what it meant more generally for their attitude toward American institutions. In practice they accepted the American common school and maintained their own Norwegian religious schools. As long as the language of the church was Norwegian, this was felt by the great majority to be natural and necessary.

Although the pastors lost the battle of the common school, they won their struggle for higher schools. Their interest in teaching and education was genuine, and their initiative and energy led to the founding of Luther College in 1863 and of St. Olaf College a decade later. These efforts fit in well with a recognized American pattern — the establishment and maintenance of higher education by private individuals and organizations, including churches — and they won the support of their countrymen. Luther and St. Olaf were modest institutions in their early years. But the establishment, growth, and progress of these colleges testify to a considerable willingness by Norwegian Lutherans to make economic sacrifices.

In the long view it is probably correct to say that the emigrants shaped their own social life and built their own institutions, while participating in the life of American society, first at the local level and subsequently at higher levels. It proceeded, in modern terms, from the periphery to the center, from congregation to church body, from local politics to state politics. Yet this explanation omits a decisive element that pointed in the opposite direction: the national crisis culminating in the Civil War. This brought national American political and moral problems into the lives of Norwegian immigrants with a powerful impact.[12]

The Civil War

There is every reason to think that the Norwegians in America were generally antagonistic to slavery. They had never been exposed to the influence the slave system had on those who were masters. They came to a section of America where a majority of the native population, whether for moral, economic, or political reasons, united during the 1850s in condemning slavery. It was easy for the Norwegians to support this view: they, too, had sought freedom in America. However, not all were immune to influence from the circles that defended slavery. A Norwegian in Texas wrote home in the late 1840s that he intended to buy a black man to help him clear his property. But to a reflective person like Elise Wærenskjold, who also lived in Texas, the immoral nature of slavery was clear.[13]

It was one thing to discuss slavery in the 1850s, but quite another to take a stand when war came and President Lincoln issued his appeal to young men to enlist. Now the problems of the larger society intruded on the most out-of-the-way Norwegian neighborhood: the question was should a son or a father go to war?

In this kind of crisis the individual and the group are subject to psychological pressure from their environments. In the early part of the Civil War there was competition between counties and townships — and between ethnic groups — to make the best showing. The ninth volunteer regiment from Wisconsin was German, the eleventh largely Irish, and the fifteenth was Scandinavian, predominantly Norwegian. The governor of Wisconsin appointed Hans Christian Heg from Muskego as colonel and commander of the regiment. From the start he was the driving force in agitating for support and in organizing the regiment. "Forward then, countrymen, let us show that we also love our new fatherland — that we, too, are prepared to defend our government, our freedom, and the unity of our country." So ran a sentence in his appeal for support in the special issue that *Emigranten* published in connection with the recruiting campaign.[14] He led the troops when they entered the field in 1862 and was renowned for his courage and resolution; he was also beloved by his men. He fell with many of them in the battle at Chickamauga, one of the bloodiest in the war. Altogether the regiment lost a third of its men before the war was over.

Norwegians also served in other regiments, and Norwegian-American historians reckon that between 4,000 and 6,000 men served in the war. A critical analysis might reduce even the lower estimate somewhat, since it may include some Swedes and Danes. But the number is still considerable for an ethnic group that included no more than 44,000.[15] The war also had its impact on those who stayed home. Subscription lists were circulated to raise money for families that needed help and for returning soldiers. Women's societies were organized, whose members made bandages and performed other humanitarian tasks. Thus the women were drawn into cooperation in the American pattern, often on American initiative and with Americans.

The Civil War meant that both soldiers and civilians identified themselves with the new country and made its cause their own. More than ever before they took part and so struck even deeper roots in American society. At the same time they gained through Colonel Heg and others who distinguished themselves militarily symbolic figures that would stand them in good stead as they sought to assert themselves and be accepted as equal partners.

THE BIG FAMILIES

Emigration was an all-European movement, which stimulated — or as some would have it, infected — Norwegians. About 1840, when only a few hundred Norwegians were migrating each year, Germans, Scots, and Irish were leaving by the tens of thousands. All in all some 40 million persons migrated overseas in the century from 1815 to 1915, three-fourths of them to the United States. Curiously, the population of Europe more than doubled in the same century. However, this was not true of all countries: Ireland lost half its population.

It is customary to regard World War I as a watershed in the history of emigration. The war obstructed civilian passenger traffic across the Atlantic, and although the numbers began to rise again in the 1920s, they were soon sharply reduced. First came the restrictions imposed by the United States, which assigned an annual quota of immigrants for each country. Then emigration was practically stopped by the world depression of 1929. For several years the current ran the other way back to Norway, and since World War II overseas migration from Europe has not attained any great dimensions.

In the history of Norwegian emigration the years to 1865 are regarded as the founding phase, the period when a tradition was created. In many communities people could follow a well-established pattern. They might even emigrate in the company of someone who had come back for a visit. Across the sea Norwegians had managed not only to win a toehold and survive but also to attain a certain prosperity. People knew this, for the letters from America told about large herds, acres, and crops. One could see it in the fine clothes of the early photographs and above all in the money that was often enclosed in the envelopes, evidence that no one could question.

Mass Emigration

The half century from 1865 to 1915 was the time of mass emigration, even though Norwegian emigrants were only a small percentage of those who came to America each year. But Norway had few people to spare. When close to three-quarters of a million persons left the country in the course of fifty years, it was a massive loss for a country that had only 1,800,000 inhabitants in 1865 and 2,500,000 in 1915. In proportion to total population only Ireland had a higher percentage emigrating.

The rate of emigration was not constant year by year over this period, nor did it continually rise to World War I. The movement consisted of three great waves. The first rolled from the latter half of the 1860s to the early 1870s. The second, the largest and longest, began rising in 1879 and continued until 1893. In this period a quarter million departed the country, leaving a population increase of only 150,000. In some years the number of emigrants was greater than the surplus of births, causing a population decrease. The record was set in 1882, when 29,000 persons emigrated, leaving Norway with 5,000 fewer people at the end of the year. An economic crisis in America in 1893 reduced the number of emigrants for a time, but about the turn of the century the third wave arose. It reached its climax between 1903 and 1907, after which the curve flattened. It was clearly going down during the years before World War I.[1]

The mass emigration may at first seem less interesting and stimulating than the early emigration. Those who do something novel, in whatever field, are especially interesting. They arouse attention, and their actions are recorded in documents that posterity can study. The first, the pioneers, are usually strong, distinctive, captivating personalities. When thousands make the same decision every year, the individual personality is submerged. The multiplicity of individual motivations, decisions, and fates cannot be captured. We must resort to statistics and group the emigrants according to places of origin, age, sex, and occupation.

Of course the migration after 1865 is worthy of attention because it was a mass movement. It spread throughout Norwegian society and left its imprint on all social classes, in town and country, indeed in virtually every family. Many a mother helped her son pack his American chest or trunk; children learned that Aunt Anne or Uncle Johan had decided to leave; or the neighbors dropped in to say goodbye. It is important to explain Norwegian emigration because it was a mass movement, and, as such, a significant part of Norway's history. In any attempt to do so it is reasonable to begin with people, the population and its growth.

Population Crisis

In earlier centuries Norway had been subject to various demographic crises. There were years, or series of years, when more people died than were born, owing to crop failure, famine, and the epidemics that followed the famine. Children were especially vulnerable in such periods, so that there were differences in the annual increment and the generations that reached marriageable age. The population grew, but by fits and starts. The last of such demographic crises involving considerable birth deficits struck Norway during the last years of the Napoleonic wars when "the poor man starved, the rich man hungered."

After 1814 Norway never experienced years when the country as a whole had more deaths than births. The natural growth was never again decimated by crop failure, famine, and epidemics, and the population grew very rapidly. In fifty years it virtually doubled. Statistics show that this was primarily due to the reduction of infant and child mortality. About 1820 it was as high as it was in India in 1960, but children born in 1840 had far greater chances to reach maturity than their parents' generation had had. So the nineteenth century became the century of big families, families with many children who reached maturity. About the turn of the century a new development began, one which has continued with minor deviations down to our time: the birth rate began to fall and the rate of population growth slackened once more.[2]

Why this noticeable difference? Why no more years of distress after 1814? Why this reduction in infant mortality? The Swedish poet-bishop Esaias Tegnér formulated a pithy answer: it was due to peace, potatoes, and the smallpox vaccine. Although the answer is an over-simplification, these are factors well worth considering.

Peace did not reign undisturbed in all of Europe between Napoleon and World War I, but as a whole this century stands out as a peaceful era in comparison with the preceding and following centuries. The number of persons lost on the battlefield before 1814 was not great enough to affect the growth of population. It was more significant that wars often brought epidemics and famine. Soldiers were roving folk who spread contagion, robbed and plundered, deprived civilians of their food, and thereby reduced their resistance. Man's three plagues — war, hunger, epidemic — often accompanied one another.

This brings us to another of the bishop's three factors — the smallpox vaccine. Smallpox was not the only epidemic disease, but it was one of the more dangerous and it took many lives. However, even before the population was fully vaccinated, the smallpox epidemics seem to have begun to disappear. There are not nearly as many accounts of severe epidemics in the early 1800s as there were in previous years. Some have therefore contended that the infections were less virulent after 1800 and were deadly only for those who had little resistance.[3]

There is reason to believe that resistance to disease increased after 1814 in part because the supply of food became better and more certain. One factor was the potato, which came to be grown through-out the country in this period. Potato crops were six times larger in 1835 than in 1809, and they continued to grow. Virtually every cottage had a small potato patch which yielded barrels of potatoes for home use. But the improvement in diet was not due solely to the potato, as the bishop suggested.

In 1809 the spring herring returned to the Norwegian coast after having been gone for many years. It came in such numbers that it was a cheap food. Herring and potatoes were staples in the diet of all Norwegians, especially of the poor. Herring was rich in protein, a nutriment almost absent in potatoes. The combination of herring and potatoes might have been monotonous, but it was healthy. It provided far better nutrition than did, for example, the Irish diet which was restricted to potatoes.

Area under cultivation and the dairy herds also increased. Even more important, better implements and methods of cultivation helped to increase productivity. Farmers got bigger yields for every barrel of seed and could cultivate a larger area than before. One scholar has calculated that the gross yield per individual in the farm population more than doubled in the years from 1809 to 1865.[4]

Decade by decade children were growing up, diligent children who were put to work at an early age. They fetched wood and water for the cook, like the Ashlad in the folktale: they picked stones from the fields and herded cattle in forests and mountains. When they were confirmed (about age fifteen), they went to work as adults, becoming hired men and servant girls, sailors or fishermen. Others made their way to the towns, where there was also a need for servants, woodcutters, and stevedores, for maids and housekeepers in the homes, and for seamstresses. Some boys got regular training as craftsmen or became store clerks, since more liberal admission to guilds and internal commerce provided new opportunities. Others left, as we have seen, for America or northern Norway.

However, aside from the rural communities that had already distinguished themselves as typical emigration districts, the countryside and the primary occupations retained most of their population growth to the 1850s and 1860s. Although mobility increased, most people stayed in the place of their birth: in 1865 more than four-fifths of the Norwegian population lived in rural areas. Industrialization came late to Norway.

The industriousness and sagacity, as contemporary sociologist Eilert Sundt describes it, of the many able-bodied men and women in this period contributed greatly to increased activity and growth in the countryside.[5] Some managed to secure a small farm of their own, either by division among sons or by the purchase of land, cultivated or uncultivated. The number of tax-listed farms grew by nearly 50 percent from 1835 to 1865. Many more became cotters under farm owners who needed more manpower to cultivate the larger fields they had brought under cultivation, or they combined work as cotters with fishing, lumbering, or handicrafts. Rural work became more specialized than before as the division of labor increased.

The good agricultural regions were now supplied with a greater number of craftsmen — blacksmiths, clockmakers, saddlemakers, tanners, and coopers, in addition to tailors, shoemakers, and carpenters. In the Romerike district just north of Christiania hauling became an occupation for many more persons — hauling planks, wood, grain, and hay for the city's many horses. More remote districts did not have such a supply of craftsmen, but here, too, specialization began. Farmers went to the craftsmen not just when they needed a fine rosepainted chest or cabinet, but for everyday objects as well. They went to the blacksmith to get iron spikes instead of the wooden nails they had made themselves and to get a new, more powerful plow. Or they found the means to obtain a cart that would carry a heavier load than the drag or the sled they had used before.

At the same time the growing population constituted a continual pressure on the resources, and a large portion of the small landowners, the cotters and the craftsmen, lived in constant struggle to gain enough from the soil and their craft to secure not only survival but a degree of security for themselves and their families. They were economically exposed and vulnerable, and they shared less in the general economic advance than the bigger farm owners. All in all the distribution of property and wealth had become more skewed during the half century after 1814, especially in the good agricultural districts of eastern Norway and Trøndelag.

In the golden prosperity of the 1850s the pressure of population and its consequences were not especially noticeable. There seemed to be plenty of opportunities, and some even declared that Norway had become an America. Good times, good crops, rising prices on grain and other farm products led to increased activity and greater job opportunities in the rural communities. Great road and railway construction jobs were undertaken by the state; wages rose considerably. Then came the 1860s with years of poor crops and falling prices. Those who had borrowed money to finance improvements, in the expectation that progress would continue, discovered that debts were burdensome. Forced farm auctions multiplied in this decade, causing farmers to lose their homes, large or small. Others had to reduce their labor force and were cautious about undertaking new enterprises, from housebuilding to ditch digging. Craftsmen and laborers found less employment and were often driven to the hard recourse of asking for poor relief from the communities. This raised the tax burden, at the same time as the school system was requiring greater outlays. Writer Aasmund Vinje believed that many of the new enterprises in the 1850s had gone too far. "We are no doubt driving people ahead so fast that we are driving them out of the country," he wrote. The reaction was especially painful in the best farm districts, the grain-producing areas of eastern Norway and Trøndelag. At the end of the decade the spring herring also disappeared, to the distress of the fishing communities.[6]

It is possible that the economic recession of the 1860s led Norway, or parts of Norway, to the brink of a demographic crisis. It became difficult for the large group of productive adults to find work and a livelihood. Finland experienced such a crisis, with more deaths than births over a number of years. In Sweden it is common to speak of the "misery years" of 1868–70. Norwegian statistics also reveal increased infant mortality in the first half of the decade: it seems that the population which progress had made possible had become *too* large.[7]

These years are the last from which there were scattered accounts of using flour made from bark as an ingredient in bread. There were also reports of wandering companies of beggars asking for help. A parish pastor in Solør reported in the spring of 1870 that well-to-do farmers were feeding thirty to fifty poor people every day and that small farmers had difficulty getting along because their grain and potatoes had frozen.

If it is true that such a population crisis threatened the rural communities, it would be one factor in an explanation of the mass emigration of the 1860s. Emigration became the safety valve that eased the pressure and provided a recourse for people who found that they were superfluous, without opportunities and prospects in Norway. Poor commissions in many communities contributed to America tickets for families and individuals who wished to emigrate and thus it may be inferred that they held the same view.

No population crisis threatened Norway later in the century, but it is clear that even then demographic development was significant. Population growth was still quite uneven. One example will suffice: during the decade of 1816 to 1825 there were an unusually large number of births. This resulted in a twenty to twenty-nine age group 40 percent larger in 1845 than it had been in 1835, which resulted in an even larger number of births, the greatest ever, in the 1850s. The maximum was reached in 1859 when nearly 55,000 children were born, a record not exceeded until 1873. These large age groups reached their twenties in the years around 1880, just when the great new wave of emigration was about to rise.

In absolute numbers, annual births continued to increase throughout the century. Children swarmed everywhere, on farms and in towns, and as infant and child mortality continued to decrease, an ever larger number of them reached maturity. Even if new jobs were created in these years, the large increase in the youthful population constituted a continual pressure on the resources of the country and the opportunities it could offer.

In America the situation was precisely the reverse. Here people and manpower were scarce, as a whole continent was being occupied, populated, cultivated, and exploited. Here immigrants were welcomed and encouraged to settle. The states of the Midwest, such as Wisconsin and Minnesota, established public offices with functionaries whose business it was to guide newcomers from Europe to their territories. Railroad companies, which had begun extending their tracks far out into unpopulated areas all the way to the Pacific Ocean, also had an interest in drawing people to these areas to provide sufficient traffic. States and companies alike turned to men of influence in the various immigrant groups to win their support in securing people and working hands. Norwegian-Americans worked in state immigration offices and in the service of the railroads, and they met with sympathy and understanding among their countrymen.[8] Norwegians in America were eager to become more numerous — in this way perhaps they could get the better of the Swedes and Irish.

More important, however, was the fact that the individual Norwegian-American farmer received his younger siblings or nephews and nieces gladly, at any rate in good times. They could perform valuable services on the farm as long as they had the patience to stay. They brought news of the home community and kin in Norway, and they made existence brighter with their Norwegian talk. Therefore the Norwegian-American gladly sent a ticket or travel money when a relative asked for it, or even on his own initiative, to secure manpower. On one side of the ocean hands were needed, on the other young people were looking for work. Therefore the demographic factor was decisively significant for mass emigration.[9]

CHANGE AND UNREST, 1865–1915

Even if the continuous population pressure is taken into account, there is something baffling about the mass emigration of the half century from 1865 to 1915. Norway was experiencing greater economic growth than in any previous period; industrialization was speeding up and machines began to take over the work that muscles had previously performed. To be sure, from a modern point of view the production and consumption of energy was still pitifully small, even in 1915. By western European or American standards the degree of industrialization was modest. Still in this period Norwegians began to use the timber in their woods to produce pulp, cellulose, and paper. They began to can sardines and mackerel, and about the turn of the century to extract electricity from high waterfalls and nitrogen from the air. Norway became a power in the shipping industry, transporting ever greater quantities of products to and from the most distant lands. Railroads cut through valleys, and steamers sailed along the coast, bringing goods and news to and from the local communities. Productivity multiplied, and laboring folk in town and country had a more comfortable living at the end of the period than at the beginning.

This progress in economic life had a counterpart in social and political life. The official class was no longer as self-recruiting: farm boys and a few sons of workingmen could make it to the university, and the most persistent of them went on to take degrees and become ministers or professors. Many more secured training beyond the common school by going to the middle school, the folk high schools, teachers' seminaries, officers' training schools, and other technical schools. A new middle class came into being consisting of public and private functionaries, from schoolteachers who often became community leaders and political figures, to stationmasters with fine, red stripes on their caps, technicians who understood the functioning of machines, and office workers who could keep accounts. The borderlines between social groups became more fluid than before. There was still a large gap between top and bottom, but the steps on the social ladder were more numerous and each was less precipitous.[1]

In political life the introduction of parliamentary responsibility for the cabinet from the middle of the 1880s was a victory for democracy, as was the introduction of trial by jury. But the most important democratic reform, universal suffrage, took longer. Not before 1898 did all grown men win the right to vote; by this time women were demanding the right to participate. This demand too was complied with before World War I.

New impulses and ideas were pressing in from abroad, leading to heated discussions of religion, literature, and social problems. In the 1880s a new crop of organizations sprang up: temperance societies, cooperative societies, youth societies, language-reform societies, and political parties; labor was beginning to organize both professionally and politically.

The state began extending its activities into new areas by prohibiting child labor and passing laws concerning safety at work. Even the question of old-age pensions was discussed, but the costs were considered too high.[2]

Economic, Social, and Political Changes

The progress is unquestionable, but it required far-reaching changes in social economy and even in political life. Whenever innovations were introduced, something old had to yield. This was felt first and most acutely in the agricultural economy. Cities and industrial concentrations provided a market for milk, cheese, butter, and meat; railroads and steamships made it easier to bring them to market. The same means of communication also brought new consumption goods to the countryside — cheap fabrics for clothing, household equipment, and inexpensive foreign grains. In sum the transformation meant that farmers changed from a system that put a premium on self-sufficiency to one of market production. The process was lengthy and affected one aspect of rural production and consumption after another, with differing rapidity and strength in various parts of the country. But it made itself felt everywhere.

The change led to a reduction in the need for manpower. Many activities that previously had provided employment were now abandoned. The farmers who hauled goods in Romerike or the skippers who sailed herring and cod along the coast, as Bjørn Kvelve had done before he went to America, could not compete with the railroad or the steamships and their low rates. People stopped raising flax to make linen thread when they could buy machine-spun cotton thread at a reasonable price. Before long machine-woven cloth also came on the market. The number of sheep was reduced, and those who still kept them, chiefly for meat production, could send wool to the factory and get back finished fabric. The sewing machine made it less laborious to sew clothes, so that a tailor or a seamstress could handle more customers than before.

Hides were now delivered to tanneries in the cities, and the country shoemaker lost his customers, who now bought at least their Sunday shoes at the country store. The woodturners, the cabinetmakers, the wheelwrights, and the makers of sheepskin blankets felt acutely the competition from the newer store goods, soon discovering that their crafts were not as highly regarded as before.

On the farms the old homemade implements were put away in a corner of the barn and stayed there until curators of folk museums poked around to gather them for their collections and to study the old handicrafts. How, for instance, had flax been prepared? Time came when vacationers bought spinning wheels to decorate their living rooms in town. Farmers acquired more efficient implements produced in factories to replace the old ones. Machinery, symbol of the new age, began to transform agriculture. First came the threshing machine, which made it unnecessary to beat the grain with a flail, week after week, in autumn. The sowing drill decreased the need for manpower in spring work, and harvest machines multiplied from the 1870s on. McCormick and later Deering became household words among Norwegian farmers as Singer did among seamstresses and housewives. Although some farmers, cotters, and hired men were still mowing by hand in the early 1900s, most medium-sized and large farms had a mower by this time. On the big farms they also had potato diggers, and a few even had self-binders.

Cheap foreign grain was a blessing for communities with a shortage of grain or an uncertain crop. Food got cheaper when one could buy flour at the store and no longer had to worry about what evening frosts might do to the harvest. In the valleys farmers stopped cultivating grain and turned their meadows and fields to fodder production. New plants like timothy and clover made it unnecessary to gather fodder in the high mountain areas at great cost of time and manpower.

But in communities where there had long been a surplus of grain for the market, farmers now faced the competition of cheap grain. In Hedmark, Gudbrandsdal, and Trøndelag the farmers had to sell at lower prices than before. The competition was noticeable in the 1860s and became increasingly severe throughout the century. The rapid increase of emigration from the "good" agricultural regions beginning in the 1860s was at least in part due to the grain prices and the problems caused by competitive imported grain.

Grain farmers were compelled to change from grain to animal husbandry, which also reduced manpower needs, since churning and cheesemaking increasingly moved from the individual farms to the community dairies. Dairies located in the neighborhood of towns took over the delivery of milk as well, thus eliminating an established contact between city dweller and farmer.

Statistics show that between 1865 and 1900 the agricultural labor force was reduced by 50,000. In 1865 there were 50,000 cotters; by 1900 less than half remained and most of them were old people. The number of adult sons and daughters helping their parents in household and agricultural work was reduced; they had become superfluous and probably did not want to stay anyway.

Even if in the long run this revolution meant higher productivity for those who continued to farm and increased prosperity and purchasing power, it proved a severe strain for the individual farmer who had to adapt to the new circumstances. Many were unequal to the strain and eventually had to give up their farms, either because they stubbornly maintained old ways of farming or because they were too adventurous in good times and incurred debts they were unable to pay off. The end of the story was the forced auction, a common occurrence in the 1860s and '80s.

This was the situation in Gudbrandsdal, wrote the local historian Ivar Kleiven to his friend Kristian Prestgard, future editor of *Decorah-Posten*, in 1888: "All who can manage it go to America, and most farmers are at the end of their rope!" Three years later he wrote ironically: "Some are forced into 'voluntary' auctions, others are leaving for America in the spring."

In valleys, many outlying marginal farms were abandoned, as people withdrew from the outposts. This was especially true of the cotters' places, where one today scarcely can see the sites of homes that once gave minimal subsistence to families hardened in drudgery. The flight from the soil had begun, a development that has continued with small interruptions to our time.

Not everyone left, and the migrants did not always go to America. Especially when times were good, many left for the cities or one of the many small towns that sprang up in the second half of the century. But during the great waves of emigration most went to America. Nearly 3,000 farmers left in the 1860s, still more in the 1880s, plus a great many more of their sons. Cotters left if they were not too old, and their children left in even greater numbers, as did craftsmen and day laborers. In the emigration statistics most of these are lumped in a category called "work not precisely determined"; but more detailed, local investigations have shown that the term "worker" includes cotters and their sons as well as some farm owner's sons.[3]

Agriculture and related occupations were not the only ones that were transformed: it happened wherever new technology was introduced. In the 1880s the transition from sails to steam in Norwegian shipping began to accelerate. A steamship needed only a small fraction of the crew employed on a sailing ship with the same carrying capacity. As a result there were several thousand fewer persons employed in shipping in 1900 than in 1875. Besides this the manpower needs were reduced in many of the livelihoods associated with sailing ships. Shipbuilding in cities and towns on the south coast of Norway was restricted, and the sailmakers' shops and the ropewalks fell silent. Even the inland farmers were affected, when the demand for timber for shipbuilding decreased. As a result emigration from the Agder region on the south coast and from the shipping districts increased rapidly, even in the 1890s when it fell off in the rest of the country. The skipper who could no longer get a profitable cargo on his ship emigrated, and so did mates, sailors, and common seamen.

The craftsmen in the cities felt the competition of machinery and the pressures of a new industrial organization. Examples of the first were the shoemakers and of the second the building trades, where contractors had many workers in their employ. In addition, the building trades were especially sensitive to economic fluctuations. In the 1870s there was a hectic building boom in the cities, e.g., in Christiania, where whole blocks date from this decade. When housebuilding nearly stopped in the economic crash of 1879, it became difficult for masons, carpenters, or woodworkers: many of them found emigration a solution. One day they were standing on the dock waiting for the boat to America. More than 1,100 carpenters left between 1881 and 1885; 5,000 craftsmen left in all. This is a large number considering that there were only about 70,000 craftsmen in the whole country according to official statistics.

Change and transformation in town and country led to the loosening of old social bonds, as is noticeable throughout the period and especially in the 1880s. In the cities the mutual solidarity of masters and journeymen was rapidly dissolving. Instead craft workers began to join in labor unions, seeking security and protection of their interests in a new kind of fellowship, which set them off from and in opposition to the masters and employers in their own craft.

In many places in the countryside, reapportionment led to the dissolution of the commonalty of labor. In other districts with larger farms the owner became more of a manager and administrator than an active and constant participant in daily work with the soil and the animals. Increasingly, well-to-do farmers stopped eating with their workers and established a social distance from them. "Sofa farmers" was the term used by some of their critics. So the workers in the country also joined in workingmen's societies, constituted of cotters, craftsmen, and other workers, especially in eastern Norway and Trøndelag. One of their topics of discussion was the problem of the cotters and the question of landownership.

The unions and the workingmen's societies were symptomatic of a social process reenforced by the political restlessness of the times. Workers in town and country began to make demands, for example that they too should have the right to vote. The winds of change which had been only a breeze in the beginning of the century had turned into a hurricane. Not only did they breathe new ideas into the heads of those who stayed home, they also caused an exodus. Thousands went across the sea, not because they did not appreciate their homeland, but because they felt that the homeland did not appreciate them and their work, and because the old social bonds could no longer hold them. "Farewell old mother Norway, I'm leaving now from thee," begins one of the better-known emigrant songs, sold as a broadside and sung throughout the country. It continues: "You are too stingy with your workers, but give a plenty to your learned sons."[4]

Changes in the Emigrant Population

In the half century from 1865 to 1915 great changes occurred in the composition of the emigrant population. In the 1860s it was primarily a family emigration, with much the same composition as the general population, aside from a slight excess in the fifteen to thirty age group, especially males, and a deficit in the age group over sixty. The typical emigrant family consisted of a man and wife thirty to forty years old with a line of children behind them and often one in the arms of both father and mother, perhaps one in the mother's womb as well. Childbirth and baptism were not unusual during the voyage, which could lead to such names for the girls as Tegneria or Atlanta Claudiana or for the boys Sirius. Families did not always travel together, for economic reasons; father or son crossed first, followed by members of the family singly or as a group. Family emigration implies a relatively even distribution of the sexes. In the 1860s 55 percent of the emigrants were men.

In the half century of mass exodus family emigration was largely replaced by individual emigration of the young and unmarried. In the wave of the 1860s about a fourth of the men were between fifteen and twenty-five; in the 1900s nearly two-thirds of them were. A similar but less marked change occurred among the women. Only 6 percent of the female emigrants between 1911 and 1915 were children under ten; in about 1870 this age group had constituted one-fourth of the total. What had begun as a family exodus ended as a migration of unmarried youth, with a marked preponderance of men, especially from the country districts.[5]

The proportions of rural and urban emigrants had also changed. Between 1866 and 1873 nine-tenths of the emigrants were rural, but in the last wave less than one-half of them were. It is a natural consequence of the economic development in Norway and America that gradually more emigrants were from the cities. From 1875 to the end of the period the cities had a higher emigration rate. Some scholars have suggested that many of these urban emigrants originally came from the country. Perhaps they had merely stayed a few years in town before they moved on. Had America been their goal when they left their rural homes, and had they thought of the city as a stopping place where they could save money for the Atlantic crossing?

Statistics disclose that the greater emigration rate in the cities does not apply to all age groups. Relatively more young people emigrated from the country than from the city, and more children as well as women and men over thirty emigrated from the cities. So family emigration must have gone on longer in the cities than in the country, in contrast to what one might have supposed. An investigation from Bergen shows that those who had come to town from the country migrated to America as families. It also suggests that the in-migrants emigrated somewhat more frequently than the established inhabitants of the city.[6] Therefore some of the urban emigrants were country folk who had stayed in the city for a time before they left. But it is not clear whether they had gone to town intending to earn money for the big trip: this does not seem to be a reasonable explanation. There were other circumstances.

First, anyone who has once left his or her childhood environment probably finds it easier to move a second time. Even migration can become a habit, and these stepwise emigrants may have moved several times before they settled in town. Second, they might have had problems adapting to the city. Perhaps they were made to feel like "hicks"; city people may have poked fun at their dialects and clothes. They may have felt like outsiders, without social moorings in the urban environment. Finally, they often worked in economically sensitive occupations, as day laborers or craftsmen, especially in the building trades. When the big building booms crashed, they were the first to be struck by unemployment.[7] Often the husband would emigrate, sending money or tickets later so that his wife and children could follow. Such mothers with their children are well known from the emigration protocols; more than half of those who left Bergen in the early 1880s had received tickets from America for themselves and their children.

Although stepwise emigration from the cities has been emphasized, it must not be overlooked that urban citizens also emigrated. But they fit more easily into the larger pattern: the young and the unmarried are dominant.

The emigrants of 1880 and later came from all parts of the country. During the last years of mass emigration they were more evenly divided, socially as well as geographically, than at the beginning. The working classes still constituted the main body of emigrants, and few officials left. Yet some did, and novelist Alexander Kielland has given us a picture of one such in his story *Arbeidsfolk* ("Working People"). Nor did shipowners or factory owners emigrate, unless they were bankrupt. Then America might be worth thinking about.

On the other hand, a modest number of physicians emigrated each year and many teachers, from private as well as public schools. Engineers and technicians left by the hundreds in the emigration wave of the 1880s, and they continued to do so in ever rising numbers in our century. Store clerks and office workers left in spite of warnings in the papers that they must be prepared to take stevedore or street-sweeping jobs in America. Intellectuals and artists wanted to try America: some of them returned disillusioned. This happened to novelist Knut Hamsun and poet Sigbjørn Obstfelder. But the editor of *Dagbladet*, Nicolai Grevstad, found employment in his profession as editor of the paper *Skandinaven* in Chicago, a post he held until his death in 1940.[8]

In 1880 the fifty-six-year-old feminist Aasta Hansteen left for America to try her hand as a portrait painter in Boston. "Of strength I still possess a bit; I turn unto the freedom of the West," she wrote in her poem "Farewell to Europe." She was enthusaistic about the feminists she met in Boston — they were far ahead of their sisters in Norway. But she, too, returned after some years. However, Agnes Mathilde Wergeland, poet and professor, the first Norwegian woman to earn a doctor's degree, left for good. She got her degree in early medieval Norwegian history, but she had to go to Munich to study and to Zürich to take her degree. She did not rapidly find a career in America, but work and unbelievable endurance sustained her and she finally obtained a professorship at the University of Wyoming.[9]

The Psychology of Emigration

Many have asked if it was the more capable, the more enterprising and energetic persons who left, or if it was those who fell behind in the struggle for bread, the losers, the maladjusted, and the deviant. Were certain personality types more predisposed to migrate than others? It is not possible to give satisfactory answers to these questions. It is reasonable to suppose that in a movement of such proportions all kinds of people were represented. Yet one must grant that the mass of emigrants was different from the Norwegian population as a whole. It represented a selection with respect to age and sex, occupation and social position. We have seen that the selection based on these criteria changed over time. The emigrants were increasingly younger, and there was a greater proportion of men and a wider spectrum of occupations and social classes.

Yet the possibility cannot be dismissed that within each age, social, and occupational group selection did take place on the basis of personality type and intelligence, and that this, too, changed over time. But it is difficult to provide information on this topic, at least using statistics. A study of a small Swedish community shows that more of those who had good marks in school emigrated than those who had poor marks.[10] But many more investigations must be done before any definite conclusions can be made about any such tendency.

Norwegian psychiatrist Ørnulf Ødegaard has studied personality types. He has shown that relatively more Norwegian-born persons in Minnesota suffered from mental illness, especially schizophrenia, in the 1920s than did members of Norway's population. He maintained that the greater frequency of illness might be due in some degree to the greater strains the emigrants were exposed to in a foreign society, but he also held that people who were disposed to this illness were more restless and found it easier than other personality types to break out of their environment.

There is not necessarily a contradiction between being restless and finding it difficult to endure a traditional environment, and being energetic and enterprising. From the earliest period of emigration we can point to such examples as Hans Barlien and Bjørn Kvelve. If we knew the people from the period of mass emigration personally, we might perhaps find more examples. There may in fact be very little difference in human potential between one who opposes early surroundings and one who succumbs to the buffetings of the world and is defeated. Rather fortuitous things may be decisive. Rarely can it be determined if the decision to emigrate was the result of a realistic evaluation of the possibilities at home in comparison with those in America, if it was basically an escape from difficulties, or if it was a desire to try one's abilities.

There were persons one could call failures or losers among the emigrants. In the 1850s a Norwegian physician wrote to a colleague in Christiania, conveying to him the gratitude "of the unhappy parents" of a boy to whom the physician in Christiania had shown special care. The boy had gone astray and was in the hands of the police, because of a misdemeanor. The father believed that it would be best to send his son to America, "to a distant continent, remote from all family aid." He was willing to expend two hundred specie dollars, a considerable sum at that time, if the voyage could be arranged. A number of "black sheep" from respectable families were sent to America. For obvious reasons we know little about them, and they can hardly have constituted any significant proportion of the emigrants.

Novelist Peter Egge tells in his memoirs about a scandal in Trondheim in the 1880s. A lieutenant and a druggist had given a young girl so much alcohol or other drugs that she got dead drunk. She was found in the street early one morning and brought into the local jail. The case was not properly investigated by the chief of police: the lieutenant left town and the druggist was not prosecuted. The result was a demonstration with jeering and window breaking at the chief of police's house, so that soldiers and firemen had to be called and the riot act read before people would go home. Investigations were made, resulting in severe punishment and prison sentences for many. "The nineteen-year-old student at the technical school who had cried 'In the gate' got forty days' arrest and a year's dismissal from school. He later came back, took his examinations, and became a respected and well-regarded industrialist." But the merchant who had written and circulated anonymous appeals for the demonstration "was judged so harshly and sat in prison so long that he gave up his business and emigrated to America as soon as he was let out. I knew him from the Working Men's Society's orchestra, where he played first violin." Was it bitterness about unjust treatment, defeatism, or a sober evaluation of possibilities that brought about this decision?

People fled to America to escape debt, child support, and paternity suits; unwed mothers emigrated, especially those who were expecting a child.

Most emigrants are anonymous: they belonged to the "simple little ones in society," it was said. But capable and energetic scholars have unearthed some of them. There was, for example, Jakob Eriksen, who emigrated from Ullensaker in 1868. He was the son of a cotter and was himself a cotter and a carpenter, married with six children. His finances seem to have been fair in the 1850s, but in the 1860s he repeatedly had to get temporary relief from the poor fund. In 1868, at age thirty-seven, he left by himself for America. His wife, Marthe Nilsdatter, and the five minor children were for a time "without means of support" and constantly needed aid from the poor fund. But in 1871 Marthe got a ticket from America and left with two sons; we do not know what happened to the rest. Another was the small farmer Amund Amundsen Borgen. He, age forty-eight, sold his farm and left with his wife and three children in 1869. Three other children had died as infants. Amund had a farm to sell and could therefore take his whole family with him. A third was a forty-year-old policeman in Bergen who emigrated in the beginning of the 1880s with his wife and six children. Both parents and four of the children were born in Sunnfjord, and the family had a precarious living in Bergen for five years before they again migrated.[11]

But from the 1880s on, there were also other types of emigrants, quite ordinary people when they left. On a July day in 1888 three young men from Stavanger boarded the boat for America. They were nineteen-year-old Birger Aasland, Andreas N. Rygg, and Herman Obstfelder. Osland, as Aasland came to be known in America, says in his memoirs that he had decided early to leave Norway, because his father, a teacher, was in economic straits — he had cosigned notes for others and had a heavy burden of debt. Young Birger had taken extra tutoring in English for two years, had studied an American conversation book, and tried to practice his language skill in conversations. His emigration was well planned. When as a well-known investment banker in Chicago he wrote his memoirs, he still had the list of things he had brought with him to America in his trunk: a Bible and a hymnal, a history of Norway in six volumes, and several dictionaries. He had two new and two old suits, an overcoat, underwear, both wool and cotton, eight pairs of hose, shoes and slippers, a clothesbrush, and a shoebrush. But his free capital on arrival in Chicago was no more than $6, and his first jobs were washing dishes, cleaning the floor, and waiting on tables in cheap restaurants. Like Osland, the two other immigrants had prosperous careers in America, Rygg as a publisher, Obstfelder as an industrialist.

In 1896 a twenty-year-old youth from Helgeland had a ticket to America in his pocket. He had been rowing to the fishing banks of Lofoten each winter since he was fourteen. Three years earlier he had written to an uncle in South Dakota and asked him for a ticket, and now it was here. When he had told the headman of his Lofot boat about his plans for emigration, the headman tried to talk him out of it. He showed the boy a boat and said: "You know I'm not stingy. If you will send the ticket back to America, I'll buy this boat for you, and then you can go to Lofoten as headman next year." The young man was Ole Edvart Rølvaag, who later achieved fame as a novelist, and he chose America.

Wanderlust

Is it possible that there was something one can call adventuresomeness, the urge to get away and go abroad, in this ever larger host of predominantly young men? Vinje, the poet, felt so: "As I began to learn, I was possessed by a desire to leave my home, go to America or wherever, just so I didn't have to stay at home. . . . 'Out, out' was the word, no matter if it led to the abyss!" We know that Bjørnson had a young farm lad express in poetry his longing to get out "over the high mountains." In one of Rølvaag's early stories a young man tells his mother he has to leave for America. "Do you have to?" asks the mother. "Yes, for life is not here." [13]

Now young people are used to getting out into the world. They hitchhike, buy an old car, or get special rates on trains and planes. They go to congresses and festivals, to developing countries as members of peace corps. It is taken for granted and encouraged, on the principle that youth is the period when one is receptive and not yet weighed down by responsibilities and should use the time to expand horizons. Our standard of living makes this possible, and it is assumed that these young people will go back to their countries and bring with them experiences that will make them better members of society.

In Norway a century ago very few young people could travel in this way, just to look around, to amuse themselves, to study, or to do research. A few poets and other artists managed to travel, to Berlin, Rome, or Paris. The urge to explore unknown territory drove Fridtjof Nansen and his group to the Arctic. Missionary calling provided others the opportunity to get to faraway countries. But they were a small minority in the large new age groups; most young people had to find employment if they wanted to leave home. No work, no travel. Craft apprentices had once been able to combine work with travel, while others took service in the neighboring community and might gradually work their way to the nearest city. The sea offered an opportunity for travel combined with hard work, and many a sailor jumped ship or signed off in foreign ports to try life abroad. This could happen in China or Australia, in South or North America, and some stayed where they landed, doing more or less well, while others shipped on a Norwegian boat and returned home after a time.

From the last decades of the century and down to 1914 America became the prime goal of the wanderlust of impecunious Norwegian young people. Transportation across the sea had become cheaper in proportion to wages. When times were good in America, it was easy to get a ticket paid from there. There are no statistics on prepaid tickets for the whole period, but for the last decade about a third of the men and 40 percent of the women had them. Scattered information suggests that in the 1880s the percentage was even higher, especially in communities with a high rate of emigration.[14]

There were few formalities connected with the journey. One had to get through Castle Garden or, later, Ellis Island. But apart from that one needed no passport, no application for admission or work permit, no registration at an office for foreign workers. The majority of emigrants about the turn of the century probably thought that their American adventure was temporary, that they would look around, earn some money, and then go back home. A good many did in fact return as time went on; the number of returnees increased constantly from the 1880s on.

The census of 1920 shows that nearly 50,000 returned Norwegian-Americans were then living in Norway. The Norwegian Bureau of Statistics has calculated that after 1880 about one-fourth of all emigrants returned to Norway. Some 30,000 came in the decade from 1911 to 1920, most of them after a relatively short period in America, an average of seven to eight years.

Most of those who returned were from the coastal districts in southern and western Norway, four-fifths of whom settled in their home communities. The county of Vest-Agder on the south coast led in absolute and relative numbers, with 6,700 returned Norwegian-Americans. Of these 4,500 were men, which meant that in 1920 every fourth man over the age of fifteen had lived at least two years in America. They had worked in Brooklyn and in midwestern cities, sailed on the Great Lakes, or fished on the west coast. Most of them had saved some money, which they could use to buy a good fishing boat, to put up a new barn on their farm, or even to buy a farm.[15]

In 1862 Gro Svendsen, "the rose of Hallingdal," had written in her diary when she left: "O merciful God, today Norway's coasts vanished before our eyes. Now I shall never again see my beloved native land." Like the other emigrants of that period she knew that her decision was final.[16] The emigrants of 1900 did not have to think so. They wished to try something different when conditions were bad at home; they wanted to see a larger society, to try their luck on this new international labor market, to tempt fortune, as some said. They assumed that if they were unlucky, there would always be a boat going home.

There was a strain of optimism in their parting: they were not saying good-bye forever.

THE FABULOUS LAND

Much has been written about the background of emigration, the social and economic factors that drove people out of their native surroundings. Authors have tried to evoke the complex of motives that caused a young woman or a man or a family to leave. Yet no one has managed to uncover the secret impulse that lay behind the whole migration. Perhaps there is none. Or perhaps the secret lies in the country to which the immigrants went. In any case we must not consider only the factors that drove people out of Norway; America offered much that was tempting.

Land

The first and most important thing, even in the age of mass emigration, was a vast expanse of soil. The land was waiting for willing hands, if one disregarded the Indians and their culture, as most people did. This land was incredibly cheap, $1.25 an acre when bought from the government ("Congress land") and $5 to $10 when bought from private persons or corporations, like railroad companies, who wanted to make a profit on the sale.

In 1862 the Homestead Act was passed, granting 160 acres without cost to any settler who promised to cultivate the land. The only charge was a modest sum to pay for the cost of surveying. When news of this law reached Norway, *Morgenbladet* refused to believe it.

There had to be some misunderstanding of the figures. But the story was true, and the Norwegians in America made it known in their letters home. Such accounts must have seemed to many a country boy without a farm like a mirage, a *fata morgana* that shimmered on the horizon. He had to pursue it and find out if it was real: was there free soil without rocks, broken not by hoe and spade and crowbar but by a pair of oxen hitched to a plow? Once the turf was turned, could you sow grain, even so precious a grain as wheat?

The prospect of becoming a landowner on what in Norway was an immense farm exerted enormous influence, as can be seen from the direction Norwegian settlement took after the Midwest opened. The Norwegians followed the northern flank of the frontier, taking land from Wisconsin to Minnesota and on into the Dakotas and Montana. They crossed the border to Canada and became farmers in the prairie provinces of Saskatchewan and Alberta. They leapfrogged to the Pacific coast and took land there, often in conjunction with fishing.

At the turn of the century, 80 percent of the Norwegians in America were concentrated in the six midwest states of Illinois, Iowa, Wisconsin, Minnesota, South and North Dakota. In the agricultural state of North Dakota they and their children constituted nearly a fourth of the population. As late as 1920 half of the Norwegian-born in America and nearly two-thirds of the second generation lived in the country and in small towns.[1] All of them did not farm, but more Norwegians farmed than did members of any other ethnic group (with the possible exception of the Icelanders). The pattern was set by small freeholders of the 1840s, and for a long time it was dominant.

"We have no fear of hunger," said a Norwegian pioneer to the jurist Munch Ræder when he visited Muskego late in the 1840s. "That is a *punctum finale*," wrote Munch Ræder, and reflected on the fact that hunger was an enemy that many a Norwegian mountain farmer could not escape. The same mentality is reflected in a letter from a farm woman in Minnesota in the 1890s, a difficult period for American farmers: "Even if times are hard, we are better off than city people. We don't show off with fancy houses, but we have plenty to eat and drink."[2]

Bjørnstjerne Bjørnson encountered the satisfaction of being one's own master when he visited North Dakota in 1881. A company of Norwegians came to speak with him, driving in the winter cold with two fine horses hitched to their sleighs and wearing buffalo skins. Most of them had been cotters in Norway, but now they had bigger farms than any landowner in Norway. They asked Bjørnson to take home with him the message that every cotter who could still put in some years of hard work should leave for America: there was space for all. Like Munch Ræder, Bjørnson had to admit they were right: as far as land and property were concerned, they had made a good exchange.[3]

Wages

Even if land was cheap or free, it was necessary to have capital to get started. But even this was easier to accumulate in America. The workers' wages in America were much higher during the emigration period than they were in Norway. In the Dakotas of 1880 one could get $2 a day plus room and board in the summer or $25 to $30 a month annually. Although this would be starvation wages today in either country, it was luxuriant pay for a Norwegian farm youth of that time. He knew that at most a hired man in Norway could get $40 to $50 a year in cash and that with American wages he could establish himself as a pioneer after a few years. American sailors' wages at the end of the last century were three to four times as high as they were on Norwegian ships. In the crafts, especially in the building trades, wages could rise to $4 or $5 a day in extremely good times.[4]

The growth of cities and high wages drew an increasing number of Norwegians to the cities. After 1880 both old and new Norwegian quarters in New York, Chicago, and Minneapolis were flooded with recent immigrants. These cities provided newcomers with great numbers of stores, bars, and boarding houses where Norwegian was spoken. Norwegian urban "colonies" sprang up on the Pacific Coast, the largest of them in Seattle. In 1920 every twentieth inhabitant of this city was born either in Norway or of Norwegian parents in America. Most of the urban colonies were populated by wage earners in handicrafts, shipping, and fishing. Norwegians in New York were closely tied to shipping, both coastal and transatlantic: barges, tugboats, luxurious yachts, all had Norwegian crewmembers. Building docks, quays, and ships gave work for ship's carpenters who wanted to go ashore. In New York's busy harbor there were always Norwegian ships, whose skippers turned to Norwegian-born ship chandlers when they needed provisions and other supplies.[5]

Those who lived in cities in America looked wherever possible for trades they were familiar with. Sailors from the south and west coasts of Norway were well represented on the east coast and the Great Lakes. People from the northwest and northern coasts of Norway (Møre, Nordland) became dominant in the rich fisheries of cod, halibut, and salmon which were centered in Seattle. In the state of Washington Norwegians worked side by side with Swedes and Finns in the forests — timbering, working in sawmills and planing mills.

Craftsmen looked first to the building trades. The extraordinary growth of the American urban population after 1865 created a great need for house building, and the development of industry called for masons, carpenters, and joiners. In general Norwegians appear to have avoided heavy industry: very few worked in coal or iron mines, in smelting or steel works. Here east Europeans were in the majority, and the unskilled got lower wages than the craftsmen.

Economic crises and depressions struck America as well, which led to hard times for wage earners in the cities. At such times they might experience what the farm woman in Minnesota was sure she would never see: a lack of food and drink. Urban immigrants faced different social problems from those of their rural midwestern countrymen. On the prairie the local communities remained strong, with their churches as focal points, severe and intolerant toward deviants, but holding their members to their work of building something new. The urban immigrants came to a society that was already built up, where they had to find a place and adapt themselves to it. They, too, sought protection by keeping together, gathering in their own section of the city, establishing and joining their own societies and clubs. Yet the social bonds were looser in the city. Some were assimilated quickly into the larger society, others lost their way: it might begin with too much to drink at Klingenberg Hall or some other bar. At worst it ended in a pauper's grave. The cities were also goals for those who did not adjust to or did not succeed in the Norwegian-American rural society. In the city they were anonymous. Reports from Norwegian consuls indicate that some Norwegians went to their destruction in American cities, but we hear little about them; they kept to themselves and did not write home.[6] The majority got along or returned home when times were hard. Often they went back to America when things improved. They knew that when the economic upswing began, it was more hectic, with a sharper rise and a stronger impact than at home in Norway.

Economic historians with mathematical and statistical training assume that mass emigration can be explained by the demographic situation and the differing economic conditions in Europe and America. They construct ingenious models and by complicated calculations figure out the weight that is to be assigned each of the variables comprising the model. A very good statistical study of Norwegian emigration seems to show that demographic and economic factors explain 87 percent of Norwegian emigration. In his description the author has also taken into account the fact that in the period of mass emigration there was a large group of Norwegians in America who could draw people after them — the "stock effect."[7]

It is easy to accept the idea that economic and demographic factors are the most significant in explaining mass emigration, that cheap land and better pay for work done were good arguments for America. This meant more substantial nutrition and better clothes, a few more furnishings in the home — a rocking chair, an organ, a piano — all in all a somewhat more comfortable economy, a more secure existence. But on both sides of the Atlantic the great majority of people were still relatively poor in 1900. Farmers, workers, and the middle class were busy meeting their basic physical needs. They did not live in an economy of affluence: they did not have baths with running water or electric equipment in their homes, they carried coal or wood from cellar and shed, and the car was still a luxury restricted to the very few (a situation that was about to change in America).

After all, the arguments for America in the age of mass migration were not just economic. The image of America, as it was sketched for people in Norway, had other features as well.

The American Image

The United States was, and continued far into the nineteenth century to be, a political and social experiment in the western world. The constitution of the United States was based on the principle of popular sovereignty; the country was a republic, a conception far more emotionally loaded than in our day. People elected those who were to rule the country at regular and frequent elections, from the local officials to the president himself. It was the land of self-government and democracy. Universal suffrage — for white men — was established in the 1820s, and at the end of the 1860s a few states were experimenting with votes for women. America was the land of freedom, in economics and religion, in speech, in assembly and organizations.

All these freedoms were granted in Norway in the age of mass emigration either in full or with very minor limitations. But suffrage was still restricted to a minority, and permanently appointed officials exerted a great influence in the local government as well as in national politics. Therefore the leaders of the political opposition, men like Ole Gabriel Ueland, Marcus Thrane, or Johan Sverdrup, occasionally pointed to America as a model of freedom. The only one who did so continually and systematically was the farmers' leader, Søren Jaabæk. In his paper *Folketidende* ("The Peoples' Times"), which had many readers in the countryside, he wrote that he regarded news from America as part of his struggle against the dominance of the official class in Norway. He wrote about economic freedom, and he explained that in America there was no compulsory military service. There the well-to-do paid for their own higher schools, and in them they did not teach such useless subjects as Latin and Greek. (A patent error on his part, of course.) There they did not support officials "to superfluity" and did not have to give them "pensioner's fees" when they retired. Hence taxes were low. There was greater activity in America, greater well-being and less poverty, wrote Jaabæk, because the self-rule of the people had been established. The people were free, while in Norway they were under the guardianship of officials.[8]

Other opposition newspapers printed letters from Norwegian emigrants, not just those that told about cows and wheat, but especially those that spoke of American conditions in general. The newspapers commented on the letters by making comparisons which, as a rule, were not favorable to conditions in Norway. In literature we find the same favorable image of America. In several of Bjørnson's and Ibsen's works the character who has been in America represents liberalism and outspokenness, an honesty which cannot be expressed until the repression of authority is gone. Not until Knut Hamsun did an entirely new view of America enter Norwegian literature. But his criticism in the book *The Cultural Life of Modern America* (1889) of the shallowness of American civilization did not in this period reach beyond literary circles.[9]

One of the most important features in the image of America was the insistence that political democracy also led to the leveling off of social differences. Many superficial circumstances could be pointed to: the maid was as elegantly clothed as her mistress, with parasol and silk dress. Some upper-class Norwegians in America scoffed at this, as when Fridtjof Meidell wrote jestingly that one would never recognize the Norwegian farm girls. He had seen them in "their natural state" among brooms and slop pails, but in their new life they minced about "in a strangely affected wriggle with parasols and fans and their lovely heads quite enveloped in veils. Åse, Berte, and Siri are transformed overnight into Aline, Betsy, and Sarah, and the same ladies are entranced at having a little 'Miss' before their names."[10] But common folk in Norway noted with satisfaction that in America there was no difference between the "upper class" and the "tramp." The workman could keep his hat or cap on even when he was talking with a minister or a judge. Even more important was the underscoring of the fact that people were respected for the work they did. No one asked, "Whose son are you?" The Norwegian arrogance was gone, and people were not rejected because their names were inelegant or "their nails were black."

"In America no occupation is vulgar," said Bjørnson in a crowded auditorium in the great hall of the Working Men's Society in Trondheim in 1882. Even a rich man would gladly sweep the street outside his own house. Others reported that both pastor and doctor cared for their horses themselves. In general there were many examples of how people conducted themselves differently from in Norway and how America was big, free, and fabulous.[11]

This image of political and social conditions in America that was sketched for ordinary people in town and in the country was of course idealized. As presented in print, in letters, in lectures, and conversations, it was an incomplete picture. Rarely was it mentioned that in industrialized America there were far greater differences between rich and poor than in Norway, that the big cities had repulsive slum areas, or that labor conflicts occurred which testified to social antagonism. Yet the picture was not entirely false. American society *was* more open than the Norwegian, the social forms were more direct and straightforward, and manual labor enjoyed greater respect.

Finally America was the land of opportunity — the land where so much could happen. There were openings, one could "do well," "make a career," if only one were persistent and watched one's opportunities. "There is more elbow room there, more prospects; that marvelous something which we call the lucky chance appears more often on one's path, and there is a possibility of seizing it on the wing." So wrote Agnes Mathilde Wergeland as late as 1906.[12]

In this image of America as the land of opportunity such events as discovering gold in California and later in Alaska were conspicuous features. The latter even stirred gold fever among some Norwegian-Americans as well as among Norwegians, especially in Sunnmøre. But this was not the most important aspect. Nor was the myth of rags to riches, as personified in Andrew Carnegie or John D. Rockefeller. The many minor careers made America a land of opportunity for Norwegians. Iver Larsen Bøe from Voss ran a clothing store in Chicago and was foresighted enough to buy up lots (his son was Victor Lawson of the *Chicago Daily News*). Christian Jevne, also in Chicago, built a flourishing retail and wholesale grocery business. A young seaman could report after a few years that he was now captain on the bridge or had managed to scrape together the money to buy his own tugboat. A fisherman owned the boat *Tordenskjold* in Seattle, another the *Brand* in Petersburg, Alaska. A man named Christiansen from Vesterålen in north Norway started a seafood business in Duluth and besides trading in fresh and frozen fish specialized in *lutefisk* (lye-treated codfish), the national culinary symbol of Norway. Schoolteachers from Norway became pastors, editors, or college professors.[13]

There were many others. Of the hundreds of engineers and technicians who emigrated some won both fame and wealth. Pioneer of skyscraper building, Joachim Giæver, metallurgist E. A. Cappelen Smith, and tunnel builders Olaf Hoff and Ole Singstad — all were leaders in their fields. Ole Evinrude's name is known by every motorboat owner.[14] It was not the big careers but the many small upward moves that meant the most, moves of people who did not rise so high that they were cut off from their fellow Norwegians. There was greater mobility in an expanding society, which might be harsh and at times brutal to the weak, but which held out high promise to those who knew they had potential.

The great majority of the emigrants became farmers or continued as wage earners and functionaries in lumbering, handicrafts, fishing, and shipping. But in all these occupations there were enough who worked their way up or founded small businesses and industries of their own to affirm the image of America as a land of opportunity. As late as 1950 the American census showed that there were relatively many, probably modest, independent entrepreneurs among the Norwegian-Americans. [15] The possibility of getting something of one's own whetted the curiosity and stimulated the imagination of young people in Norway, especially of the young men. They had better opportunities than young women, and their prospects were more varied. What we call sex roles today were very apparent in the emigration of young people: women were discriminated against on both sides of the ocean with regard to occupations and wages.

Agencies for Emigration

The image of America was also constantly polished and held up to the public by those who were economically interested in keeping the movement alive — the midwestern states, the railroad companies, and above all the steamship lines. The Allan Line, the White Star Line, Cunard, the Danish Thingvalla Line, and many others were represented by offices and agencies in Norway. Around 1870 a Norwegian translantic steamship company was founded, but it had to give up after a few years. Not until 1913 could the *Kristianiafjord* of the Norwegian-America Line start on its maiden voyage.

Outside the offices of the steamship companies waved the Star-Spangled Banner. In the windows were placards and exhibits, sometimes of golden ears of wheat from the prairie. "Export houses for people" is what Vinje called them, maintaining that they had "disguised runners" who caught hold of people when they got off the train in Christiania, almost as a lumberjack used a boat hook on logs. No doubt such descriptions are exaggerated, but the steamship companies did advertise their activities, in the papers as well as in little handbooks for the guidance of emigrants.

The head agencies had representatives throughout the country: merchants, storekeepers, and innkeepers got a little extra income by acting as agents; at the same time they thereby drew extra customers to their own business. Their places of business were marked with the signs and markers of the company and with colorful placards. An indignant letter writer claims that he had seen such "gaudy decoys" hung up as wall decorations in the old log houses in the countryside.

The steamship companies also worked in America. The Norwegian-American press carried just as many advertisements for the various lines as did the Norwegian newspapers. In the United States also there were head agents and local agents who sold tickets and found willing buyers. The sale depended of course on the general business conditions and on the economic circumstances of the buyers.[16] A husband whose wife and children were in Norway and who wanted to get them over had a harder time scraping together the travel money in bad times than in good, and for the farmers there might be many considerations. In 1878 a farm woman in Minnesota wrote to her friend in Norway: "I see by your letter that many would like to come here to us, but lack travel funds. We cannot at this time send tickets to anyone." One reason, she went on, was that the grasshoppers had taken last year's wheat crop. In a few days they had stripped the fields. For another, she and her husband were buying more land, so that they had no free money to send to fellow dalesmen bound for America. But when times were good and the farmers needed help, they sometimes sent tickets on their own initiative to people in the home community whom they did not even know personally.[17]

One method often used by representatives of the steamship companies in America was to offer a Norwegian-American a free trip back to Norway in return for his efforts to bring with him a number of new emigrants. He may even have gotten the same fee per emigrant as the local agents in Norway. There are indications that such "Yankee agents" were among the more effective.[18]

It is hard to judge the extent to which steamship companies influenced the rate of emigration. It is probable that the economic, social, and other factors mentioned above were more important, the considerations that pushed people out of the country and pulled them to America. But considerable sums were invested in this commercial enterprise, which was well developed by the end of the century. Norway could not afford to invest corresponding capital to keep the emigrants at home. The government did expend considerable sums developing better means of communication, but these sums were trifling compared to the capital at the disposal of the steamship companies. No one conceived of using government funds to create new jobs; the concept of government-subsidized industrial development was unknown as was the concept of regional planning. No one thought of developing local industry to keep people from moving. Not until the last decade before World War I did the first tentative efforts begin. The State Workers' and Housing Bank was then established to give low-interest loans to landless people who wished to become farm owners.

Not everyone in Norway accepted the positive image of America. Some maintained that the American form of democracy led to tyranny by the majority, and they even used the term "mob rule." In the 1880s there were conservatives who were afraid that the liberals intended to "Americanize" Norwegian society, and they kept asserting that Americans were materialists.

There were writers who tried to give a balanced evaluation of America in books, articles, magazines, and newspapers; their number was growing. At the same time some of the features in the common man's image of America were becoming less clearly marked. They were gradually fading because the differences between Norway and America were diminishing. This was true, for instance, of universal suffrage and political democracy. Nevertheless the image remained effective throughout the period of mass emigration. "There is now only one country I would like to see," wrote Ola Thommesen, leading Norwegian editor, in 1908, "the great land of the future, where so many of my countrymen have found a home." America was still in the eyes of many the land of the future — the land of the great possibilities.

NORWAY IN AMERICA

Using the American census of 1920 the Norwegian Bureau of Statistics has calculated that some 1,200,000 people of unmixed Norwegian descent were then living in the United States, almost half the population of Norway. In addition it was estimated that there were about 700,000 persons who were part Norwegian.

The American census also indicated that to the turn of the century most Norwegian immigrants married one another. Subsequently the number who married native-born Americans increased. The Bureau estimated that the overwhelming majority of these mates were of Norwegian or part Norwegian ancestry, which would mean that until 1920 about 90 percent of the Norwegian-born married people who were Norwegian or part Norwegian.

When Norwegian immigrants did marry people from other ethnic groups, they usually chose them from other Scandinavian groups, especially Swedes. Over half the marriages contracted with non-Norwegians from 1890 to 1920 were with Swedes. Norwegians were by far the most exclusive group in the marriage market, even of the Scandinavian nationalities. Danes were more cosmopolitan in their choice of mates, and the Swedes were intermediate.

This difference is probably due primarily to the pattern of settlement. Norwegians lived closer together than the others: in 1900 many more than half of them still had their homes in three states, but the

Danes were spread over many. No doubt this pattern also explains why there were so many more Norwegian-Swedish than Norwegian-Danish marriages. It was easier to meet Swedes in the Midwest, especially in Minnesota; the law of supply and demand also applies to the marriage market.

To be sure, the statistics report only the marriages of the first generation; no printed statistics are available for the second and third. In the compact Norwegian settlements, where Norwegian language and customs were maintained, they no doubt continued to marry one another. Those who moved out, got an education, and entered new occupations were more likely to marry outside the group.[1]

Det norske Amerika

The figures for marriage indicate the extent to which Norwegians stayed together, and it is probable that the solidarity in this crucial sphere of life extended to others as well. The historical evidence confirms the suggestion: the period from the Civil War to World War I saw the flowering of a Norwegian immigrant society, *det norske Amerika*, a Norway in America. The early institutions were expanded and new ones were founded.

The first and most important reason was the mass emigration that made Norwegians a numerically significant element in certain states, while bringing a steady stream of new impulses from Norway. The newcomers of this period were, generally, more conscious of their Norwegian heritage than the preceding generation, to whom the local community had been more important. Finally, American midwestern attitudes were still largely favorable toward or at least tolerant of preserving ethnic groups. To be sure, native Americans were not especially eager to admit foreigners into their private lives, and they often moved out of districts when foreign groups moved in. Natives took it for granted that immigrants would do the hardest work and get the least pay. But they did not carry on a systematic policy of Americanization. The public school was a major factor in Americanizing the children, but in most states private schools with foreign-language instruction were not forbidden. Discrimination against immigrants undoubtedly did occur, and at the end of the period antipathy to foreigners was growing. But the antipathy was directed far more toward immigrants from south and east Europe than toward those from the north and west, who were considered more acceptable by Anglo-Saxon Americans. For these reasons the Norwegians could continue to build up institutions of their own while they were entering and slowly being absorbed by American society.[2]

The Church

Group solidarity did not imply internal agreement, as the ecclesiastical development shows: here strife and disunion were the order of the day. From the beginning of the Civil War and for many years after, the high-church leaders of the Norwegian Synod carried on a purely theological (and German-inspired) debate about whether slavery was sinful *in and of itself.* They agreed that slavery in America was an evil, but was it sinful according to the word of the Bible everywhere and under all circumstances? Such hairsplitting discussions of theological dogma led to the secession of minorities and the founding of new religious bodies.

A number of university-trained pastors were quite unwilling to adapt themselves to American circumstances and found it difficult to see beyond their own circle. By virtue of their education they constituted a Norwegian cultural elite in America, and many were strong and gifted personalities. The Norwegian Synod underscored the authority of the clergy, opposed religious teaching by laymen, and emphasized dogmatic orthodoxy as well as strict organizational discipline. They kept common people at a distance. This uncompromising stand alienated many who were not pietists of the Elling Eielsen type and diminished the pastors' leadership role in the Norwegian ethnic group.[3]

Toward the turn of the century interest in pure dogma lessened, and the high-church position lost ground within the Norwegian Synod as well. Norwegian- and American-born farm boys and schoolteachers were trained for the pastorate at the Synod's college and theological seminary, Luther College in Decorah and Luther Seminary in St. Paul. These pioneer pastors found it easier to associate with their parishioners on equal terms and to cooperate with their congregation in religious and secular matters. The pastors of the Synod continued to be theologically orthodox and became, if anything, more severe in their condemnation of wordly pleasures. The pioneer pastors opposed drunkenness, but they had no objection to a glass of wine on a social occasion, sometimes wine imported from Norway. By the end of the century no alcohol was served when Synod pastors gathered. On this issue, as well as on card playing and dancing, the differences between the Synod and the low-church groups diminished as years passed.

The low-church groups were moving from the bleak pietism of Elling Eielsen. Eielsen had looked on this world as a vale of sorrow and held that the gift of grace could be conferred only after repentance and conversion. For him the congregation consisted only of the converted, gathered around the preacher. His uncompromising stand led to endless splits and splintering.

A more moderate view held that the congregation was the basic unit in the church and that it alone represented God's kingdom on earth, all superstructure being the work of men. The new leaders encouraged the activity of laymen but suggested that education was also needed for the pastoral calling. So they, too, erected theological seminaries, where a democratic ministry was to get its training.

The low-church people in the 1880s and 90s believed that the world could be improved, and they were eager to help. They participated not only in missionary activity, but also in educational work of various kinds and in popular movements, above all the temperance movement. They were inspired by American protestantism as well as by the low church in Norway to take radical points of view on social and political problems.[4]

In the 1870s two academically trained Norwegians came to the college of the low-church group, Augsburg College in Minneapolis, where they became professors and exerted great influence. One of them was Sven Oftedal, member of a well-known family associated with the low-church movement in Norway. The other was Georg Sverdrup, a nephew of the liberal leader Johan Sverdrup. He was president of the school for a generation, guiding it under the slogan of "life and spirit," in opposition to "dead orthodoxy" and dogmatism.

Oftedal was a crusader in the movement for total abstinence, a leftist in politics, and he defended both trade unionism and the right to strike. He had a bent for practical politics, becoming a member of the Minneapolis school board, where he worked for the development of a public school system. He was also one of the driving forces behind the establishment of a public library. Oftedal and Sverdrup edited the weekly *Folkebladet* ("The People's Paper"), which brought its readers secular and religious news. They also maintained close relations with the low-church milieu in Norway.[5]

Both branches of the Norwegian Lutheran Church were culturally conservative, as is evident from their frenetic attacks on the writer Bjørnstjerne Bjørnson when he lectured in the Midwest in the winter of 1880–81. All Norwegians in America had loved and honored the Bjørnson of the country novels, beginning with *Synnøve Solbakken* (1857). But when Bjørnson announced that he was a freethinker and told his audiences that most of the Old Testament was myths and fables, the pastors denounced him as a pagan and advised their parishioners not to attend his lectures. Bjørnson in turn did not hesitate to provoke and offend, and not just on religious matters. In his letters to Norwegian newspapers he wrote about the cotters' sons who had acquired splendid farms in America. He told Norwegian-Americans that these farmers in their fine buffalo-hide coats were ever so orthodox, but they were also "a little bit drunk." Often, and especially in his last lecture, he made critical comments about his Norwegian-American hosts that were provocative and not always factual. He lumped together all the immigrants, accusing them of drunkenness or claiming that they were opposed to the American school system and were abjectly dominated by their pastors. He had heard of Norwegian-American schools, he said, where they did not permit instruction in natural science because they were afraid the students would begin to doubt the story of creation. One result was that even Bjørnson's supporters gradually stopped defending him as he went from town to town amid snowstorms and icy blasts.[6]

There were more than a dozen different Norwegian Lutheran Church bodies among the immigrants in the period from the Civil War to the turn of the century. But by this time a movement had begun that looked to their union. In 1917 the three largest synods joined in the Norwegian Lutheran Church in America, with more than half a million members distributed in several thousand, mostly small, congregations. At the time of union eight high schools became the property of the new church, and twelve others received subsidies. This was nearly twice as many members and several more schools than the Swedish-American Church, the Augustana Synod, had.[7] No doubt the long and bitter doctrinal conflicts that had riven the Norwegian-American churches were evidence of an intense commitment to religious institutions. The controversies stirred the interest of average Norwegians and made them more aware of questions of faith. Congregational splits were reflected in the building of rival churches; it was said that if one saw a white-painted church on each side of a road, one could be sure of being in a Norwegian community. Even those who might wish to remain neutral had to take sides.

Devotion to the church stimulated an interest in higher education, which called for economic sacrifices. Thousands of small contributions and a few large ones made it possible to construct academies, colleges, and seminaries. These schools were at first poor in resources and staff but severe in their discipline of students, whether their conduct or their faith. The spiritual climate gradually became gentler, the resources more abundant, and the standards higher, until the best of them could provide a tolerant and intellectually superior environment. The best of the schools became centers for the study of Norwegian language and literature, which helped to stimulate an interest in Scandinavian studies in American universities as well.[8]

Higher Education

As early as 1869 the young and dynamic Rasmus B. Anderson persuaded the University of Wisconsin to introduce a course in Scandinavian studies. In 1875 the university established a chair in Scandinavian languages and literature with Anderson as its first occupant. His writings included translations of Bjørnson's stories, a book on Scandinavian mythology (1875), and one on the Norse discovery of America with the provocative title *America Not Discovered by Columbus* (1874). He urged Norwegians in America to be aware of their ties with the Viking past and did what he could to make them known to other Americans. Even though he had rebelled against the strict discipline at Luther College and had been expelled, the college did give him an insight into Norwegian history and literature.[9]

Welfare Organizations

Most initiatives to found special Norwegian welfare organizations came from the church bodies, which could call on their members for cooperation and support. Norwegian-Americans founded some twenty to thirty hospitals, of which the Norwegian Hospital in Chicago was especially known as a well-organized institution with excellent service. Old-age homes, orphanages, and other welfare institutions were even more numerous. Private clinics were also founded by Norwegian physicians. The best-known were in Wisconsin — Dr. Midelfart's in Eau Claire and Dr. Adolf Gundersen's in LaCrosse. The latter virtually created a medical dynasty, with six of his seven sons becoming physicians.[10]

The Norwegian-Language Press

The Norwegian-language press had an almost explosive development: a thorough investigation has revealed that between 1865 and 1914 no fewer than 565 papers and magazines existed. Most were short-lived and either disappeared or were absorbed by other papers. In this way *Emigranten* became a part of *Fædrelandet og Emigranten* ("The Fatherland and the Emigrant"). Others had circulations that would have been envied by the largest contemporary newspapers in Norway. In Chicago *Skandinaven*, a loyal supporter of the Republican Party, first appeared in 1866. *Decorah-Posten* in Decorah, Iowa, started in 1874 as a strictly nonpolitical newspaper. Its founder, B. B. Anundsen, was so "hard up" in the early years that he occasionally had to go out on construction work. Then in 1884 he bought a story by H. A. Foss called *Husmandsgutten* ("The Cotter's Son") which he ran as a serial. This proved to be a stroke of genius that quickly enlarged the subscription list. People were eager to read this success story about themselves, a simple tale of the poor cotter's son and the rich farmer's daughter who fell in love. The father rejects him as a suitor, and the young man leaves for America, earns much money, and returns just in time to buy the estate which the farmer is about to lose through drinking and neglect. And of course the chosen one has been faithfully waiting all the years he has been gone.

By the 1880s Norwegian-language newspapers had been founded in all the major centers where Norwegians lived and in some minor ones as well. Minneapolis had four or five papers, the most long-lived of them being *Minneapolis Tidende* 1887–1935. Another was *Budstikken*, which for some years was edited by Luth Jæger, a radical Democrat. He also founded the Norwegian-American Liberal Society to support Johan Sverdrup and the Liberal Party in Norway during the 1880s, when they were locked in bitter struggle with the conservatives over the veto power of the king.

Newspapers were founded on both coasts. In 1891 *Nordisk Tidende* began appearing in Brooklyn, but it did not become a leading newspaper until it was taken over by A. N. Rygh about 1910. In Seattle *Washington-Posten* kept Norwegians informed of news in America as well as from "the old country." In 1915 there were sixty-two Norwegian-Danish newspapers with a total circulation of 490,000.[11]

Journalism provided work and a meager living for people with various backgrounds, nearly all of them adults when they emigrated. Some of them had training as printers, others as teachers; some were folk high-school graduates or students who had not completed their professional studies (one of them wrote that "poverty and mathematics" were the reasons for his emigration). Some, like Nicolay Grevstad, had journalistic experience in Norway. Others were Paul Hjelm Hansen, who had been associated with the Thrane movement and who had composed the workingmen's petition of 1850; Svein Nilsson, who had been a kind of snoopy reporter for the conservative editor Friele in *Morgenbladet* and showed some flair for political intrigues in America as well; and O. S. Hervin, who used the pseudonym "Herm. Wang" in *Verdens Gang* in the 1870s and later in America. As an essayist and commentator he wrote entertainingly about his countrymen and their activities, delivering waspish thrusts right and left, and he was a literary critic as well. Olav Kringen, a cotter's son and lumberjack from Sel, took the opposite course: he began his journalistic career in America and returned to continue it in Norway — as editor for many years of the Labor Party's newspaper and also working for the movement as an organizer and contributing to various foreign reviews and periodicals.

Some of the academic liberals moved to America and found employment in the Norwegian-American press. In the list of several hundred people who worked part-time or full-time in journalism there are "upper-class," usually foreign, names like Arctander,

Brandt, Fleischer, Sartz, Wesenberg, and Wist, as well as native farm names like Bothne, Hande, Prestgard, and Skørdalsvold.[12]

The great number of newspapers meant that in the 1880s the Norwegian-American press developed a rich variety of views and attitudes. To be sure, those that became large and lasted a long time were either nonpolitical or Republican. But there was room for others as well: when Marcus Thrane retired, other radicals succeeded him. They often discovered that the number of subscribers was too small to provide the editor with a living, but many of them persisted. The number of left-wing papers was considerable, and some survived for a long period. Names such as *Reform*, *Rodhuggeren* ("The Radical"), *Gaa Paa* ("Go Ahead") testify to their controversial aims.

Gaa Paa was socialist and *Reform* a temperance paper, though it was also much more. The editor, after the mid-1890s, was Waldemar Ager from Fredrikstad. He was not afraid of controversy and expressed independent and unconventional opinions about many fields. He was deeply interested in literature, printed literary contributions by Norwegian-American authors, and wielded one of the best pens in the literature of Norwegian America, as a novelist and short-story writer.

Norwegian Literature

The newspapers offered possibilities for developing an environment marked by greater cultural broadmindedness and perspective than the one provided by the church. The larger newspapers opened bookstores and sold contemporary Norwegian literature, especially *Skandinaven's* and Relling's (i.e., the newspaper *Norden's*) bookstores in Chicago. Ibsen's *A Doll's House* was discussed by two correspondents in *Norden* in 1880, a year after its appearance. Literary societies sprang up in smaller cities, for example in Madison, Wisconsin, where the society "Ygdrasil," founded in 1896, is still flourishing. In Decorah, Iowa, the Symra Society is a continuing reminder of a literary journal named *Symra* ("Anemone") which was published between 1905 and 1914. The editors, Johannes B. Wist and Kristian Prestgard, also edited *Decorah-Posten* in collaboration with faculty members at Luther College. Many valuable articles and poems were published in this magazine, which was described in its pages as a cultural periodical "for Norwegians on both sides of the sea."[13]

Norway in America also had a literature of its own in prose and verse. As is often true, the most popular works were not always the best. *The Cotter's Son* by H. A. Foss went into almost as many editions in Norway as in America. Nor is it strange that the most popular song began with the words, "Can you forget old Norway? Never can I forget it," or that it had a melody with such flourishes that, in Ager's words, "one thought one had heard it before even though one had never heard it before." In the midst of the workaday world there was a vigorous poetic strain revealed in the thousands of poems printed in the newspapers. In 1903, 250 poems were collected by Knut M. Teigen in an anthology containing forty-five authors. Bjørnson's rural tales were models for a number of early prose narrators, whose work did not compare with his. The temperance movement inspired both verse and prose, and a wide circle of readers appreciated a book like H. A. Foss's *The American Saloon*, mostly those who were already convinced. But perhaps a few were won over by its portrayal of the destructiveness of alcohol.[14]

In the end the emigrant became the chief character, as his or her problems in the new society were given literary treatment. Authors wrote to vent their nostalgia, to picture the toil and drudgery that could deaden their spirits, to flay the superficial Americanization that hollowed out one's personality, to decry the generation gap and the conflict between old and new values. The tales often emphasized the costs of being an immigrant in a foreign land more than the America letters did. Most authors tended to moralize and underline a little too obviously how they believed the immigrants should handle their problems: it was harder to create figures that would live on in their readers' hearts.

There were not many really gifted writers among them, but a few can be favorably compared with contemporary authors in Norway. Hjalmar Hiorth Boyesen won fame in American literary circles. The most extraordinary as well as the most nearly impenetrable was Jon Norstog, a nephew of Aasmund Vinje; he allowed his vast visions, which tumbled out and nearly overwhelmed him, to find expression in biblical dramas written in New Norwegian (Landsmaal) verse. Norstog was a self-sustaining poet, who printed his books on his own handpress, bound them himself, and then wandered about selling them, though with no great economic success.

In a sometimes biting essay written in 1914 about Norwegian-American literature, Waldemar Ager wrote that "the great Norwegian-American family had only two children, and they were both nursed abundantly: the church and politics. When anyone prophesied about a Norwegian-American literature, Sarah laughed in her tent: that was sheer nonsense." Ager portrayed a cadre of poets who did not find their public, who wrote just one book because they could not afford to publish any more. He described poets with abilities and talents that struggled to find expression, but who in their efforts "to get air whistle and wheeze instead of breathing."

But Ager took special note of one book that had recently appeared anonymously with the title *Amerika-Breve* ("America Letters"): it was O. E. Rølvaag's first book. He, too, had felt the pressure of his confining environment, but at length he did manage to breathe freely. He had the dream of giving poetic form to the story of Norwegian "land-taking" in America, and in *Giants in the Earth* he succeeded in doing so. He gave his readers a low-key, gently humorous, tender portrayal of the pioneer Per Hansa and his wife Beret and the other people of Helgeland in north Norway settling on the South Dakota prairie. He gave voice to the joy of conquering new land and of building while battling the wilderness. This joy possessed Per Hansa and drove him on to ever new and ingenious improvements of all kinds. But Rølvaag also portrayed the costs of conquest: Beret became a symbol of all the longing, the losses, and the sacrifices that the struggle had exacted. The prairie filled Beret with terror: it became for her a wild beast that wanted to devour her, and it almost drove her mad.[15]

The Norwegian Heritage

Rølvaag and other Norwegian-American intellectuals were at this time — in the 1920s — intensely concerned about the cultural situation of the immigrants. Rølvaag organized a society "For the Ancestral Heritage" in 1918 to counteract the new war-inspired attack on "foreign" ethnicity and "hyphenated" Americans. Kristian Prestgard analyzed the tragedy of the emigrants and their sense of rootlessness: they were not completely at home anywhere, not entirely at ease in their new existence, not even in relation to their own children, who had grown into American society more intimately than they. If they tried to find their way back to the old country, they were strangers, different, and in spite of everything influenced by conditions in the country they had chosen. These writers and most other culturally conscious Norwegians in America agreed that in time one should and would become wholly American: they were loyal to the new country. But they did not wish to come empty-handed to the feast and believed that one did not become a good citizen by denying one's origins or traditions. They wished to preserve the ancestral heritage, maintain and cultivate the Norwegian language, and keep in touch with the old country. As Rølvaag put it as early as 1907: "If a man is to realize in full measure the potentialities of his own being, he must first of all learn to know the people of his own kin and his own people's history and literature. This knowledge constitutes our cultural roots. Without it we become drifting vagrants, scrubs, or tramps, culturally speaking." [16]

They did not always meet with understanding among their countrymen either in America or in Norway. One may ask with Theodore C. Blegen whether the majority of emigrants felt the conflict of the old and the new as intensely. Everyday life at work and at home, constantly changing and developing, made the transition more gradual and less perceptible for most people — less tragic and less schizophrenic. [17]

Even if this was true, culturally conscious Norwegian-Americans helped to maintain an interest in what they called "Norsedom," to build a nobler arch over the cultural tradition than one consisting only of traditional foods like *lutefisk* and *lefse*, and to win the loyalty of some of the young people growing up in America. Behind them they had myriad societies and organizations founded by Norwegians and for Norwegians in America.

POLITICS
AND ORGANIZATIONS

I t may be said, without much exaggeration" William Ellery
Channing observed, "that everything is done now by
societies." His remark echoed Alexis de Tocqueville, who in
1839 had told European readers of the "immense assemblage of associations" in the United States — "religious, moral, serious, futile,
general or restricted, enormous or diminutive. The Americans make
associations to give entertainment, to found seminaries, to build inns,
to construct churches, to diffuse books, to send missionaries to the
antipodes; in this manner they found hospitals, prisons, and schools.
If it is proposed to inculcate some truth or to foster some feeling by
the encouragement of a great example, they form a society."[1]

During the 1840s Norway also became acquainted with this "principle of association" — missionary and temperance societies were the
first to develop. The majority of the early immigrants were untouched
by this new development. The Quakers were an exception, and to
some extent the Haugeans were also. The Haugeans surely had a
feeling of community, but very little formal organization, and in
Norway they stayed within the state church.

In the period of mass emigration this changed as more newcomers
had had experience with associations in the homeland. They were
prepared to found and join associations and societies, some of which
grew into Norwegian-American institutions like the various Lutheran
synods or into larger organizations covering the Middle West or all

144

parts of America where Norwegians lived. In the 1880s there was a new surge of organizing among Norwegians in both Norway and America: the old neighborhoods were losing their all-encompassing social functions in favor of societies with specialized ones.

There were more types of Norwegian-American societies than we can treat in a brief survey.[2] There were womens' societies ("ladies' aids"), young people's societies, and mission societies in practically every one of the four or five thousand congregations. From the 1870s on a great number of singing societies were created and in 1886 a federation of United Scandinavian Singers of America, which, however, later foundered on the rock of nationalism. The Norwegian Singers' Federation in America that emerged from the split had in its golden age from 1900 to 1914 1,500 singing members and excellent directors and soloists. In 1914, the centennial year of the Norwegian constitution, a great many of them visited Norway, where their concerts were warmly applauded.[3]

Other societies devoted themselves to sports, gymnastics, and skiing, the last especially popular after the brothers Hemmestveit came from Norway in the late 1880s. Interest then slackened, but it revived at the turn of the century. Ski jumping at *Norge Hill* near Chicago attracted thousands of spectators. The most picturesque of all societies must have been the Rifle Club in Minneapolis organized in the 1880s, after the model of rifle clubs in Norway, which in the heated political atmosphere of that time were the supporters of parliament against king and cabinet. The Minneapolis club is said to have attracted attention when two or three hundred men in Norwegian chasseurs' uniforms marched through the streets under a Norwegian flag, "of course with an American flag beside it."[4]

Others founded literary and dramatic societies to advance knowledge of Norwegian literature and perform Norwegian plays. At the colleges, in the towns, and even at places in the country, debating societies were founded. Birger Osland helped to organize such a society, the Arne Garborg Club in Chicago, named after the renowned author. Here the members discussed current topics such as capital and labor, pacifism, the death penalty, and the race problem, or they took up the theme of the position of Norwegians in America. In the larger cities well-to-do Norwegians even managed to build their own club houses.[5]

Rural traditions were carried on through folk dance and fiddlers' groups; there were about 100 active fiddlers when they organized a national society in 1914. The so-called *bygdelag* were associations for people who came from the same district in Norway. The first was Valdres Samband in 1901, but after that they multiplied rapidly: people from Telemark, Gudbrandsdal, Nordland, and many others. The regional differences of the rural culture in Norway reappeared in America. The meetings of the people from Rogaland were characterized by hymn singing and pious devotion, but the *bygdelag* from the inland valleys enjoyed themselves with old-time dancing to the Hardanger fiddle. Young and old could meet at these gatherings, but they must have meant most to the elderly, who could chat about the old days and refresh their memories of home. Several of the *bygdelag* published yearbooks with articles on pioneer history, personal reminiscences, and local traditions from Norway. Much valuable historical material that would otherwise have been lost is collected in these annuals.

There were thirty-eight such *bygdelag* in 1914, when the able and diligent editor Carl G. O. Hansen surveyed them in a volume published by Norwegian-Americans in honor of the Norwegian centennial. A short time later they united in a common council, which took the initiative for the celebration of the Norwegian-American centennial in Minneapolis in 1925. In spite of some obvious differences, these societies were comparable to the rural societies that sprang up in Norwegian cities during the same period.[6]

The largest and most enduring purely Norwegian-American organization was the Sons of Norway, founded in Minneapolis in 1896 after the model of American fraternal lodges. Starting as a mutual aid fund and locally organized as lodges with elaborately titled officers and ornate ceremonies, it has grown into a large insurance company with a cultural program. In 1907 the insurance in force stood at 1 million dollars; by 1936 (in spite of the 1929–30 Depression) it had passed 10 million. After World War II a change in promotional philosophy led to even more rapid expansion. A field staff of professionally trained full-time personnel was employed, with training courses for new employees. Between 1964 and 1968 the new insurance written increased over 350 percent, and in 1970 the insurance in force had reached $63,260,231, more than double that of 1960. The Daughters of Norway developed a separate organization, but eventually the two joined forces. Lodge names like Wergeland, Ueland, Garborg, Grieg, and Terje Vigen in the Sons of Norway, and Freya, Hjørdis, and Camilla Collett in the Daughters of Norway bear witness to their Norwegian origins. The Sons of Norway also publishes a membership magazine that brings news from Norway as well as from the American lodges. Both organizations have worked actively for Norwegian cultural interests, conducting language classes and giving fellowships for study in Norway. They have arranged tours for numerous Norwegian and Norwegian-American lecturers and artists.[7]

All the societies and associations mentioned had as one of their goals to create solidarity among Norwegians in America by establishing Norwegian institutions and increasing Norwegian ethnic awareness. In one way or another they all wished to protect their Norwegian cultural heritage, at the same time as they served the social function of bringing together people who wanted to cultivate one or another special interest. Although they were not intended to isolate the immigrants from American society, there was a certain tendency in this direction. There were Norwegians in America who pointed this out and looked with some disapproval on the multiplication of such societies, e.g., Judge Andreas Ueland in Minneapolis, a son of the Norwegian agrarian political leader Ole Gabriel Ueland.[8]

There were other Norwegian associations that worked for more general purposes in the larger American society. Some were interest groups within which Norwegians organized societies of their own, such as local unions of typographers, masons, painters, and the like. Norwegian fishermen on the west coast formed a "Fishermen's Union," and several times in the 1880s and '90s held back their products to get higher prices on the fish they sold to the canneries. There were Norwegian workingmen's societies in some cities from the 1870s on, and in 1893 a Scandinavian labor organization was formed, with 100 local unions and nearly 5,000 members — nine-tenths of them Norwegian-American women and men.[9]

The Norwegian-American branch of the temperance movement had an even greater popularity. In the mid-1880s there was a Norwegian temperance organization modeled after that of the home country with a great number of local societies, as well as Norwegian lodges within the International Order of Good Templars. As in Norway, the temperance movement acted as a pressure group in political life, sometimes in the form of special temperance parties.[10] Through their involvement in this idealistic, popular movement many Norwegian-Americans became interested in politics, and relations between the movement in Norway and Norwegians in America were very close.

Political Parties

Since the Civil War the majority of Norwegians had supported the Republican Party, Lincoln's party. Even though they had gained experience in politics at the local level, they were still grossly underrepresented on county and state levels as late as 1880. No one had yet been elected to congress, and no one was admitted to the inner councils of the Republican Party. Therefore, they had little influence on nominations at the state and national levels: Yankees dominated the party.

Interest and participation in politics, the will to make themselves felt as a group, was rapidly growing among Norwegian-Americans about 1880. In 1882 Norwegian-born Knute Nelson was nominated for congress in an electoral district where there were many Scandinavians. The Republican Party split on this nomination, and Nelson met a competitor from his own party and a Democrat in the election. The ensuing campaign was hard-fought. The question of whether a "foreigner" could be entrusted with such a task was much debated at party rallies and in the newspapers. Nelson won by a wide margin. Norwegians and Swedes had turned out in large numbers. Among politicians the district was long known as "the bloody fifth."

This election was the beginning of a long and illustrious political career for Knute Nelson.[11] After another hard-fought campaign ten years later he became the first foreign-born governor of Minnesota, and from there he again went to Washington, this time to the senate. He was re-elected repeatedly, and when he died in 1923 he was one of the most highly regarded members of the senate, although he was very conservative during his later years.

The election of 1882 was the first breakthrough for Norwegian candidates and it whetted their appetite. In the field of politics Norwegians usually worked with other Scandinavians, especially the Swedes in Minnesota, but they also worked by themselves and were generally more active than their fellow Scandinavians. They succeeded in getting more of their members elected to responsible offices than did the Swedes or Danes; in Minnesota they got more officials elected than did the much more numerous Germans. Between 1882 and 1924 five senators and nineteen congressmen of Norwegian origin were elected in Wisconsin, Minnesota, and the Dakotas, and many more were elected to important state offices, including eleven governors, in these states.[12]

There is no reason to suggest that Norwegians had a greater talent for politics than, for example, Swedes. When trying to explain the differences in political activity during the 1880s among Scandinavian groups it is important to note again that Norwegians had a more compact settlement pattern and that their settlements were older. Thus in the 1880s they had more candidates for political office, more people who had worked and gained experience on the local level. They could point to their many Civil War veterans — an asset in the Republican Party. More Norwegians than Swedes lived in the country, and it was easier to get ahead and win elections in rural areas than in the cities. To this may be added impulses from political activity in Norway. In the later decades of the nineteenth century nationalism in Norway was linked to liberalism and democracy, but in Sweden it was associated with aristocracy and conservatism. The Liberal Party that won power in Norway in 1884 agitated for democratic ideas that could easily be fitted into American political life.

Beginning in the 1880s many Norwegians cut loose from the Republican Party, some to join the Temperance Party, still more to join a new political movement, populism, and its party, the People's Party. This was an agrarian party, formed by dissatisfied midwestern farmers, especially wheat farmers, who complained about falling prices. Even with good crops they had a hard time paying interest and repaying the principal on their debts, and in the late 1880s crops were not good. The populists maintained that the middlemen were appropriating more than their just share of the values created by the farmers through their work. Such middlemen were the railroad companies that shipped the grain and owned the silos where it was stored; also the mill owners who ground it to flour, the exporters who sold it, and the banks which exacted a high rate of interest. The populists were alarmed at the rapid growth of industrialization and the growing size of the units in industry, transportation, and banking. They called for public control and regulation of transportation and industry. It is no exaggeration to say that they were anticapitalistic and that they had much in common with the "green socialism" of our day.[13]

This movement won wide support among the Norwegians in America, especially in western Minnesota and the Dakotas. As a farm woman in Minnesota wrote to her home in Norway, "We cannot blame God for these hard times, for he has blessed the land with rich fruit. The blame is with the president and his government and the capitalists."[14]

The party split gave Norwegians new alternatives and the possibility of new political advances. They formed their own party clubs within both the People's Party and the Republican Party, on occasion with the Swedes. They called them "Viking leagues" or "Scandinavian leagues," and they worked hard to get their candidates elected, often in opposition to the established party organization, e.g., in the Republican Party. Sometimes they operated anonymously and secretly to mobilize supporters and organize coups at the party primaries. They were successful in breaking the monopoly of Anglo-Americans in the parties and in major political offices. In a state like Minnesota it soon became a political advantage to have a Scandinavian name or to be able to point to an ancestor from Norway or Sweden.

In the period before 1914 the majority of Norwegians held opinions to the left of center. They supported populism until it disappeared with the good times about the turn of the century, and they joined the liberal wing of the Republican Party. They were strong supporters of Robert La Follette, the reform governor of Wisconsin, and were proud that he knew some Norwegian. Radical agrarian movements in the Dakotas and later the Farmer-Labor Party in Minnesota had many Norwegian-American supporters.

With few exceptions the men who made careers in major political offices were born in America or, like Nelson, had grown up and been educated there. In political life it was a bonus to speak the language of the land fluently and preferably without an accent: one could not appeal only to Norwegian or Scandinavian voters. It was said of one candidate that he was acceptable because he spoke fine English; if his

Norwegian was somewhat deficient that was of less consequence, for the Norwegian voters would gladly overlook it.

To have a chance to win support and get results politicians had to have a thorough knowledge of American conditions and American political problems. They had to deal with matters that concerned a whole state or the whole nation. At the same time this lively political activity quickened the pace of assimilation among the voters. Although their work on behalf of Norwegian-American candidates was an expression of self-assertion, voters were gradually growing more concerned about the issues for which the various parties and politicians stood. In this way the distinctly Norwegian aspect of political life gradually receded into the background and became something that one brought forth in wholly Norwegian surroundings and on festive occasions.

The success of Norwegian-American politicians naturally filled their countrymen with pride and joy, and we may suppose — without succumbing to chauvinistic self-satisfaction — that the heritage they brought with them benefited the Norwegian community in America and also the larger American society. Their rapid integration into this society, of which their political activity was one indication, may lead one to question the inner strength of Norwegian ethnicity which was so much in evidence in the first decade of the century. In any case this strength was soon to be exposed to a severe test.[15]

THE
IMMIGRANTS
BECOME AMERICANS

In 1925 the Norwegians in America celebrated the centennial of the sloop *Restauration's* voyage across the ocean. For three sunny days in June tens of thousands of Norwegian-Americans gathered on the huge state fairgrounds in St. Paul, Minnesota. They had crowded the trains from Wisconsin and the Dakotas. Some had come all the way from the east and west coast, spending days traveling. Those who lived nearest loaded the family into the Ford, their new "status symbol." Minneapolis was festively decorated, with American and Norwegian flags on buildings and in store windows. The city council had even decreed that June 8 should be a "folk holiday."

The Norwegian-Americans enjoyed a program demonstrating the best their group could offer of choral singing and instrumental music, exhibits of various kinds, meetings of *bygdelag*, historical pageants, and speeches. The old country honored its countrymen who had emigrated by sending representatives of the cabinet, the parliament, the church, the university and the colleges, and a number of organizations — from the Authors' Society to the League of Farm Youth. Each brought greetings and homage. The high point in the festivities was reached on the day when Calvin Coolidge, president of the United States, appeared at the fairgrounds. He spoke to 80,000 listeners, and a new invention known as a loudspeaker carried his voice to all. He had handsome words for the work of Norwegians in America, emphasizing that they had been good citizens, loyal to their new country in peace and war, and he did not fail to make the connection with Leif Ericson and the discovery of Vinland.[1]

These were days when it felt good to be a Norwegian-American. The pioneers of 1840 were long since gone, but some of the younger people from the wave of the 1860s and many of the later pioneers sat on the platform and listened. They might let their thoughts wander back in time and nod: Yes, it was true. They had worked hard. They had contributed something to the building of this country. They had seen vast changes since the time they tramped westward with a pair of oxen hitched to a covered wagon in the burning sun of the prairie looking for a piece of land they could till. But this was a festival and the words were festive. The everyday task was something else, at least for those who were working actively for the maintenance of Norwegian language and culture, the "ancestral heritage," as they put it. This work gradually became more laborious.

The first faint signs that the process of Americanization was causing the basis of Norwegian culture in America to crumble had appeared long before. "Norsedom" had begun to "dry up at the roots," just when the press and cultural life were having their strongest and finest flowering.[2] The interest in politics had drawn some into the larger society, but these were a minority and they had to maintain some contact with their Norwegian electorate. However, larger numbers of young people were educated and drawn from their original environment to new occupations and locations. They were no longer interested primarily in becoming pastors in Norwegian churches or teachers at Norwegian colleges. They became university professors and scientists in many fields — lawyers and doctors, technicians and nurses, office workers — and they got their jobs and their livelihood from American institutions and enterprises. Two men, in very different ways, influenced the development of the larger American society. One was Andrew Furuseth, who devoted his life to the improvement of the sailors' miserable lot. The other was Thorstein Veblen, whose incisive analysis of the American economic and social system left an enduring impact.

The current flowed into the cities, even though the Norwegians as a group remained in the country and the small towns more than other immigrant groups. Farm boys and girls moved away, and the old folks settled in the nearest small town when they no longer had the strength to operate the farm. Statistics as well as personal accounts tell the same story. "Well, now I'll tell you that we have rented our farm to a family for three years, and for this we'll get one-half of the crop," wrote a sixty-year-old farm woman from Minnesota. "We are now so old and weak that we could no longer run the farm ourselves." The children had moved to town: one son had a photography business and earned good money, for both "rich people and working people" wanted pictures and were willing to pay up to $12 a dozen. Another son was a druggist in Minneapolis. When the children were gone, the old folks no longer enjoyed their life on the farm.

When the young Norwegian-Americans moved into town, they were less particular about marrying other Norwegians than the first generation had been. The farm woman from Minnesota refers to marriages with people of Swedish, Danish, and German origin among her children and grandchildren. In such cases the English language naturally crept in, and the sense of solidarity with a distinct Norwegian background was diluted.[3]

The Norwegian Language

There were still compact settlements where the Norwegian-American country dialect was the language of home and work, where *Skandinaven* and *Decorah-Posten* were read thoroughly, and where churchgoing was associated with the older, bookish Norwegian of the Bible. American teachers still discovered to their despair — at the beginning of this century — that children knew only a few words of English when they entered school and that they turned to Norwegian as soon as recess began. If an outsider tried to find a place in such an environment, he or she had to learn Norwegian, become a Lutheran, and drink coffee in the afternoon. Gradually these districts were restricted to a few in Wisconsin, Minnesota, and the Dakotas: flatbread and *lefse* were still being baked in southern Minnesota in the 1920s (and later).[4]

Historically, attempts on the part of authorities to suppress a language have in fact promoted its survival for generations. The situation among Norwegians in America was quite different: Norwegian was never forbidden, either in speech or writing, not even during World War I, though Governor Harding of Iowa tried to do so.[5] The Norwegian language disappeared because young people refused to use it. There are many reports from our century of children and young people who replied in English when their parents addressed them in Norwegian. Norwegian gradually became a language for old people; the young were concerned about speaking English without the accent that would reveal their "foreign" origin. In Norwegian-American literature the language conflict between generations is a central theme.[6]

Teachers and journalists worked together with other culturally concerned persons in the Norwegian-American group to preserve and cultivate the Norwegian language. In 1903 they founded a society, the Norwegian Society, which had this work as its only goal, and they wrote articles in the quarterly published by the Society. But they never succeeded in gaining mass support for their program. And so other organizations founded by and for Norwegians in America had to adapt if they wished to survive.[7]

The church was the first to face the problem. The Norwegian Synod had wanted to found Norwegian common schools to secure Norwegian as the "language of the heart." By 1900 the Synod as well as other churches had to consider whether they could keep their young people if Sunday school, confirmation, and services were to be in Norwegian only. In the long run a church body in a country without a state church, competing for souls with other churches, could take just one course. Church interests had to come before ethnic and cultural ones. In 1915 nearly a fourth of the sermons were given in English as was more than a fourth of the instruction in Sunday schools and for confirmation. Fifteen years later Norwegian had practically disappeared in the instruction of children and young people, and only one-tenth of the congregations (with one-twentieth of the members) had all-Norwegian sermons. In 1946 the church dropped "Norwegian" from its name: it was now the Evangelical Lutheran Church and made its appeal to all Lutherans in America regardless of origin or ancestry. In 1960 it joined with other Lutheran synods to become the American Lutheran Church; most of the former Norwegian Lutheran congregations are members of this body. Its president is David W. Preus, a great-grandson of Herman A. Preus, one of the founders of the Norwegian Synod in the 1850s.[8]

A similar development began at the colleges about the turn of the century and for the same reasons: young people wanted to be instructed in English. A man like Rølvaag discovered to his sorrow that Norwegian had to be taught as any foreign language was taught, because most of the students knew only the Norwegian they had "picked up" from grandpa and grandma. The colleges had to consider the competition and offer instruction of a type and quality comparable with that of other colleges. The study of Norwegian language and literature, which had been required of all students with a Norwegian background, became voluntary and gradually assumed a more modest position in the work of the colleges, thus making them more American and less Norwegian.[9]

World War I

The drying up of the roots began to affect the flowering branches under the stress of World War I and the years immediately after it. Young men who were drafted could hardly gather in regiments of their own with Norwegian-speaking officers as they had in the Civil War. This time men of all backgrounds were brought together in the armed forces, and the soldier's life leveled their differences: in the barracks and in the trenches all became American. The young women who took jobs as nurses, secretaries, and war workers encountered new conditions and new people: they were all working for their country.

As in the Civil War, the effect of the national crisis spread from the center to the periphery, the local community. Each citizen had to show loyalty and support for the war, for example by buying government bonds, "Liberty Bonds." Certain ethnic groups, especially the Germans, were suspected of disloyalty, and this suspicion might be directed at other groups that tried to preserve their ethnic individuality. No one wished to be accused of being a "hyphenated" American, and young people were exposed to the pressure that had been exerted on them from the moment they entered public school: they often made a point of being monolingual, in order to be American like everybody else.

The pressure from the center at times caused conflicts of conscience for some. The progressive Republicans in the Midwest had been among the least war-minded in the period before America's entry into the war; they were pacifists at heart, and many of them looked on the war propaganda of activists as the nefarious work of the armament industry and the capitalists. Norwegian-American senator Asle Gronna from North Dakota voted (as one of six senators) with Robert La Follette against American entry into the war in 1917. The conflict is reflected also in Rølvaag's work and that of several Norwegian activists: their loyalty was unquestionable, but they disapproved of the kind of Americanism they now saw emerging.[10]

Restricting Immigration

The Russian revolution triggered a fear of the "reds" and intensified the demand for full Americanism, "100 percent." This demand was in sharp contrast to the political and social climate that had existed earlier. In the years right after the war, immigrants who espoused dissident political opinions were occasionally deported if they had not become American citizens. The opponents of free immigration got the upper hand, and the United States began to close its door to newcomers, the door it had kept open to Europe throughout its history. Several laws restricting immigration were passed in the years 1921 to 1929: the last of these gave Norway an annual quota of 2,377. In the biggest postwar year, 1923, 18,000 Norwegians emigrated, 16,000 of them to the United States.[11]

The restriction of immigration put an end to the continual rich inflow of Norwegian language, cultural impulses, and personal news. Besides, the newcomers of the 1920s were children of a new age: the aggressively nationalistic mood of the nineteenth-century liberals was gone. The new immigrants were Norwegian but not necessarily enthusiastic patriots. They were attracted more by possibilities of employment than by political conditions or social opportunities.

Societies and Newspapers

A general survey of the development of Norwegian societies and newspapers for the period since 1914 has not yet been made. But it is obvious that activity was reduced, that associations gradually disintegrated or were dissolved. Even earlier the great organizer of seamen's unions, Andrew Furuseth, had found that he had to work entirely as an American to get results. Members of Norwegian unions and political clubs must have learned the same in the 1920s. The temperance movement reached its goal when prohibition was introduced in 1919 and never again succeeded in winning a place in the affections of the common people. Sports-minded young people cultivated their talents at schools and colleges, or professionally, and most of the Norwegian societies were dissolved. The most famous Norwegian-American sportsman in American history, coach Knute Rockne, trained his football team at Notre Dame University, a Catholic school. When a Norwegian sports club in New York was dissolved, all the loving cups and prizes it had won were given to the Emigrant Museum in Norway.[12]

The largest of the Norwegian organizations, the Sons of Norway, had its economic base in the insurance business. But even this was not entirely stable, because of the age distribution of its members. Beginning in 1942 the membership magazine appeared in English, which helped to promote a renewed interest among younger members. In this way it continued to work on behalf of Norway and Norwegian culture.[13]

This recourse was not readily available to newspapers. At the time of the centennial in 1925 the larger ones were still doing well, but the opposition papers had given up. The socialistic *Gaa Paa* in Minneapolis closed down in 1920; *Normanden* in North Dakota struggled to stay alive; and *Reform* went on as a one-man enterprise until Waldemar Ager's death (1942). Even the larger papers had to depend on their faithful subscribers as they watched the circulation falling off year by year. The depression of the 1930s delivered the death blow to several of them: *Minneapolis Tidende* stopped in 1935 and *Skandinaven* survived only until 1941. Their subscription lists were taken over by *Decorah-Posten*, and yet it had no more than 35,000 subscribers in 1950, about one-half of *Skandinaven's* list at its peak. In 1972 *Decorah-Posten* also had to give up, leaving only *Nordisk Tidende* in Brooklyn, *Vinland* in Chicago, *Minnesota Posten* in Minneapolis, and *Western Viking* in Seattle.[14]

This development was part of a more general process that occurred among all immigrant groups but at different speeds, depending on the pattern of settlement and the time span of mass immigration. The immigrants became Americans, and their descendants were not Norwegian-Americans in the sense that the immigrants had been.

They were Americans of Norwegian descent, or were part Norwegian, shaped by America with respect to their work, social life, political affiliations, the causes they supported, and the interests they pursued.

Solidarity

Even so there are small Norwegian enclaves here and there in the Middle West, in Coon Valley and Stoughton, Wisconsin, and in the Red River Valley, on the Minnesota and the North Dakota sides, where a knowledge of Norwegian has been transmitted from parents to children down to our own time, and where people are still conscious of being "Norskies." Two or three years ago a young Norwegian historian went from Land, an east Norwegian district, to America to study emigration. The trip cost him little more than airfare and a round-trip Greyhound bus ticket. From the moment he met the descendants of emigrants from the Land district, he was taken care of. He was fed and lodged, and given information on where to go next.

One may meet second and third generation descendants who speak Norwegian, and the town of Stoughton has made the celebration of May 17 a major civic enterprise. In major cities, there are still Norwegian-American societies, even though the members are fewer and generally older than before. In places like Brooklyn, New York, San Pedro, and Los Angeles, there is even today a small but steady influx of young people, especially from the coastal districts of southern Norway. Some are "birds of passage" as their parents were, some come to stay.

There is solidarity in larger groups as well, for example in education. In the 1920s the smaller and less effective schools were consolidated, and support was concentrated on the major ones to bring them up to standard. Anyone who saw one of the Norwegian-American colleges (St. Olaf, Luther, Augsburg, Concordia, or Pacific Lutheran) in the 1930s and has seen them recently cannot help but be impressed by the expansion of the postwar period and the high academic standards that have been achieved. This progress has been made possible by thousands of contributions from average middle-class people and rarely from the wealthy. These donors have the sense that the schools are theirs, and that it is their common task to support them.[15]

There is still an indefinable feeling of togetherness and solidarity, of kinship and intimacy among many of the descendants of Norwegian immigrants, vague in some, strong and vital in others. It is rooted in common childhood memories, whether it be the celebration of Christmas or parental attitudes toward life. From this sense of fellowship arises a wish and a determination to maintain an identity in the great American society with its many ethnic groups. From it arises also an interest in the past, in genealogy and Norwegian-American history, and beyond these in the old country itself.[16]

It is significant that the Norwegian-American Historical Association, which was founded in connection with the centennial of 1925, has been a growing organization. For a great many years the scholarly work of the association was directed by the distinguished pioneer in research on Norwegian-American history, Theodore C. Blegen. The strict demands he made on himself and his younger collaborators established a tradition that has resulted in the more thorough study of Norwegian emigration and Norwegian-American settlement and cultural history than that of most other ethnic groups. Contemporary descendants of Norwegians have united in a great cultural and historical task — developing the old Norwegian-American museum in Decorah, Iowa, into a modern Norwegian folk museum for Americans, a display of settlement history and pioneer life. Named "Vesterheim" (Western Home), it has become a focus of the new ethnic revival, one phase of which is an annual Nordic Fest.[17]

World War II helped to stir interest in Norway, which was fighting with America for the same ideals. Social developments since the war have also stimulated an interest in the social and political system of the Nordic countries, including Norway.

In the 1960s a new interest in the lands of their origin sprang up among all ethnic groups in America, what has been called the "ethnic revival." Among Norwegians it has led to a reawakening of interest — let us hope it is not just a passing fad — in the study of Norwegian language and literature at colleges and universities and in new activity in the organizations that have survived. The museum in Decorah has noted a new and growing interest in Norwegian folk art since it initiated courses in woodcarving, rosepainting, Hardanger embroidery, and the like.[18]

At the same time the airplane has made it possible to travel quickly and relatively cheaply, a possibility eagerly seized by thousands of Americans of Norwegian descent every summer. Some visit Norwegian museums and mountains and fjords like regular tourists. Others have kept up contact with their kinsmen in Norway and know exactly where they are going to visit with relatives. Some are hunting in archives and elsewhere for a place, a family, or a name that may throw light on their roots. Young Americans of Norwegian descent constitute a large percentage of the students at the annual summer school of the University of Oslo. In this way descendants of those who once were drawn from the harsh struggle for daily bread to the great republic in the West now make pilgrimages to the land of their ancestors. Some of them discover it is a remarkably interesting country, not just for its scenery but even more for its people, its social structure, and its political system.

THE EMIGRANTS
AND THE HOMELAND

When emigration began in the 1840s poets and writers — as well as authorities — were appalled. "Alas! The Black Death now must I recall with terror," wrote Henrik Wergeland. "Now as then are farms abandoned in our valleys."[1] Two decades later people had grown accustomed to it and looked on it with a kind of sober resignation. Many even suggested that given the difficult economic circumstances of the 1860s, emigration was advantageous for the country: Norway had too many people in proportion to its capital resources. This view was widespread until the end of the century, when opinion changed. Increasingly people maintained that it was a national misfortune for the country to lose its best manpower, those who had been supported and educated by parents and society, just when they were prepared to do productive work. Immediately after the turn of the century a number of business organizations took steps to counteract emigration by founding the Society for Limiting Emigration. Population loss was now regarded as a serious social problem.[2]

It is impossible to know how Norway would have developed economically and socially had there been no mass emigration. One can suggest conflicting hypotheses: the productive capacity of the emigrants would have speeded up economic growth and made the country richer; or their presence might have been burdensome, keeping wages down and creating a mass proletariat in town and country.

We do not even know if the population would have developed in the same way without emigration; perhaps there would have been depression years with a high mortality rate or people might have begun limiting the birth rate sooner than they did.[3]

What we do know is that emigration affected demographic conditions: actual population growth was much smaller than the surplus of births over deaths; and the proportions of younger people and of men were reduced. Some said Norway was becoming a nation of babies and graybeards, forgetting that children generally have parents. Others worried about "the abnormal surplus of women," which led an increasing number of women to look for work outside their homes. This sometimes led to their taking jobs from men, thus causing more emigration. Worse yet, it was a threat to "the physical and moral development of the race," for woman's place was still in the home — as housewife or maid.[4]

But if the demographic development in the entire country with respect to age and sex groups is to be explained, other facts must be taken into account, above all the internal migrations. The surplus of women was greatest in the cities, and the deficit of young people was in the country. It is quite possible that the social environment was impoverished in communities where emigration was heaviest, that life lost some of its movement and energy where there were few young people — in short, a foretaste of the rural problems of our own time. On the other hand, it is a reasonable hypothesis that the maintenance and even increase in wages in the 1880s was due to the reduction in manpower caused by emigration, just as the emigration of sailors helped to raise wages on Norwegian ships.

Money from America to Norway

The emigrants carried with them not only the capital that had been invested in their education but also some cash. The sums involved can hardly have been great, although some, especially among the early emigrants, were relatively well-off. In the 1860s they were among the poorest immigrants to arrive in the Midwest, and even later there are a number of accounts indicating that many were penniless on arrival. In the 1880s the average was about twenty-five kroner ($6) per emigrant, a sum that should be regarded as a minimum figure. Not everyone is willing to declare one's holdings to inquisitive authorities.[5]

But surprisingly the emigrants were soon sending money home, and not just for tickets or other travel expenses. They sent considerable sums to their families, as reports indicate beginning in the 1850s. The flow of money increased with the years, transmitted as money orders and bank drafts, or by the steamship companies. A calculation from 1905 suggests that 20 million kroner (some 5 million dollars) was sent that year. This may have been a record year, but 12 to 15 million kroner must have been sent every year between 1905 and World War I. These were gifts to relatives and the savings of people who intended to return. The sums were considerable at a time when the total annual imports from the United States were valued at 15 to 18 million kroner, and the Norwegian national budget was only about 90 to a 100 million kroner. But this is not all: immigrants often sent cash in ordinary letters, e.g., special cards with a slot into which a silver dollar could be inserted were put in envelopes and mailed. Mail clerks occasionally took these envelopes when they could feel money inside, but no doubt most of the cash reached its destination. It was welcome indeed; as Ingeborg Refling Hagen described it in a poem: "Hush, don't fight, kids; tomorrow the America boat will come with a dollar bill for us."[6]

Norwegian-Americans collected money for people in Norway who had been victims of disaster — crop failure, bad fishing, a city fire, or a destructive landslide. In 1872 they helped raise money for the millennial monument to King Harald Fairhair, founder of the Norwegian dynasty. In 1905 they gave the big bell that rang out for peace and freedom from Akershus Fort in 1908. Norwegian academics in America made a donation to the university centennial in 1911, and all Norwegian-Americans united in giving a memorial at the centennial of the Norwegian constitution in 1914. The American *bygdelag* collected funds for local causes, old-age homes, or church organs. The Nordland Norwegians in America raised money for a rescue vessel.

Emigrants who had done unusually well in America sometimes set up endowments; the most generous donor was perhaps engineer Tinius Olsen of Kongsberg, who established endowments of nearly a half million kroner for young people in his hometown who wished to get a technical education. In this way Norwegian-Americans tried to express their love for home and family, for the community and the country they had left. Around 1910 they made a decisive contribution to the founding of the Norwegian America Line, incorporated in Christiania, at that time a major national effort. The one who undertook the task of persuading his Norwegian-American countrymen to take shares in the enterprise was Birger Osland, who twenty-five years earlier had arrived in Chicago with $6 in his pocket. The result of his and others' work was that shares for more than a million dollars were sold in America.[7]

When in 1940 Norway experienced the national disaster of Nazi occupation, which would last five years, Norwegian-Americans again showed that they had not forgotten the old country. They organized a large-scale Aid to Norway operation, supported by churches and secular organizations and channeled through state committees. Even during the war the leaders succeeded in making contacts with Norwegians in Sweden who passed contributions of food and provisions on to Norway, some openly and some secretly. In 1944 Aid to Norway sent goods and money to the recently liberated but ravaged Finnmark area. During the whole war they assisted the Norwegian training program for fliers in Camp Little Norway in Toronto. Individuals also supported the welfare programs for Norwegian seamen instituted by the Norwegian government exiled in London. A survey of aid sent to Norway during the war and immediately afterward shows that Norwegians received from Aid to Norway 156 million kroner in money and goods.[8]

Emigrants subscribed to Norwegian-American newspapers for their relatives at home: thousands of copies of *Skandinaven*, as well as *Decorah-Posten* and others, crossed the seas. *Decorah-Posten* was still mailing nearly 4,000 copies to Norway in 1950, and that figure can safely be doubled for the end of the preceding century. Emigrants sent photographs that adorned many living rooms in Norway. Sometimes they sent products that were rare, perhaps unknown, in remote districts in Norway, e.g., a woman in Minnesota sent baking powder to her friend in Dovre in the 1880s.[9]

America Letters

Above all, many sent letters: there are America letters from the beginning. The early letters show clearly that the writers were making a special effort to describe general conditions in America, especially those that differed from conditions in Norway. One wrote that a letter from America should be meaningful, saying that many had asked him to report on the country. "But since it is too elaborate to write to so many, I request that you let this letter circulate or make a copy of it so that anyone who wishes can learn from it." Sometimes there was too much interest in a letter. As late as 1889 one farmer reminded his children in America: "Don't write about everything in one letter. You know how it is: one wants to read it, another wants to borrow it, and not everybody should see everything."[10]

Letter writing was a novel means of communication in the Norwegian rural society of the 1840s. Hans Nielsen Hauge had used it to create and maintain contact within his religious movement; but in many families the America letter was the first they received in the mail, and for a long time it was the most common type. The introduction of stamps around 1850 in Norway and America made it much cheaper than it had been before. Norwegians on both sides of the Atlantic were also becoming more skilled in writing, even if they were not all equally diligent correspondents. Norwegian postal statistics give no information on the number of letters from America, only on letters from abroad. But in 1881 the 37,000 inhabitants of Sogn district got nearly 10,000 letters from abroad, while the neighboring South and North Nordfjord district with 50,000 inhabitants got only 4,000. It seems likely that most of the foreign letters to Sogn came from America, since many emigrated from Sogn.[11]

Later letter writers were not as concerned about giving thorough surveys of American conditions as the early writers had been, and they naturally tended to write more about their personal circumstances. They usually took more things for granted, but even so they did not limit themselves to telling about their cows, their crops, or their children. They emphasized again and again that in America one had to work harder than in Norway: money did not grow on trees, and if anyone worked for two days and drank for three, he would hardly have enough to pay for the clothes on his back.

Sometimes they commented on conditions or events in Norway. "I suppose you're glad to have annual parliaments," wrote one. "It's a good thing you have Johan Sverdrup," wrote another. "Further I can report that this fall I have forsworn King Oscar of Norway and Sweden," reported a man from Gausdal in January 1885, "so now I can vote. Last fall we had a presidential election, and I took part in voting for president, as did everyone else, high or low." He, too, noted that there was no class distinction in America; everyone was respected according to his abilities. "No one will ask: was your father a farmer or a businessman; they will consider what you are, and your previous life has no significance. But anyone who drinks whiskey is considered a vulgar person." In November 1913 a politically interested Norwegian in Nebraska wrote that Woodrow Wilson looked as if he would be a good president. The writer had been a Republican and a supporter of Teddy Roosevelt, but now he was happy to see that Wilson was stopping the financiers and capitalists of the East.[12]

It is impossible to measure exactly what this direct contact with America meant for those who stayed in Norway, transmitted as it was by newspapers, visits, and especially by letters. In any case it was unique, different from other impulses reaching the country, because it came straight into the homes of common people from their nearest and dearest kin. No doubt the contact was stimulating: to know that one's brothers and sisters were doing well could strengthen one's own self-confidence, proving that one was of good stock, and that one only needed a chance. Many were delighted to see that a Norwegian-American greeted and conversed with the bailiff and the pastor as their equal.

Even children could feel these impulses. "When I was a boy, I learned the name of America before I heard of any other country," reports Professor Didrik Arup Seip, who was born in 1884 and grew up in the remote rural district of Åseral in southern Norway. "I heard about New York and Chicago before London and Berlin. Names like Dakota and Minnesota were better known to me than Spain and France. This was due to the fact that I grew up in a mountain community which had sent many of its young men and even some of its women to America. Letters as well as Norwegian-American newspapers came all the time. Far up in that mountain valley we were in lively cultural contact with America, receiving reports that gave life a wider horizon and nourished our imaginations."[13]

Evidence indicates that many observers were aware that America letters and other reports provided common people with widening horizons. Eilert Sundt, who knew the Norwegian countryside better than most, said that the America letters were one of the "motivating forces" of the age, in addition to other novelties like agricultural schools, folk high schools, farmers' societies, congregational meetings, and newspapers. I mentioned previously how Søren Jaabæk used America in his agitation. The most vivid picture of the significance of the America letters is drawn by Alexander Kielland in his novel *Fortuna*. The common people, he said, are great readers, and they read "what hardly any of us think about, they read over and over again the thousands of letters that flow in upon us every year from the Norwegians in America. You see, that is a better educational resource than all the books and newspapers. For here the people learn for the first time from their own people, in their own language, from their own thinking, the only thing a person can understand all the way through. And just imagine all the criticism implied in these letters of our conditions here from top to bottom — clear, comprehensible judgments and comparisons, from a cousin, or from Uncle Lars who was so trustworthy and well-acquainted with everything." "Common people," wrote Kielland, did not read "the newspapers of the pillars of society," "the daily repetition of the ancient truths that in America live the scoundrels, in Paris the communards, in Christiania wisdom, and in Stockholm virtue. This they do not read."[14] The criticism that Kielland mentions provided a growing self-consciousness and a stimulus to opposition. If universal suffrage could carry the farm boy Knute Nelson to the national assembly of the United States in 1882, should not universal suffrage be introduced in Norway, too, so that common people might have something to say? The America letters did not create the policies of the Liberal Party, but they supported its agitation for political democracy. One can only imagine what effect it would have today if some hundreds of thousands of Norwegians living in China sent money home to their parents and wrote letters in praise of Chinese social conditions: one would certainly hear about it.

Attitudes toward Norwegian-Americans

Let us try to follow these impulses further. Norwegian-Americans rejoiced when news reached them that the union with Sweden had been dissolved in 1905. They tried to influence the American government to recognize Norway as an independent state. In November 1905 came a significant plebiscite after the union with Sweden was dissolved: should Norway become a republic or a monarchy? More than one-fifth of the voters wanted a republic, a surprising number when one considers the long tradition of monarchy. No doubt stories of how well Norwegians were getting along in the American republic meant more to the voters than, for example, the model of the third French republic.

This contact with America was broad and popular, and it did not include the upper class, the "aristocrats." The educated and official classes had little fondness for the Norwegian-Americans returning to visit Norway. They looked on them as show-offs, boasting upstarts, with fur coats and gold teeth, often caricatured in the humorous papers of the time. They noted that although many of the Norwegian-Americans appeared to be well-off, they regrettably lacked "culture." "But who are these people?" wrote a Norwegian who had lived some years in America. "Poor farm boys, perhaps from the most remote districts, cotters' sons with the least possible schooling." And with whom are they being compared? "Because they are well-dressed and usually have a well-filled pocketbook, they are compared with city people and those who are known as the educated class, i.e., people who have been given a good education and have lived life in more cultivated circles in general." But this comparison is based on false premises, maintains the writer. "One must place these people in their own environment, and I think they will measure up both in one and the other respect in comparison with our average farmers."

Only the district physicians occasionally expressed a different view from the one prevalent among the "cultivated." One of them wrote that Norwegian-American women visiting back home had taught people to value cleanliness and neatness in the household. Other observers reported that returned Norwegian-Americans were experimenters who introduced novelties in agriculture: they drained marshes, were quick to buy machinery, and in general succeeded in getting their fellows out of "old ruts." [15]

The "cultivated" class in Norway, what would now be called "the establishment," showed little interest in "Norwegian America" and had few connections there; some businessmen in Bergen might have been exceptions. This lack of interest offended Norwegian-Americans, especially those who were active in organizational and journalistic life. When in 1884 Johan Sverdrup wrote to Norwegian-American organizations to thank them for their support, he got a letter back from editor Nicolay Grevstad saying that this was the first sign Norwegians in America had received from Norway, not only of recognition, but even of common courtesy.[16]

About the turn of the century this attitude was slowly changing, as newspapers and magazines published articles on Norwegians in America and books began appearing. These books told Norwegians in statistical terms what their countrymen had succeeded in building up in the new country. In 1903 *Aftenposten* asserted that Norwegians had to stop being so haughty, should no longer say they would have nothing to do with the "plebeians and upstarts" in America. At this time politicians also began discovering that the emigrants were interested in the movement for national independence.[17]

Then came the exciting year 1905. That fall, when it appeared that the negotiations with Sweden might collapse and war would break out, Norwegians "discovered" their emigrated countrymen in America and elsewhere. They received abundant testimonials that the emigrants had not forgotten Norway and that they supported her national cause. This spontaneous reaction led Bjørnson to make a broadside appeal, calling on Norwegians to "make Norway larger." "The liberation of 1905 has united the Norwegian family as never before. The desire for tying lasting bonds and encouraging all possible cooperation between Norwegians at home and abroad is now strong on both sides of the ocean. On this concept we should be able to found an organization."[18]

New Contacts

In 1906 Norwegians in America, church as well as secular representatives, were invited to the coronation of King Haakon and Queen Maud. Thousands of other Norwegian-Americans had also come to participate. A special festival was held for them at St. Hanshaugen park in Christiania, where Carl Berner, president of the *Storting*, spoke. He repeated Bjørnson's idea of forming an organization, a league that would work to keep alive the contacts among Norwegians and their descendants, not only in America, but around the world. A year later *Nordmanns-Forbundet* ("The League of Norsemen") was founded.

The new league won support from a number of national associations and from several thousand individuals. It also became the connecting link in the more official recognition of Norwegians in America which now followed. In 1908 The League of Norsemen sent representatives to a memorial celebration of the birth of poet Henrik Wergeland held in Minneapolis. The delegates brought with them as a gift a bronze casting of Gustav Vigeland's statue of Wergeland. They also bore greetings from King Haakon and conferred the order of St. Olav on the leaders of the Norwegian-American Church bodies.

On the occasion of the 1914 centennial of the Norwegian constitution, celebrated with an exhibition at Frogner Park in Christiania, a special Norwegian-American exhibit was sponsored by the League of Norsemen. The thousands of Norwegians who visited the exhibition were treated to pictures and statistical displays, models and objects, showing what the emigrants had been doing in their new country. This was a novel sight for many.

Since that time *Nordmanns-Forbundet* has expanded its organizational contacts by cooperating with Norwegian-American institutions and organizations, and by establishing local branches wherever there are Norwegians, of whom there are many more in America than anywhere else. Norwegian lecturers, as well as musicians and singers, have been sent to America; in exchange choruses and orchestras the best of them from the colleges, have been sent to Norway from America. The *bygdelag* have come to visit, collectively and individually. As personal contacts weakened, organized contact became more significant.

Ties that bound family to family became less strong. Old letter writers died, and there were fewer to keep up the tradition, because they could no longer communicate in the same language and because they had forgotten their ties. During the depression of the 1930s there were fewer good tidings to report, and not many could afford to send money back home. Then World War II and the German occupation closed off all possibilities for normal contact.

The impulses that crossed the Atlantic from home to home until 1914 are gone. Even if they did now exist, the image of America could no longer be drawn in the clear strokes characteristic of the newspapers, letters, and books in the age of mass migration. Insofar as Norway and the other Scandinavian countries can point today to their political and social democracy as one that in spite of its shortcomings awakens interest in other countries, not least in America, it is surely appropriate to recall the impressions, ideas, and impulses communicated by the emigrants who had made their new homes in America to their countrymen at home.

Many Americans of Norwegian ancestry still feel they have an identity, a history of their own. They share this feeling with many other ethnic groups in this country. In 1975 many Norwegian-Americans joined in celebrating the 150th anniversary of the sloop *Restauration* and the fifty-two men, women, and children who led Norwegian migration West. Norwegians at home did the same, not only because this migration is a part of their history but also because their American countrymen and their descendants have given Norway material and spiritual values. They have contributed by their labors to creating respect for Norway, and Norwegians would be poorer if these bonds should break.

Norwegians still feel that the Icelanders are their near kinsmen even though it is more than a thousand years since their ancestors settled in Iceland. Norwegians still feel kinship when they visit the Shetlands or the Orkneys. So they surely have good reason to hope that the solidarity which results from having common historical memories, a common tradition, and perhaps also a common outlook and values, will continue to exist for a long time between Norwegians at home and the descendants of those who left Norway in the days of migration to America.

NOTES

NOTES

(NAHA stands for the Norwegian-American Historical Association)

Chapter 1: Migration

1. The most up-to-date history of Norway in the English language is T. K. Derry, *A Short History of Norway*, 2nd ed. London: Oxford University Press, 1968. More important is *A History of Modern Norway, 1814–1972*, by the same author, Oxford: Clarendon Press, 1973, which also contains a chapter on Norwegians abroad. Karen Larsen, *A History of Norway*, 2nd ed. Princeton, N.J.: Princeton University Press, is also useful.

2. Emigration to the Netherlands is the subject of Oddleif Hodne's unpublished thesis "Fra Agder til Amsterdam," University of Oslo, Institute of History, 1976. (mimeographed)

3. J. O. Evjen, *Scandinavian Immigrants in New York, 1630–1674*, Baltimore: Genealogical Publishing Co., 1972 (reprint). See also Paul Knaplund, "Norwegians in the Selkirk settlement 1815–1870," *Studies and Records*, v. 6, Northfield, Minn., 1931, pp. 1–11, and Hjalmar R. Holand, "An early Norwegian fur trader of the Canadian Northwest," *Studies and Records*, v. 5, Northfield, 1930, pp. 1–13.

4. For the image of America in Norway, see Sigmund Skard, *The United States in Norwegian History*, Oslo: Universitetsforlaget, 1976.

5. John Quincy Adams, *Writings*, ed. by Worthington Chauncey Ford, v. 3, N.Y.: Macmillan, 1914, pp. 343–45, letter dated Christiansand, Norway, September 29, 1809, to the secretary of state.

6. Ingrid Semmingsen, "A shipload of German emigrants and their significance for the Norwegian emigration of 1825," *The Swedish Pioneer Historical Quarterly*, July 1974, pp. 183–92. The hypothesis propounded in the article that some of the German emigrants were Rappites has since been verified. See Semmingsen, De tyske emigranter i Bergen 1817–18, *Bergens historiske forenings skrifter*, 1976, pp. 120–38. More detailed information on the Rappites among them is given by Karl J. R. Arndt, "George Rapp's Harmonists and the beginnings of Norwegian migration to America," *The Western Pennsylvania Historical Magazine*, v. 60, July 1977, pp. 143–263.

Chapter 2: The Sloop *Restauration*

1. The great authority on early Norwegian emigration is the late Theodore C. Blegen. His *Norwegian Migration to America, 1825–1860*, v. 1, Northfield: NAHA, 1931, contains

the most scholarly, detailed and accurate account of the movement in this period as well as of the Sloopers. In chap. 2 he discusses the history of the Sloopers up to their settlement in Kendall. Recent research has provided some new information: see Richard Canuteson, "A little more light on the Kendall colony," *Studies and Records*, v. 19, Northfield, 1956, pp. 82–101, on the distribution of property in Kendall, and two articles by Mario S. DePillis on a letter, which he discovered, from some of the Norwegian settlers, and endorsed by Cleng Peerson, to Frederick Rapp: "Still more light on the Kendall colony: a unique Slooper letter," *Studies and Records*, v. 20, Northfield, 1959, pp. 24–31, and "Cleng Peerson and the communitarian background of Norwegian immigration," *Norwegian-American Studies*, v. 21, Northfield, 1962, pp. 136–57. In the second article DePillis discusses the content of the letter, which is an application for a loan from the Rappites, and its significance in relation to the communitarian ideas of the Sloopers. Frederick Rapp's negative answer to the request of the Norwegian settlers is published in Arndt's article "George Rapp's Harmonists." A new and shorter history of Norwegian emigration which is very reliable and contains much factual information is Arlow W. Andersen, *The Norwegian-Americans*, Boston: Twayne Publishers, 1975.

2. A much more detailed account of the difficulties of the Quakers and their conflicts with Norwegian authorities is found in Blegen, *Norwegian Migration*, v. 1, chap. 2.

3. Blegen, *Norwegian Migration*, v. 1, p. 29.

4. Blegen, *Norwegian Migration*, v. 1, p. 51.

5. Blegen *Norwegian Migration: American Transition*, v. 2, Northfield: NAHA, 1970, pp. 599–628.

6. Quoted from Rasmus B. Anderson, *The First Chapter of Norwegian Immigration (1821–1840)*, Madison: The author, 1906, pp. 79–80.

7. Copies of the Hovland letters have been found in these communities. In all of them the exodus began during the years 1836 to 1838. Norsk historisk kjeldeskrift-institutt, Oslo, has a large collection of America letters. Copies of most of them are in the archives of the Norwegian-American Historical Association, St. Olaf College, Northfield.

8. Henry J. Cadbury, "The Norwegian Quakers of 1825," *Studies and Records*, v. 1, Minneapolis, 1926, pp. 60–94, and "Four emigrant shiploads of 1836 and 1837," *Studies and Records*, v. 2, Northfield, 1927, pp. 20–52.

9. Letter from Tønnes Willemsen to Elias Tastad of November 18, 1836. Here quoted from Gunnar Malmin, "Norsk Landnàm i U.S.," *Decorah-Posten*, December 5, 1924.

10. Theodore C. Blegen, ed., *Land of Their Choice: The Immigrants Write Home*. Minneapolis: University of Minnesota Press, 1955, pp. 27–31.

Chapter 3: Pioneers

1. Blegen, *Norwegian Migration*, v. 1, chaps. 2–7, provides detailed information on pioneers and the spread of settlements.

2. Blegen, *Norwegian Migration*, v. 1, pp. 26–27, in which earlier research and sources concerning the early life of Cleng Peerson are also listed.

3. Blegen, *Land of Their Choice*, p. 42 (letter from Ole Rynning). See DePillis, "Cleng Peerson."

4. D. G. Ristad, "A doctrinaire idealist," *Studies and Records*, v. 3, Northfield, 1928, pp. 13–22. Ole S. Aavatsmark, *Hans Barlien. En norsk bondefører*, Trondheim: Nidaros & Trøndelagens boktr., 1954, gives much new information on Barlien. Even in America, Barlien unsuccessfully tried to invent. See Blegen, *Land of Their Choice*, p. 82. A letter from Barlien appears in Blegen, *Land of Their Choice*, pp. 52–54, and in H. F. Swanson, "The Sugar Creek Settlement," *Studies and Records*, v. 9, Northfield, 1936, pp. 38–44.

5. For further information on the development of freedom of trade in Norway see Derry, *Modern Norway*, pp. 31–37 and 106–11.

6. Quoted from Semmingsen, *Veien mot vest: Utvandringen fra Norge til Amerika*, v. 1, Oslo: Aschehoug & Co., 1942, p. 58.

7. Arne Odd Johnsen, "Johannes Nordboe and Norwegian immigration," *Studies and Records*, v. 8, Northfield, 1934, pp. 23–38. Einar Hovdhaugen, *Frå Venabygd til Texas*, Oslo: Det norske samlaget, 1975, provides new information on Nordboe and tells about his own contacts with Nordboe's descendants in California.

8. Anderson, *The First Chapter*, p. 155.

9. Henrik Wergeland (1809–1845) was the cosmic poet who became a national symbol because of his rebellious opposition to entrenched privilege and his advocacy of the popular cause. For further information see Harald Beyer, *The History of Norwegian Literature*, New York: New York University Press, 1956, translated by Einar Haugen.

10. Blegen, *Norwegian Migration*, v. 1, p. 93.

11. "The seventeenth of May in Mid-Atlantic: Ole Rynning's emigrant song," *Studies and Records*, v. 8, Northfield, 1934, p. 22. Also in Theodore C. Blegen and Martin B. Ruud, *Norwegian emigrant songs and ballads*, Minneapolis: University of Minnesota Press, 1936.

12. *Ole Rynning's True Account of America*, translated and edited by Theodore C. Blegen, Travel and Description Series, v. 1, Minneapolis: NAHA, 1926. The historical introduction, pp. 1–22, contains an excellent biographical sketch of Ole Rynning. The quotation is from a contemporary letter. See *Land of Their Choice*, pp. 67 and 81–82, and *A Chronicle of Old Muskego. The Diary of Søren Bache 1839–1847*, translated and edited by Clarence A. Clausen and Andreas Elviken, Northfield: NAHA, 1951, pp. 10–11.

13. Information on Reiersen is found in Einar Haugen, "J.R. Reiersen's indiscretions," *Norwegian-American Studies*, v. 21, Northfield, 1962, pp. 169–77. See also Derwood Johnson, "Reiersen's Texas," pp. 252–74, in the same volume; Theodore C. Blegen, "Norwegians in the West in 1844. A contemporary account," *Studies and Records*, v. 1, Minneapolis, 1926, pp. 110–25; Sverre Steen, *Kristiansands historie i fredens århundre, 1814–1914*, Oslo: Grøndahl, 1948, pp. 152–57.

14. The letters of Elise Wærenskjold have been published in *The Lady with the Pen: Elise Wærenskjold in Texas*, edited by Clarence A. Clausen, Minneapolis: NAHA, who has also written an excellent biographical sketch.

15. Eva L. Haugen and Ingrid Semmingsen, "Peder Anderson of Bergen and Lowell: artist and ambassador of culture," *Americana-Norvegica*, v. 4, Oslo and Boston, 1973, pp. 1–20. Eva L. Haugen, "The story of Peder Anderson," *Norwegian-American Studies*, v. 26, Northfield, 1974, pp. 31–48.

16. Blegen, *Land of Their Choice*, p. 36.

Chapter 4: Exodus

1. The earliest printed data on the number of emigrants are found in the quinquennial reports from the county governors (*Amtmændenes femaarsberetninger*). They quite obviously are minimum figures. Professor Gerhard B. Naeseth of Madison has gathered a great amount of information on Norwegian immigrants up to 1850 based on American passenger lists and Norwegian parish registers. This material, when printed, will surely revise earlier figures. Canadian passenger lists exist from 1865; from 1867 on, Norwegian statistics are based on passenger lists and should be considered reliable. Statistics on emigration are published in a separate volume of Norges offisielle statistikk (Norwegian official statistics) NOS VII, 25 Kra. 19. For a discussion of early American official statistics on immigration see Blegen, *Norwegian Migration*, v. 1, pp. 349–52.

2. On Norwegian emigration in its Scandinavian context, see Semmingsen, "Emigration from Scandinavia," *Scandinavian Economic History Review*, 1972, v. 20, pp. 45–60, and in the same issue, Birgitta Odén, "Scandinavian emigration prior to 1914," pp. 89–94. Emigration from Tinn parish in Telemark is discussed by Andres Svalestuen in *Tinns emigrasjonshistorie, 1837–1907*, Oslo: Universitetsforlaget, 1972. Arvid Sandaker describes "Emigration from Land Parish, 1866–75," *Norwegian-American Studies*, v. 26,

Northfield, 1974, pp. 49–74. See also Arnfinn Engen, "Emigration from Dovre: a microstudy," and Semmingsen, "Norwegian immigration in Nordic perspective: recent migration research," both in *Norwegian Influence in the Upper Midwest*, edited by Harald S. Naess, Duluth: University of Minnesota, 1976, pp. 13–15 and 6–12, respectively.

3. Halvdan Koht, "Bonde mot borgar i nynorsk historie," in *Historisk Tidsskrift*, Series 5, v. 1, pp. 29–85. Also reprinted in *Hundre års historisk forskning. Utvalgte artikler fra Historisk Tidsskrift* (Historical research through a hundred years. Selected articles from *Historisk Tidsskrift*), Oslo: The University Press, 1970, pp. 197–229.

4. Eilert Sundt (1817–75), demographer and sociologist. See Martin S. Allwood, *Eilert Sundt, a Pioneer in Sociology and Social Anthropology*, Oslo: O. Norli, 1957, and Arthur Hillman, "Eilert Sundt, social surveyor, extraordinary," *The Sociological Review*, v. 43, 1951, pp. 49–56. The information is found in Sundt's works *Om giftermaal i Norge* (On Marriage in Norway) and *Om Pipervigen og Ruseløkbakken. Undersøgelser om arbeidsklassens kaar og saeder* (On the living conditions and morals of the working class in Christiania). Both were reprinted in Oslo by Gyldendal in 1967 and 1968, respectively.

5. Blegen, *Norwegian Migration*, v. 1, p. 123.

6. Sundt, *Marriage in Norway*, p. 145.

7. Vilhelm Moberg, *Utvandrarna* (The Emigrants) v. 1, Stockholm: Bonniers, 1949, pp. 43–44.

8. Blegen, *Land of Their Choice*, pp. 26 and 44.

9. Blegen, *Norwegian Migration*, v. 1, p. 148.

10. Blegen, *Norwegian Migration*, v. 1, pp. 149–50.

11. On America Fever see Blegen, *Norwegian Migration*, v. 1, pp. 64–71, 86–87, and 103.

12. Svalestuen, *Tinns emigrasjonshistorie*, pp. 153–57.

Chapter 5: Land of Freedom and Opportunity

1. Arthur E. Bestor, *Backwoods Utopias*, Philadelphia: University of Pennsylvania Press, 1950, is the best account of communitarian societies in America. George M. Stephensson, *The Religious Aspects of Swedish Immigration*, Minneapolis: University of Minnesota Press, 1932 (1961 reprint), discusses the Bishop Hill colony. Carl Wittke, *We Who Built America*, New York, 1932, p. 340, says seventy-eight communistic societies in the United States, "a number considerably smaller than 25 years earlier, when social experimentation seems to have reached a peak."

2. Both Mack Walker, *Germany and the Emigration*, Cambridge, Mass.: Harvard University Press, 1964, and W. S. Shepperson, *British Emigration to North America: Projects and Opinions in the Early Victorian Period*, Minneapolis: University of Minnesota Press, 1957, discuss emigration plans of that kind. René Remond, *Les États-Unis devant l'opinion française*, v. 1–2, Saint Just-La Pendue: Fondation Nationale des Sciences Politiques, is a classic.

3. Letter from Barlien quoted in Aavatsmark, *Hans Barlien*, pp. 162–63.

4. Blegen, *Norwegian Migration*, v. 1, pp. 335–36, discusses the Tank experiment. See also A. M. Iversen, *A Brief Account of the Activity of the Evangelical Moravian Church among Scandinavians in Wisconsin*, Madison: Wisconsin State Historical Society (manuscript division), and Carlton C. Qualey, *Norwegian Settlement in the United States*, Northfield: NAHA, 1938, pp. 222–24.

5. Blegen, *Norwegian Migration*, v. 1, discusses the Oleana experiment and the migration to California in chaps. 12 and 13. Mortimer Smith, *Life of Ole Bull*, published for the American-Scandinavian Foundation by Princeton University Press, 1960. On the Thrane movement see Derry, *Modern Norway*, pp. 41–43, and Blegen, *Norwegian Migration*, v. 1, pp. 325–29. Torstein Jahr, "Oleana. Et blad av den norske indvandrings historie," *Symra*, Decorah, 1910, v. 6, pp. 3–37, 129–62, and 195–216, is a detailed study.

6. Blegen and Ruud have included both the song from *Arbeiderforeningernes Blad* and the Oleana ballad in their collection of Norwegian emigrant songs and ballads.

7. Some unpublished masters theses based on material from local districts in which the Thrane movement was strong support this conclusion.

8. Ingrid Semmingsen, *Veien mot vest*, v. 1, pp. 375–76.

9. Blegen, *Land of Their Choice*, pp. 224, 252–54, and Kenneth Bjork, *West of the Great Divide*, Northfield: NAHA, 1958, pp. 166 and 169.

10. Bjork, *West of the Great Divide*, pp. 274–99. Also in *Studies and Records*, v. 19, Northfield, 1956, pp. 62–88.

11. *Beretning om Kongeriget Norges økonomiske Tilstand, 1851–55* (Report on the economic conditions of the Kingdom of Norway, 1851–55), NOS (CBS) No. 2, Christiania, 1858, Nordre Bergenhus Amt, pp. 10–12; and *1856–60*, Christiania, 1863, p. 8.

Chapter 6: The Long Journey

1. Finnish emigration is discussed by Reino Kero, *Migration from Finland to North America in the Years between the United States Civil War and the First World War*, University of Turku, 1874, pp. 16–23.

2. Blegen, *Norwegian Migration*, v. 2, pp. 3–36, provides a detailed account of the Norwegian emigrant traffic and the voyage across the Atlantic.

3. Semmingsen, *Veien mot vest*, v. 1, p. 106.

4. Blegen, *Norwegian Migration*, v. 1, pp. 136–37.

5. Aasmund Olavsen Vinje (1818–70), Norwegian poet and journalist. Quoted from *Drammens Tidende*, 21 April 1857, in *Veien mot vest*, v. 1, pp. 101–2.

6. *Skilling-Magazin*, March 21, 1868, quoted in *Veien mot vest*, v. 1, pp. 110–11.

7. Semmingsen, *Veien mot vest*, v. 1, pp. 120–22. See also *Norse Immigrant Letters*, Minneapolis, 1925.

8. Semmingsen, *Veien mot vest*, v. 1, pp. 132–33.

9. Blegen, *Norwegian Migration*, v. 2, p. 32.

10. Letter in the Østerud collection in the archives of the NAHA.

Chapter 7: Years of Trial

1. *A Chronicle of Old Muskego*, pp. 165 and 209. Blegen, *Norwegian Migration*, v. 2, pp. 37–68, gives a vivid description of frontier conditions.

2. Blegen, *Land of Their Choice*, p. 68. The letter was also published in *Studies and Records*, v. 14, Northfield, 1944, pp. 41–53. The quotation is on p. 14.

3. Knut Gjerset and Ludvig Hektoen, "Health conditions and the practice of medicine among the early Norwegian settlers 1825–1865," *Studies and Records*, v. 1, Minneapolis, 1926, pp. 1–59; Peter T. Harstad, "Disease and sickness on the Wisconsin frontier," *Wisconsin Magazine of History*, v. 43, Winter 1959–60 and Spring 1960, pp. 83–96, 203–20, 253–63, and 959–60.

4. Gjerset and Hektoen, "Health conditions," p. 20; *Chronicle of Old Muskego*, p. 99. See also Blegen, *Norwegian Migration*, v. 2, p. 59.

5. Blegen, *Norwegian Migration*, v. 2, p. 58.

6. *Land of Their Choice*, pp. 191–94.

7. For a discussion of leprosy among Norwegian immigrants see Eva L. Haugen and Ingrid Semmingsen, "Peder Anderson of Bergen and Lowell."

8. Gjerset and Hektoen, "Health conditions," p. 32, provide mortality statistics from the parish registers of Coon Valley, a settlement that escaped severe epidemics. The statistics show that of the total of 194 deaths in the years 1855 to 1865, 94 were children 0 to 5 years old. On tuberculosis see Blegen, *Norwegian Migration*, v. 2, p. 60. On mortality at the end of the century see Niles Carpenter, *Immigrants and Their Children*.

Census monograph VII, Washington, 1927, pp. 196–210, especially pp. 203–4, and Julie Backer, *Dødeligheten og dens årsaker i Norge* (Trend of mortality and causes of death in Norway), 1856–1955, Samfunnsøkonomiske Studier 10 (CBS), Oslo, 1961, p. 46, Table 15.

9. Gjerset and Hektoen, "Health conditions," pp. 10–11, and *Studies and Records*, v. 6, Northfield, 1931,pp. 12–29. Carlton C. Qualey, *Claus L. Clausen: Pioneer Pastor and Settlement Promoter*, Northfield: NAHA, 1931. Also Qualey, *Norwegian Settlement*, pp. 86–92, a thorough study based on census records and descriptive material that very effectively illustrates the concentration of Norwegian settlement.

10. The so-called Wisconsin Ballad is translated and discussed by Einar Haugen in "A Norwegian-American pioneer ballad," *Studies and Records*, v. 15, Northfield, 1949, pp. 1–19.

11. *America in the Forties. The Letters of Ole Munch Ræder*, translated and edited by Gunnar Malmin, Minneapolis: University of Minnesota Press for the NAHA, 1929, p. 6.

12. Frank G. Nelson, *Following the Pathfinder. A Norwegian's Account of Western Missouri in 1848*. (Forthcoming)

13. Semmingsen, *Veien mot vest*, v. 1, pp. 317–19.

Chapter 8: A Pioneer Society

1. *The Diary of Elisabeth Koren, 1853–1855*, translated and edited by David T. Nelson, Northfield: NAHA, 1955.

2. Translated from *Fra pionertiden. Uddrag af Elisabeth Korens dagbog og breve fra femtiaarene*, Decorah, Iowa: Udgiverens forlag, 1914, p. 150. Cf. *Diary* p. 187. Blegen, *Norwegian Migration*, v. 2, chaps. 6 and 7, gives further details of the social life and to some extent the social organization of the Norwegian settlements. Rigmor Frimanslund, "Farm community and neighborhood community," *Scandinavian Economic Historical Review*, v. 4, 1956, pp. 62–81, discusses the rural social organization in Norway.

3. Probate Court archives, Hillsboro, North Dakota, "Papers in the matter of the estate of John Engebretsen." The only food that was bought for the funeral was nutmeg candy (naatmens kendy) costing 25¢. There was also an auction after the funeral of a few agricultural and household items: a hay fork, scythe, spade, ax, straw bed, stove and stove pipe, lamp, four milk dishes, four tin dishes, four cups, picture frame (malerifraim), and some personal belongings including a trunk, a coat, and a pair of boots. The improvement of the land was sold separately and brought $495.

4. Blegen, *Norwegian Migration*, v. 1. pp. 120–22. Blegen, *Norwegian Migration*, v. 2, chap. 4, discusses the religious development and specifically the religious impulse and the American churches on pp. 100–31, and in chap. 5, the emerging church, pp. 131–74. The latest book on the subject, Andersen, *The Norwegian-Americans*, does the same on pp. 101–22. The most recent work on Lutheran churches is E. Clifford Nelson and Eugene L. Fevold, *The Lutheran Church among Norwegian-Americans: A History of the Evangelical Lutheran Church*, Minneapolis: Augsburg, 1960. See also Eugene L. Fevold, "The Norwegian Immigrant and His Church," *Norwegian-American Studies*, v. 23, Northfield, 1967, pp. 3–16. Fevold stresses the importance of the church as "the cohesive social force." On Puritanism among the immigrants see Frederick Hale, "Marcus Hansen, puritanism and Scandinavian temperance movements," *Norwegian-American Studies*, v. 27, Northfield, 1977, pp. 18–40.

5. Blegen, *Norwegian Migration*, v. 2, p. 143, note 24.

6. Blegen, *Land of Their Choice*, p. 194. E. Clifford Nelson, ed., *A Pioneer Churchman. J. W. C. Dietrichson in Wisconsin, 1844–1850*, Boston: Twayne Publishers, 1973, pp. 192 and 195. Nelson in his introduction, pp. 1–38, provides an excellent biographical sketch of Dietrichson and an analysis of his views on church organization and pastoral authority.

7. *The Strange American Way. Letters of Caja Munch from Wiota, Wisconsin, 1855–1859*

with an American Adventure, Excerpts from "Vita mea," an Autobiography written in 1903 for His Children by Johan Storm Munch, Translated by Helene Munch and Peter A. Munch, and an Essay on Social Class and Acculturation by Peter A. Munch, Carbondale: Southern Illinois University Press, 1970. The quotation is from "Vita mea," p. 118. Munch's essay has been very valuable to me because of its sociological viewpoints.

8. Einar Haugen, *The Norwegian Language in America: A Study in Bilingual Behavior,* 2 v. Philadelphia: University of Pennsylvania Press, 1953, v. 1, p. 34 (2nd ed., 1 v., Bloomington: Indiana University Press, 1969). Haugen's historical introduction on Norwegian immigration is the best and most analytical short survey I know of.

9. Blegen, *Norwegian Migration,* v. 2, discusses the press on pp. 277–300 and 301–30. Andersen provides an account of political debate in the 1850s in *The Norwegian Americans,* pp. 59–71. The concept of an "old society" in which the family is the primary group and the neighborhood a *"Gemeinschaft"* (*Tonnies*) with face-to-face contact has influenced my reasoning in this chapter. See, for instance, Peter Laslett, *The World We Lost,* 2nd ed., London: Methuen, 1971; Karl Polanyi, *The Great Transformation,* Boston: Beacon, 1971; C. Wright Mills, *The Sociological Imagination,* Gretna, La.: Pelican, 1970; *Sociology of the Family,* ed. by Michael Anderson, Baltimore: Penguin, 1971; George Dalton, ed., *Primitive, Archaic, and Modern Economies. Essays of Karl Polanyi,* New York: Beacon, 1971.

Chapter 9: Encountering Americans

1. I am greatly indebted to Einar Haugen, *The Norwegian Language in America,* and to Peter A. Munch, "Social adjustment among Wisconsin Norwegians," *American Sociological Review,* v. 14, 1949, pp. 780–87, and "Segregation and assimilation of Norwegian settlements in Wisconsin," *Studies and Records,* v. 18, Northfield, 1954, pp. 102–40, as well as to the pioneer study of Merle Curti, *The Making of an American Community: A Case Study of Democracy in a Frontier County,* Philadelphia: University of Pennsylvania Press, 1953, v. 1, chap. 5. Kenneth O. Bjork, *West of the Great Divide,* cites examples of Norwegians moving into the middle class.

2. Einar Haugen, "A Norwegian-American pioneer ballad," pp. 1–19.

3. Haugen, *The Norwegian Language,* v. 1, chap. 5.

4. Haugen, *The Norwegian Language,* v. 1, p. 54. The original letter is translated in *Frontier Parsonage. The Letters of Olaus Fredrik Duus, Norwegian Pastor in Wisconsin, 1855–1858,* Northfield: NAHA, 1947, pp. 28–29, dated July 9, 1956.

5. Haugen, *Norwegian Language,* v. 1, pp. 59–60.

6. Kristofer Janson, *Amerikanske forholde,* Copenhagen: Gyldendalske, 1881, p. 110.

7. *Nordlyset,* April 6, 1848. Quoted from Semmingsen, *Veien mot vest,* v. 1, p. 324.

8. *Norsk-amerikanernes festskrift,* Decorah, Iowa, 1914, pp. 34 and 37. Also quoted in Blegen, *Norwegian Migration,* v. 2, p. 404.

9. Curti, *American Community,* p. 318. See also Laurence M. Larson, *The Changing West and Other Essays,* Northfield: NAHA, 1937. The convention riot at Benson Grove, Iowa, in 1876 is discussed on pp. 39–48.

10. Blegen, *Norwegian Migration,* v. 2, pp. 241–76, on the school question and conflict. See also Laurence M. Larson, "Skandinaven, professor Anderson and the yankee school," *The Changing West,* pp. 116–47. For the view of an outsider see Nicolas Tavuchis, *Pastors and Immigrants,* The Hague: Martinus Nijhoff, 1963, pp. 37–54; the author is a perceptive sociologist. The most recent account is Frank C. Nelsen, "The school controversy among Norwegian immigrants," *Norwegian-American Studies,* v. 26, Northfield, 1974, pp. 206–19.

11. On pastors and female servants see Munch, *The Strange American Way,* pp. 49, 71, 75, 181, and 187, and *Frontier Parsonage,* p. 62. The drunken man in the parlor, Munch, p. 76.

12. Blegen, *Norwegian Migration,* v. 2, pp. 383–417, discusses Norwegian attitudes

toward and participation in the Civil War. He has also edited *Hans C. Heg. The Civil War Letters of Colonel Hans and Christian Heg*. Northfield: NAHA, 1936. Other publications of Civil War letters are: Knute Nelson, "Some Civil War letters of Knute Nelson," *Norwegian-American Studies*, v. 23, Northfield, 1974, pp. 17–50; Mons H. Grinager, "The letters of Mons H. Grinager, pioneer and soldier," *Norwegian-American Studies*, v. 24, Northfield, 1970, pp. 29–77; and C. A. Clausen and Derwood C. Johnson, "Norwegian soldiers in the Confederate forces," *Norwegian-American Studies*, v. 25, Northfield, 1972, pp. 105–41. An introduction by Clausen and Johnson on Norwegians in Texas precedes the letters. A more condensed treatment of Norwegian attitudes toward slavery and the Civil War is given by Andersen, *The Norwegian-Americans*, pp. 72–83.

13. On Norwegian slaveowners in Texas see Clausen and Johnson, "Norwegian soldiers in the Confederate forces"; Elise Wærenskjold is quoted on p. 108. On the Norwegian who wanted to buy a black man see Frank G. Nelson, *Following the Pathfinder*, chap. 7, note 12.

14. Semmingsen, *Veien mot vest*, v. 2, pp. 467–68.

15. Blegen, *Norwegian Migration 1825–1860*, v. 2, pp. 389–90. Andersen, *The Norwegian-Americans*, p. 77, estimates that "Norwegian soldiers alone, nationwide, probably numbered close to 6000" and the total of Scandinavians "approached 9000."

Chapter 10: The Big Families

1. Norwegian population statistics are found in two series: Folketellinger (population censuses) and Folkemengdens bevegelse (population movement). The last includes emigration statistics. A separate volume on emigration statistics (Utvandringsstatistik) CBS (Central Bureau of Statistics) was published in 1921 as Series VII, No. 25, Kra. 1921. A very convenient survey is *Historisk statistikk 1968* (Historical statistics 1968) Oslo, 1968, with text in both Norwegian and English. Very useful is Julie Backer, *Ekteskap, fødsler og vandringer i Norge 1856–1960* (Marriages, births and migrations in Norway) Samfunnsøkonomiske studier 13, published by Statistisk Sentralbyrå CBS, Oslo, 1965. The study has a summary in English and English text to tables and diagrams. Norway has no immigration statistics before World War I. Statistics on the birthplace of the population when the censuses and calculations were made by the Central Bureau of Statistics show, however, that apart from overseas emigration, Norway had a slight surplus of immigrants, most from Sweden.

2. The best study in English of Norwegian population development in the first two-thirds of the nineteenth century is Michael Drake, *Population and Society in Norway 1735–1865*, Cambridge: the University Press, 1969. See also Backer, *Trend of Mortality*. On life expectancy at birth see pp. 245–46 (English summary). On the influence of the demographic factor on emigration see Thorvald Moe, "Demographic Developments and Economic Growth in Norway 1740–1940," PhD thesis, Stanford University, 1970.

3. Drake, *Population*, pp. 41–74, especially pp. 50–53.

4. Fartein Valen-Sendstad, *Norske landbruksredskaper i 1800–1850-årene* (Norwegian agricultural tools), Lillehammer: De Sandvigske Samlingers Skrifter, v. 4, 1964 (English summary).

5. Sundt, *Marriage in Norway*, p. 145, note 6. Semmingsen, *Veien mot vest*, v. 2, p. 61.

6. For a more detailed account see Semmingsen, *Veien mot vest*, v. 2, pp. 42–85. Quotation is from Vinje, p. 62.

7. For a comparative survey of population development in the Nordic countries in the nineteenth century see Andres Svalestuen, "Nordisk emigrasjon," *Emigrationen fra Norden indtil I verdenskrig. Rapporter til det nordiske historikermøde i København 1971* (Emigration from the Nordic Countries until World War I. Report to the Nordic Historical Congress Copenhagen 1971).

8. Blegen, *Norwegian Migration*, v. 2, discusses the question of American promotion of immigration on pp. 383–88. A very thorough and detailed study is Lars Ljungmark,

For sale— Minnesota. *Organized Promotion of Scandinavian Immigration*. Stockholm: Studia historica Gothoburgensia, 1971.

9. Louis Henry, "La population de la Norvège depuis deux siècles," *Population* v. 25, 1970, translated by William Petersen in *Readings in Population*, pp. 16–27, New York: Macmillan, 1972, pp. 16–27, argues that "broadly speaking, the principal features of the demographic history of Norway over the past two centuries have been precocity in the control of deaths and retardation in the control of births. It is therefore one of the countries where the lag between the decline of mortality and that of fertility has been most marked." This lends importance to the role of the demographic factor in emigration. But extensive emigration could be seen as a factor retarding the "demographic transition," that is, the control of fertility.

Chapter 11: Change and Unrest

1. Derry, *History of Modern Norway*, gives a short account of "social reactions to economic change," pp. 129–35, and discusses emigration, pp. 206–24. Industrialization is treated rather shallowly by Sima Lieberman, *Industrialization of Norway, 1800–1920*, Oslo: Universitetsforlaget, 1970, and more ably by Lennart Jörberg, "The Nordic countries, 1850–1914," in Carlo Cipolla, ed., *The Fontana Economic History of Europe*, v. 4, pt. 2, 1976, pp. 375–485. See also Ingrid Semmingsen, "The dissolution of Estate society in Norway," *Scandinavian Economic History Review*, v. 2, 1954, pp. 166–203; Peter A. Munch, "A study of cultural change. Rural-urban conflicts in Norway," *Studia Norvegica*, Oslo, 1956, No. 9.

2. See Derry, *History of Modern Norway*, passim; Edvard Bull, *The Norwegian Trade Union Movement*, Brussels: I.F.C.T.U. Monographs on national trade union movements, No. 4, 1966; Walter Galenson, *Labor in Norway*, Cambridge, Mass.: Harvard University Press, 1949; O. B. Grimley, *Co-operatives in Norway*, Oslo: Norwegian Cooperative Union and Wholesale Society, 1950. On the temperance movement: Per Fuglum, *Kampen om alkoholen i Norge, 1816–1904* (the temperance and prohibition movement in Norway), Oslo: Universitetsforlaget, 1972. Einar Molland, *Church Life in Norway, 1800–1950*, Minneapolis, 1957.

3. Kleiven is quoted in Semmingsen, *Veien mot vest*, v. 2, pp. 91–92. For internal migration see Hallstein Myklebost, *Norske tettsteder* (Norwegian Population Agglomerations), No. 4, Oslo: Universitetsforlaget, 1960, with English summary, and in the same work, Thorvald Moe, "Demographic developments," pp. 120–31; Sivert Langholm, "Short distance migration, circles and flows: movement to and from Ullensaker according to the population census list of 1865," *Scandinavian Economic History Review*, 1975, v. 23, pp. 36–62, and by the same author, "On the scope of micro-history," *Scandinavian Journal of History*, 1976, v. 1, pp. 1–24, and "The Christiania project: historians investigate the making of urban society," *Research in Norway 1976*, ed. by The Norwegian Research Council, Oslo, 1976.

4. See Blegen and Ruud, *Norwegian Emigrant Songs*, p. 341.

5. For the importance of family ties across the Atlantic as a factor explaining the emigration of unmarried youth from the countryside, see Arnfinn Engen, "Emigration from Dovre," *Norwegian Influence in the Upper Midwest*, p. 14

6. For the discussion of "stage migration," see Fred Nilsson, *Emigrationen från Stockholm, 1870–1894*, pp. 61–64, English summary pp. 362–75. Kristian Hvidt, *Flight to America. The Social Background of 300,000 Danish Emigrants*, New York: 1975, Academic Press, pp. 55–62. Ingrid Semmingsen, "Family emigration from Bergen," *Americana-Norvegica*, v. 3, pp. 38–63, and "Emigration from Scandinavia," *Scandinavian Economic History Review*, v. 20, 1972, pp. 52–54.

7. Semmingsen, "Family emigration," p. 59.

8. Occupations of emigrants are given in the printed statistics, (CBS) NOS VII, 25. Kenneth Bjork, *Saga in Steel and Concrete*, Northfield: NAHA, 1947, is a well-

documented study of the emigration of Norwegian engineers and of their careers in America. Similar studies of other professions have not been done.

9. Aasta Hansteen, see Semmingsen, *Veien mot vest*, v. 2, pp. 190–91. Maren Michelet, *Glimpses of Agnes Mathilde Wergeland's Life*, Minneapolis: Folkebladet Publishing Co., 1916. Øystein Ore, "Norwegian emigrants with university training 1830–1880," *Norwegian-American Studies*, v. 19, Northfield, 1956, pp. 160–88.

10. The "study of the small Swedish community" by Kjell is forthcoming. The results are mentioned in Sune Åkerman, "From Stockholm to San Francisco," *Annales Academiae Regiae Scientiarum Upsaliensis*, v. 19, 1975 (presented as a report to the XIV International Congress of Historical Sciences, San Francisco, August 22–29, 1975). For personality types see Ørnulf Ødegaard, "Emigration and insanity. A study of mental disease among the Norwegianborn population of Minnesota," *Acta Psychiatrica et Neurologica*, Suppl. IV, Copenhagen, 1932.

11. Emigrant biographies, Institute of History, University of Oslo. (mimeographed)

12. Birger Osland, *A Long Pull from Stavanger: The Reminiscences of a Norwegian Immigrant*, Northfield: NAHA, 1945, pp. 6, 7, and 13.

13. Quoted from Gudrun Hovde Gvåle, *O. E. Rølvaag. Nordmann og amerikanar*, pp. 63 and 66–67.

14. See, for instance, Engen, "Emigration from Dovre"; Sandaker, "Emigration from Land Parish"; and Semmingsen, "Family emigration from Bergen."

15. Information on returned emigrants is from NOS (CBS) VII, 25, pp. 74–80, and NOS (CBS) VII, 81, pp. 72–79 (Survey of Census, 1920). Knut Gjerset, *Norwegian Sailors on the Great Lakes*, Northfield: NAHA, 1928, and *Norwegian Sailors in American Waters*, Northfield: NAHA, 1933, provide information on sailors. Bjork, *West of the Great Divide*, also has information on fishermen.

16. *Frontier Mother. The Letters of Gro Svendsen*. Translated and edited by Pauline Farseth and Theodore C. Blegen. Northfield: NAHA, 1950, p. 14.

Chapter 12: The Fabulous Land

1. The standard work on the spread of Norwegian settlement is the thorough study of Carlton C. Qualey, *Norwegian Settlement in the United States*. Bjork's important book *West of the Great Divide* covers settlement in California and the Pacific Northwest and also topics like the press, church, societies, occupations, and social life. Bjork has also treated Norwegian settlement in Canada in several articles: "Bella Coola," *Americana-Norvegica*, v. 3, Oslo, 1971, pp. 195–222; "The founding of the Quatsino colony," *Norwegian-American Studies* v. 25, Northfield, 1972, pp. 80–125; and "Scandinavian migration to the Canadian prairie provinces," *Norwegian-American Studies*, v. 26, Northfield, 1975, pp. 3–30. Richard K. Vedder and Lowell E. Gallaway, "The settlement preferences of Scandinavian emigrants to the United States," *Scandinavian Economic History Review*, v. 18, 1970, pp. 159–76, try to explain the pattern of settlement using a multivariable model incorporating seven factors. Job opportunity seems to be the most important. See Niles Carpenter, *Immigrants and Their Children*, Census Monographs VII, Washington D.C., 1927. Of 50 ethnic groups, "foreign-born whites," the Norwegian-born was at the bottom of the list with 47.2 percent urban in contrast to, for example, people from eastern Europe with 85.7 percent urban.

The *Immigration Report* (Washington D.C., 1911), v. 28, p. 177, shows the main occupational groups of Norwegian emigrants and their offspring in the United States in 1900.

	Male Breadwinners	
	Norwegian-Born	Norwegian Parentage
Agricultural pursuits	49.8%	63.0%
Professional services	1.8	2.2

Trade and transportation	12.5	14.1
Manufacturing and mechanical	23.2	11.1
Building trades	7.9	2.7

The building trades group is a subdivision of the manufacturing and mechanical group. Note the decline of agriculture and the growth of industry among Norwegian-born immigrants, presumably the most recent ones. The trade and transportation group does not include sailors. The *Immigration Report* says (p. 181) that of the total number of Norwegian male breadwinners of the first generation, 4,023, or 2.4 percent, were classified by the census as boatmen and sailors, "a larger number than was reported for any other class of immigrants." In New York state the number of Norwegian boatmen and sailors, 1,062, constituted 16.8 percent of the total number of male breadwinners in the first generation, and the number engaged in the building trades, 1,753, constituted 27.6 percent (p. 179). These two occupation groups together comprised nearly 45 percent of all Norwegian-born, male breadwinners in New York state.

See also Blegen, *Norwegian Migration*, v. 2, pp. 331–56.

2. A slightly different and less accurate translation is given in Malmin, *America in the forties. The Letters of Ole Munch Ræder*, p. 64, and in Blegen, *Land of Their Choice*, p. 212. Thomter collection of America-letters, NAHA, Marie Killie, Sacred Heart, Minnesota, to Marie Thomter, Dovre, February 7 and December 10, 1893, July 15, 1896, and May 29, 1898.

3. Semmingsen, *Veien mot vest*, v. 2, p. 218.

4. Bjork, *West of the Great Divide*, has the most information on wages in various occupations. Sailors' wages are given in Gjerset's two volumes on Norwegian sailors. On wages in Norway see *Historisk Statistikk, 1968*.

5. See Qualey and Bjork references, note 1 this chapter, and Andrew N. Rygg, *Norwegians in New York, 1825–1925*, New York: The Norwegian News Company, 1941.

6. Knight Hoover provides a good analysis of the cohesiveness of the Norwegian colony in Brooklyn in *Norwegians in New York,*" *Norwegian-American Studies*, v. 24, Northfield, 1970, pp. 221–34. Elizabeth Fedde's diary, translated and edited by Beulah Folkedahl in *Norwegian-American Studies*, v. 20, Northfield, 1959, pp. 170–96, with a valuable introduction, provides insight into the conditions of the less fortunate among the Norwegians in Brooklyn.

7. Thorvald Moe, "Demographic Developments."

8. For a more detailed analysis of Jaabæk see Franklin D. Scott, "Søren Jaabæk, Americanizer in Norway: a study in cultural exchange," *Norwegian-American Studies*, v. 17, Northfield, 1952, pp. 87–107.

9. Knut Hamsun, *The Cultural Life of Modern America*, translated by Barbara Morgridge, Cambridge, Mass., Harvard University Press, 1969. On the reception of the book in Norway see Arlow W. Andersen, "Knut Hamsun's America," *Norwegian-American Studies*, v. 23, Northfield, 1967, pp. 175–203.

10. Blegen, *Land of Their Choice*, pp. 306–7, provides a slightly different translation. A serious study of names and name changes is Marjorie M. Kimmerle, "Norwegian-American surnames," *Studies and Records*, v. 12, Northfield, 1941, pp. 1–32. A still more thorough and extensive treatment is found in Haugen, *Norwegian Language*, pp. 191–232.

11. Jørund Mannsåker, *Emigrasjon og diktning*, Oslo: Det norske samlaget, 1971, treats the theme of emigration and the image of America in Norwegian fiction. Bjørnson in Trondheim is mentioned in Peter Egge, *Minner fra barndom og ungdom*, pp. 38–39.

12. "Hvorfor folk udvandrer" (Why people emigrate), *Nylænde* (Women's rights periodical) Kra. June 1906.

13. Blegen, *Norwegian Migration*, v. 2, pp. 542–96, has information on academic careers. See also John A. Hofstead, *American Educators of Norwegian Origin*, Min-

neapolis: Augsburg, 1931, and Andersen, *The Norwegian-Americans*, chap. 12. A good study is Laurence M. Larson, "The Norwegian pioneer in the field of scholarship," *Studies and Records*, v. 2, Northfield, 1927, pp. 62–77.

14. Bjork, *Saga in Steel*, pp. 171–185, 196, 222–27, 244–64, and 338.

15. Edward Hutchinson, *Immigrants and Their Children, a Census Monograph*, New York, 1956, pp. 241–42 and tables 41A and 41B.

16. Blegen, *Norwegian Migration*, v. 2, chap. 12, provides some information on the activities of emigration agents in the early period and during the Canadian interlude, and early in chap. 8 on the era of the Civil War. Semmingsen discusses the subject in *Veien mot vest*, v. 2, pp. 86–139. Kristian Hvidt, "Danish emigration prior to 1914," *Scandinavian Economic History Review*, v. 14, 1966, pp. 158–78, cites the activity of agents as a third independent factor in addition to "pull" and "push." A different view is held by Sune Åkerman and Berit Brattne in the article "The importance of the transport sector for mass emigration," *From Sweden to America*, Minneapolis: University of Minnesota Press, 1976, pp. 176–200. Ljungmark, *For Sale — Minnesota*, stresses the work of agents through the Scandinavian ethnic groups. Osland, *A Long Pull from Stavanger*, pp. 56–101, relates the story of Norwegian-American support for the founding of the Norwegian-American steamship line.

17. Thomter letter collection, NAHA, letter dated June 1, 1878. Semmingsen, *Veien mot vest*, v. 2, p. 400.

18. Åkerman and Brattne, "The importance of the transport sector," and Kristian Hvidt, "Trends," *Scandinavian Economic History Review*, v. 18, pp. 158–78.

Chapter 13: Norway in America

1. NOS (CBS) Ragnvald Jønsberg, "Nordmenn i utlandet" (Norwegians Abroad) *Statistiske meddelelser* (Statistical Reports) v. 42, pp. 421–39, Kra. 1924. Kristian Hvidt, *Flight*, pp. 167–69, provides tables on concentration of settlement, intramarriage, and intermarriage for the Scandinavian ethnic groups which confirm these statements. Sture Lindmark, *Swedish America 1914–1932. Studies in Ethnicity with Emphasis on Illinois and Minnesota. Studia Historica Upsaliensia*, v. 37, Stockholm, 1971, pp. 50–63, reaches the same conclusions: "religious barriers were more difficult to overcome than the national" (p. 54); "the geographical concentration strengthened the cultural isolation far more than the melting-pot advocates could ever have imagined" (p. 55).

2. John Higham, *Strangers in the Land*, New Brunswick, N.J.: Rutgers University Press, 1955.

3. Nelson and Fevold, *The Lutheran Church*, v. 1, pp. 169–80; Blegen, *Norwegian Migration*, v. 2, pp. 418–53; Nicholas Tavuchis, *Pastors and Immigrants*. Andersen, *Norwegian-Americans*, pp. 101–22, also includes a description of non-Lutheran church bodies.

4. See references in note 3 this chapter and Haugen, *Norwegian Language*, v. 1, pp. 33–36.

5. Carl H. Chrislock, *From Fjord to Freeway, 100 Years*, Minneapolis: Augsburg, 1969, pp. 34, 107, 123–24. Nina Draxten, *Kristofer Janson in America*, Boston: Twayne Publishers, 1976, pp. 59–60. (This book, unfortunately, was not available to me when I wrote the Norwegian version of this history.)

6. Arthur C. Paulson, "Bjørnson and the Norwegian-Americans," 1880–81 *Studies and Records*, v. 5, Northfield, 1931, pp. 85–109. See also Blegen, *Norwegian Migration*, v. 2, pp. 565–67, and Lloyd Hustvedt, *Rasmus Bjørn Anderson. Pioneer Scholar*, Northfield: NAHA, 1966, pp. 164–71.

7. Haugen, *Norwegian Language*, pp. 34–35.

8. For the history of the various colleges, see Chrislock, *From Fjord to Freeway*; David T. Nelson, *Luther College 1861–1961*, Philadelphia: University of Pennsylvania Press, 1961; Joseph M. Shaw, *History of St. Olaf College 1874–1974*, Northfield: NAHA, 1974.

9. Hustvedt, *Rasmus Bjørn Anderson*, is an excellent biography of this colorful personality.

10. Blegen, *Norwegian Migration*, v. 2, pp. 578–79. Nicolay Grevstad, *The Norwegian-American Hospital*, Chicago, 1930; Leon M. Bowes, *A History of the Norwegian Old People's Home*, Chicago, 1940; Andreas N. Rygg, *The Norwegian Children's Home 1909–1949*, New York, 1949.

11. Blegen, *Norwegian Migration*, v. 2, chap. 17, discusses the press; see especially pp. 546–52. Andersen, *Norwegian Americans*, chap. 7, is relevant. Information on the press after the Civil War is from an article by Johannes B. Wist, "Pressen efter borgerkrigen" (The [Norwegian-American] press after the Civil War), *Norsk-amerikanernes festskrift, 1914*, Decorah, Iowa: The Symra Society, pp. 41–203. The number 564 papers and periodicals from the beginning of *Nordlyset* in 1849 until 1914 is given there. Blegen, *Norwegian Migration*, v. 2, p. 547, says, "between four and five hundred Norwegian papers were established." The circulation of 1815 is quoted from Lindmark, *Swedish America*, p. 226. The source is N. W. Ayers, *Newspaper Annual and Directory 1915–1932*. See also *The Norwegian-American Press and Nordisk Tidende. A Content Analysis* by Inga Wilhelmsen Allwood, Knud K. Mogensen, Carl Nesjar, and Martin S. Allwood, ed. by the Institute of Social Research, Marston Hill, Mullsjö, Sweden 1950 (mimeographed). *Facts about the Norwegian-American Colony in Brooklyn, N.Y. and Nordisk Tidende*, New York, 1941. Agnes M. Larson, "The editorial policy of Skandinaven 1900–1903," *Studies and Records*, v. 8, Northfield, 1934, pp. 112–35. Odd S. Lovoll, "The Norwegian press in North Dakota," *Norwegian-American Studies*, v. 24, Northfield, 1970, pp. 68–101, and "Decorah-Posten: the story of an immigrant newspaper," *Norwegian-American Studies*, v. 27, 1975, pp. 77–100.

12. Wist, *Norsk-amerikanernes festskrift*, Beulah Folkedahl, "Norwegians become Americans," *Norwegian-American Studies*, v. 21, Northfield, 1962, pp. 95–135, has information on the political activities of Svein Nilsson (pp. 124–30). See also "Immigration as viewed by a Norwegian-American farmer in 1869," a letter translated and edited by Jacob Hodnefield in *Studies and Records*, v. 2, Northfield, 1927, pp. 53–61, especially pp. 59–61.

13. On Marcus Thrane see Blegen, *Norwegian Migration*, v. 2, p. 550; Waldemar Westergaard, "Marcus Thrane in America: some unpublished letters from 1880–1884," *Studies and Records*, v. 9, Northfield, 1936, pp. 67–76; Andersen, *The Norwegian-Americans*, pp. 89–91; Wist, *Festskrift, passim*, on the various editors. On Ibsen: see Arthur C. Paulson and Kenneth Bjork, "A Doll's House on the prairie: the first Ibsen controversy in America," *Studies and Records*, v. 11, Northfield, 1940, pp. 1–16; also Blegen, *Norwegian Migration*, v. 2, pp. 563–64; Einar Haugen, "Ibsen in America: a forgotten performance and an unpublished letter," *Journal of English and German philology*, v. 33, 1934, pp. 396–420. On Ager: *Norsk-amerikanernes festskrift, 1914*, pp. 119–20; Kenneth Smemo, "The Norwegian ethnic experience and the literature of Waldemar Ager," *Norwegian Influence*, pp. 59–64. On Symra: Einar Haugen, "Symra: a memoir," *Norwegian-American Studies*, v. 27, Northfield, 1977, pp. 101–10.

14. The Anthology: Knut M. Teigen, *Vesterlandske digte*, Minneapolis: Gode venners forlag, 1905. The standard work on Scandinavian-language literature in America is Dorothy B. Skårdal, *The Divided Heart: Scandinavian Immigrant Experience through Literary Sources*, Lincoln, Nebraska: University of Nebraska Press, 1974; Blegen discusses the subject in *Norwegian Migration*, v. 2, pp. 585–96. Clarence A. Glasrud, *Hjalmar Hjorth Boyesen*, Northfield: NAHA, 1963. See also Per E. Seyersted, "Hjalmar Hjorth Boyesen, outer success, inner failure," *Americana Norvegica*, v. 1, Oslo, 1966, pp. 106–238, and "The drooping lily. H. H. Boyesen as early American misogynist," *Americana Norvegica*, v. 3, Oslo, 1971, pp. 74–87.

15. The standard biography on Rølvaag in English is Theodore Jorgenson and Nora O. Solum, *Ole Edvart Rølvaag. A Biography*. N.Y.: Harper, 1939. The literature on Rølvaag in articles is overwhelming. See Ager's essay in *Nordmændenes festskrift*, pp. 307–29.

16. Rudolph J. Vecoli, "An outsider's view of the association," *Norwegian-American Studies*, v. 27, Northfield, 1977, p. 277. See Eva L. and Einar Haugen, *Land of the Free: Bjørnson's Letters from America, 1880–1881*. (Forthcoming, NAHA)

17. Blegen, *Norwegian Migration*, v. 2, pp. 69–72. See also *Cultural Pluralism versus Assimilation*, edited by Odd S. Lovoll, Topical studies, v. 2, Northfield: NAHA, 1977.

Chapter 14: Politics and Organizations

1. William E. Channing quoted from John M. Blum et al., *The National Experience*, 2nd ed., New York: Harcourt, 1968, p. 257. Alexis de Tocqueville, *Democracy in America*, v. 2, New York: Knopf, 1948, p. 106. On Norway and the "principle of association," see Sverre Steen, "De frivillige sammenslutninger og det norske demokrati," *Historisk tidsskrift*, 1946–48, v. 34, pp. 581–600. Also Derry, *A Short History*, pp. 36, 49, 155–56, 175–77, 225–28.

2. The basic information on the various kinds of societies upon which all subsequent authors have drawn is the article by Carl G. O. Hansen, "Det norske foreningsliv i Amerika," *Norsk-amerikanernes festskrift, 1914*, pp. 266–91. Blegen's discussion in *Norwegian Migration*, v. 2, pp. 543–96, is very insightful; see especially pp. 560–62, 567–71, 573–83. Haugen, *Norwegian Language*, v. 1, pp. 33–35. Andersen provides much factual information in *Norwegian-Americans*, pp. 138–56. For the Pacific coast see Bjork, *The Great Divide*, pp. 178–90 and *passim*.

3. On singers, in addition to sources already mentioned, see *Norwegian Singers' Association 1892–1942. Golden Jubilee*, Minneapolis, 1942, and *Norwegian Glee Club, Minneapolis. History of the Norwegian Glee Club of Minneapolis 1912–1937*, Minneapolis, 1937. Bjork, *The Great Divide*, pp. 617, 620, and 627.

4. The Rifle Club, quoted from Hansen, *Festskrift*, p. 273. Derry, *Modern Norway*, has a short but clear survey of Norwegian immigration, pp. 206–36, including a section on contributions to American society, pp. 216–22.

5. On literary and dramatic societies, in addition to references given in notes 2 and 13, chap. 13, see Napier Wilt and Henriette C. Koren Naeseth, "Two early Norwegian dramatic societies in Chicago," *Studies and Records*, v. 10, Northfield, 1938, pp. 44–75, Arne Garborg Club in Osland, *Symra Society. Fiftieth Anniversary 1907–1957*, Decorah, Iowa, 1957, pp. 34–40. Harald S. Naess, "Ygrasil literary society 1896–1971," "*Americana Norvegica*, v. 4, Oslo, 1973, pp. 31–45. *Chicago Norske Klub. Historical Sketch Published on the Occasion of the Dedication of Its New Club House*, Chicago, 1917. Andrew N. Rygg, *The Norwegian Club. A History of the Club, 1904–1944*, New York, 1944. Ralph Enger, *The History of the Norwegian Club in San Francisco*, San Francisco, 1947 (reprinted 1970).

6. The *bygdelag* movement is ably analyzed by Odd S. Lovoll in his *A Folk Epic. The bygdelag in America*, Boston: Twayne Publishers, 1975.

7. The fullest and most up-to-date account of the history of the Sons of Norway is Sverre Norborg, *An American Saga. Sons of Norway, 1895–1970*, Minneapolis: Sons of Norway, 1970. See also Blegen, *Norwegian Migration*, v. 2, p. 578, and Andersen, *Norwegian-Americans*, pp. 146–48.

8. Andreas Ueland, *Recollections of an Immigrant*, N.Y.: Minton Balch, 1929, pp. 48–49, 150–51, 192–204, and by the same author, *A Minor Melting Pot*, reprint from *Samband*, March and June 1931, Minneapolis.

9. Hansen, *Festskrift*, pp. 272 and 289; Bjork, *The Great Divide*, pp. 543–44, 553–55, 575–76, 587–95.

10. Duane R. Lindberg, "Men of the Cloth and the Social Cultural Fabric of the Norwegian Ethnic Community of North Dakota," PhD thesis, University of Minnesota, 1975, pp. 160–68.

11. Martin W. Odland, *Life of Knute Nelson*, Minneapolis: Lund Press, 1926, especially chaps. 5 and 6.

12. Jon Wefald, *A Voice of Protest*, Topical studies v. 1, Northfield: NAHA, 1971, pp. 26–27.

13. In addition to Wefald, see Odd S. Lovoll, "The Norwegian press in North Dakota"; David L. Brye, "Wisconsin Scandinavians and progressivism 1900–1950," *Norwegian-American Studies*, v. 27, Northfield, 1977, pp. 163–93; Sten Carlsson, "Scandinavian politicians in Minnesota around the turn of the century, a study of the role of the ethnic factor in an immigrant state," *Americana-Norvegica*, v. 3, Oslo, 1971, pp. 237–71; Michael P. Rogin, *The Intellectuals and McCarthy*, Cambridge, Mass.: M.I.T. Press, 1971; Theodore C. Blegen, *Minnesota. A History of the State*, Minneapolis: University of Minnesota Press, 1975, pp. 387–90, and on Floyd B. Olson, pp. 523–29. The classic study of populism is John D. Hicks, *Populist Revolt*, Minneapolis: 1931. See also James M. Youngdale, *Populism. A Psychohistorical Perspective.* N.Y.: Kennikat Press, 1975.

14. Marie Killie to Marie Thomter, April 28, 1899, NAHA letter collection.

15. Citizenship is often pointed to as an index of assimilation. Carpenter, *Immigrants and Their Children*, p. 250, notes, however, that naturalization is not "tantamount to Americanization." Lindmark, *Swedish America*, discusses the question on pp. 40–49. He shows that the "number naturalized and the time of arrival were quite dependent on each other" and that more rural people applied for citizenship than did urban dwellers. See also Carpenter, *Immigrants and Their Children*, pp. 250–59, who indicates that 76 percent of the Norwegians were naturalized in 1920, a few more Swedes and Danes, and Germans were on top with 80 percent. The difference is easily explained by the fact that a larger percentage of Norwegians had arrived during the years 1900–1915, when Swedish and Danish immigration was lower and German immigration dwindled. See Lindmark, *Swedish America*, Tables 7 and 8, pp. 46–47.

Chapter 15: Immigrants Become Americans

1. My account is based mainly on reports in Norwegian newspapers. See, however, Odd S. Lovoll, *A Folk Epic*, pp. 164–73.

2. Haugen, *Norwegian Language*, v. 1, p. 247. I am heavily indebted to this work for the discussion in this chapter. See especially pp. 233–60 and 261–94.

3. Marie Killie to Marie Thomter, May 29, 1898, December 6, 1901, March 10, 1904, and January 30, 1912, NAHA collection.

4. Haugen, *Norwegian Language*, v. 1, p. 236. "Flatbrød" and "lefse," oral information, 1974, from an American woman who grew up in southern Minnesota.

5. Haugen, *Norwegian Language*, v. 1, p. 257.

6. Skårdal, *Divided Heart*, pp. 273–79 and 317–25.

7. On the Norwegian Society see Lovoll, *Cultural Pluralism*, and Blegen, *Norwegian Migration*, v. 2, p. 579.

8. Haugen, *Norwegian Language*, v. 1, pp. 254–55, 262–74; Nelson and Fevold, *The Lutheran Church*, v. 2, pp. 3–225, on the movement toward union, and pp. 242–54, on the language transition. See also E. Clifford Nelson, *Lutheranism in North America 1914–1970*, Minneapolis: Augsburg, 1972.

9. Chrislock, *Fjord to Freeway*, pp. 139 and 151; Nelson, *Luther College*, p. 93 and 214; Shaw, *St. Olaf*, pp. 79, 138–39, 241–44, and 296–297. Lovoll, *A Folk Epic*, p. 228.

10. Jorgenson and Solum, *Rølvaag*, pp. 228–35. Wefald, *Protest*, pp. 73–78.

11. NOS (CBS) *Folkemengdens bevegelse 1921–1930*, Oslo, 1932, and Backer, *Marriages*, p. 158.

12. Osland, *Long Pull*, pp. 47–53. Carl M. Gunderson, "Historie om Knute Kenneth Rockne," unpublished manuscript in the Norwegian-American Collection of the University Library, Oslo.

13. Sons of Norway, see Norborg, *Saga*, pp. 97–107 and 197.

14. Newspapers: Haugen, *Norwegian Language*, v. 1, p. 279.
15. Consolidation of schools: Blegen, *Norwegian Migration*, v. 2, pp. 539–42. See also the various school histories mentioned earlier.
16. Haugen, *Norwegian Language*, v. 1, pp. 279–94, on language retention and persisting loyalties.
17. Odd S. Lovoll, *The Norwegian-American Historical Association, 1925–1975*, Northfield: NAHA, 1975, and Rudolph J. Vecoli, "An outsider's view of the association," pp. 272–79.
18. For an assessment of the activities of the various Scandinavian institutions and organizations in the 1970s, see *The Scandinavian Presence in North America*, edited by Erik J. Friis, New York: Harpers, 1976.

Chapter 16: Emigrants and Homeland

1. Blegen and Ruud, *Norwegian Emigrant Songs*, p. 78, gives a somewhat different translation.
2. Arne Hassing, "Norway's organized response to emigration," *Norwegian-American Studies*, v. 25, Northfield, 1972, pp. 54–79.
3. See chap. 10, note 8 (Louis Henry).
4. "Indstilling fra den departementale komite som i 1912–13 blev nedsat for at behandle utvandringslovgivningen." Bilag II til Ot. prp. nr. 24 i Stortingsforhandlinger 1921, b. 8, pp. 17–25 (Report of the committee on the emigration laws, printed in Parliamentary Records, 1921, v. 8, pp. 17–25).
5. Curti, *American Community*, pp. 176–97. Semmingsen, *Veien mot vest*, v. 2, p. 177.
6. Semmingsen, *Veien mot vest*, v. 2, pp. 454–57. The special cards and the mail clerks: oral information from Professor Sverre Steen who served as a mail clerk in his youth.
7. Semmingsen, *Veien mot vest*, v. 2, pp. 457–59. Osland, *A Long Pull*, pp. 70–96.
8. Andrew N. Rygg, *American Relief for Norway. A Survey of American Relief Work for Norway during and after the Second World War*. N.Y.: Arnesen Press, 1949.
9. *Decorah-Posten*: Einar Haugen, *Norwegian Language*, v. 1, p. 277, says 3,897 copies outside the U.S. and Canada. Baking powder: Marie Killie to Marie Thomter, May 29, 1889, NAHA collection.
10. Nelson, *Following the Pathfinder*, letter from Peter Nelson, July 19, 1948. Letter from Ole Evensen Sundby, third day of Christmas 1889.
11. Norwegian postal statistics 1881, NOS, Ny Række. F. Nr 2. (CBS. New Series, F. No. 2) Kra. 1882.
12. Hans Johansen Wold to relatives in Gausdal, Norway, Brohead, January 18, 1885. John Steen to Thv. (Thorvald Steen), Wahoo, Nebraska, November 25, 1913. See Carlton C. Qualey, ed. and trans., "Three America Letters to Lesja," *Norwegian-American Studies*, Northfield, 1977, v. 27, 41–54.
13. Ingrid Semmingsen, "Kontakt med Amerika," *Amerika och Norden*, publications of the Nordic Association for American Studies. Stockholm: Almqvist & Wiksell, 1964, pp. 65–74. The quotation is on p. 67.
14. Kielland, *Fortuna*, pp. 366–67, in *Samlede verker*, v. 2 (Collected Works) Oslo: Gyldendal, 1941. Both quotations are also found in Semmingsen, "Emigration and the image of America in Europe," *Immigration and American History. Essays in honor of Theodore C. Blegen*, p. 41, edited by Henry S. Commager, Minneapolis: University of Minnesota Press, 1961. Eilert Sundt: Semmingsen, *Veien mot vest*, v. 2, p. 475.
15. Semmingsen, *Veien mot vest*, v. 2, pp. 458–68, 478–79. Quotation from district physician, p. 467 and pp. 478–79. On 1905, see Derry, *A Short History*, pp. 160–71; Raymond E. Lindgren, *Norway-Sweden, Union, Disunion, and Scandinavian Integration*, Princeton, N.J.: Princeton University Press, 1959; H. Fred Swansen, "The attitude of the United States towards Norway in the crisis of 1905," *Studies and Records*, v. 4,

Northfield, 1929, pp. 43–53; Terje I. Leiren, "American press opinion and Norwegian independence," *Norwegian-American Studies*, v. 27, Northfield, 1977, pp. 224–42. P. E. Storing, "United States recognition of Norway in 1905," *Americana Norvegica*, v. 2, Philadelphia, 1968, pp. 160–90.

16. Semmingsen, *Veien mot vest*, v. 2, p. 482. On Sverdrup's first ministry: Derry, *A Short History*, pp. 53–59.

17. *Aftenposten* quoted in Semmingsen, *Veien mot vest*, v. 2, p. 490. On information about America: Paul Knaplund, "H. Tambs Lyche: propagandist for America," *Norwegian-American Studies*, v. 24, 1970, pp. 102–11, and Skard, *The United States*, pp. 119–26.

18. The appeal of Bjørnstjerne Bjørnson is quoted from *De tok Norge med seg. Nordmanns-Forbundets saga gjennom 50 år* (They took Norway along with them. The saga of the League of Norsemen through 50 years), Oslo: Dreyer, 1957, p. 14. This book is also my main source for the founding and the work of the League of Norsemen. See also Johan Hambro, "The League of Norsemen," *The Norseman*, v. 5, 1964, pp. 113–17.

SELECTED BIBLIOGRAPHY

SELECTED BIBLIOGRAPHY

Migration Theory and Research

Åkerman, Sune. *From Stockholm to San Francisco, Annales Academiæ Regiæ Scientiarum Upsaliensis*, Uppsala, 1975, and Report to the XIVth International Congress of Historical Sciences, San Francisco, August 22–29, 1975.

———. Theories and methods of migration research. In Harald Runblom and Hans Norman, eds., *From Sweden to America*. Minneapolis: University of Minnesota Press, 1976, pp. 19–75.

Lee, Everett S. A Theory of migration, *Demography*, 1966, 3, 47–57.

Mangalam, J. J. *Human Migration. A Guide to Migration Literature in English, 1955–1962*. Lexington: University of Kentucky Press, 1968.

Moe, Thorvald. Demographic developments and economic growth in Norway, 1740–1940: An econometric study. PhD thesis, Stanford University, 1970.

Odén, Birgitta. Ekonomiska emigrationsmodeller och historisk forskning (Economic emigration models and historical research), *Scandia*, 1970, 37, 1–70.

Petersen, William. *Population*. New York: Macmillan, 1975. (3rd ed.)

———. Migration. Social aspects. *International Encyclopedia of the Social Sciences*. Vol. 10. New York: Macmillan, 1968, pp. 286–92.

Thomas, Brinley. *Migration and Economic Growth, A Study of Great Britain and the Atlantic Economy*. Cambridge: The University Press, 1954. (2nd ed., 1972)

———. Migration. Economic aspects. *International Encyclopedia of the Social Sciences*. Vol. 10. New York: Macmillan, 1968, pp. 292–99.

———. *Migration and Urban Development. A Reappraisal of British and American Business Cycles*. London: Methuen, 1972.

Thomas, Dorothy Swaine. *Research Memorandum on Migration Differentials*. New York: Social Science Research Council, 1938.

———. *Social and Economic Aspects of Swedish Population Movements, 1750–1933*. New York: Macmillan, 1941.

Emigration from the Nordic Countries

Andersen, Arlow W. *The Norwegian-Americans*. Boston: Twayne Publishers, 1975.

Bjork, Kenneth O. *Saga in Steel and Concrete: Norwegian Engineers in America*. Northfield: NAHA, 1947.

——. *West of the Great Divide: Norwegian Migration to the Pacific Coast*. Northfield: NAHA, 1958.

Blegen, Theodore C. *Norwegian Migration to America, 1825–1860*. Northfield: NAHA, 1931.

Evjen, John O. *Scandinavian Immigrants in New York, 1630–1674*. Minneapolis: Holter, 1916. (Reprint, Baltimore: Genealogical Publishing, 1972)

Hvidt, Kristian. *Flight to America. The Social Background of 300,000 Danish Emigrants*. New York: Academic Press, 1975.

Janson, Florence F. *The Background of Swedish Emigration, 1840–1930*. Chicago: University of Chicago Press, 1931.

Kero, Reino. *Migration from Finland to North America in the Years between the United States Civil War and the First World War*. University of Turku, 1974.

Koivukangas, Olavi. *Scandinavian Immigration and Settlement in Australia before World War II*. University of Turku, 1974.

Lindberg, John S. *The Background of Swedish Emigration to the United States. An Economic and Sociological Study in the Dynamics of Migration*. Minneapolis: University of Minnesota Press, 1930.

Ljungmark, Lars. *For Sale—Minnesota. Organized Promotion of Scandinavian Immigration, 1866–1873*, vol. 8. Göteborg: Läromedelsförlaget, 1971.

Mulder, William. *Homeward to Zion: Mormon Migration from Scandinavia*. Minneapolis: University of Minnesota Press, 1957.

Runblom, Harald, and Hans Norman, eds. *From Sweden to America. A History of the Migration*. Minneapolis: University of Minnesota Press, 1976.

Semmingsen, Ingrid. *Veien mot vest: Utvandringen fra Norge til Amerika* (The Way West: Emigration from Norway to America). Oslo: Aschehoug & Co. (vol. 1, 1942; vol. 2, 1950)

Svalestuen, Andres, Sune Åkerman, Reino Kero, and Kristian Hvidt. Emigrationen fra Norden indtil 1. verdenskrig in *Rapporter til det nordiske historikemøde i København 1971* (Emigration from the Nordic countries to World War I. *Reports to the Nordic Historical Congress in Copenhagen, 1971.*)

Emigration from Other European Countries

Carrothers, William A. *Emigration from the British Isles, with Special Reference to the Overseas Dominions*. London: King & Son, 1929.

Erickson, Charlotte. *American Industry and the European Immigrant, 1860–1885*. Cambridge, Mass.: Harvard University Press, 1957.

——. *Invisible Immigrants. The Adaptation of English and Scottish Immigrants in 19th Century America*. Miami: University of Miami Press, 1972.

Foerster, Robert R. *Italian Emigration of Our Times*. Cambridge, Mass.: Harvard University Press, 1919.

Hansen, Marcus Lee. *The Atlantic Migration, 1607–1848*. Cambridge, Mass.: Harvard University Press, 1940.

Jones, Madlwyn Allen. *American Immigration*. Chicago: University of Chicago Press, 1960.

Saloutos, Theodore. *They Remember America. The Story of the Repatriated Greek-Americans*. Berkeley: University of California Press, 1956.

Schrier, Arnold. *Ireland and the American Emigration, 1850–1900*. Minneapolis: University of Minnesota Press, 1958.

Shepperson, Wilbur S. *British Emigration to North America: Projects and Opinions in the Early Victorian Period*. Minneapolis: University of Minnesota Press, 1957.

Taylor, Philip. *The Distant Magnet. European Emigration to the U.S.A.* New York: Harper & Row, 1971.

Thistlethwaite, Frank. Migration from Europe overseas in the nineteenth and twentieth century. *Reports*, vol. V, XIth *International Congress of Historical Sciences*, Uppsala, 1960.

Walker, Mack. *Germany and the Emigration, 1816–1885*. Cambridge, Mass.: Harvard University Press, 1964.

Immigrants in America

Andersen, Arlow W. *The Immigrant Takes His Stand: The Norwegian Immigrant Press and American Public Affairs, 1847 to 1872*. Northfield: NAHA, 1953.

———. *The Salt of the Earth: A History of Norwegian-Danish Methodism in America*. Nashville, Tenn.: Parthenon Press, 1962.

———. *The Norwegian-Americans*. Boston: Twayne Publishers, 1975.

Beijbom, Ulf. *Swedes in Chicago*. Stockholm: Läromedelsförlaget, 1971.

Bergmann, Leola N. *Americans from Norway*. Philadelphia: Lippincott, 1950.

Blegen, Theodore C. *Norwegian Migration*. Vol. 2. *The American Transition*. Northfield: NAHA, 1940.

———. *Land of Their Choice. The Immigrants Write Home*. Minneapolis: University of Minnesota Press, 1955.

Carlsson, Sten. Scandinavian politicians in Minnesota around the turn of the century. A study of the ethnic factor in an immigrant state. *Americana Norvegica*, 1971, 3, 237–71.

Carpenter, Niles. *Immigrants and Their Children*. Census monograph. Washington, D.C., 1927.

Chrislock, Carl. *From Fjord to Freeway: 100 Years of Augsburg College*. Minneapolis: Augsburg Publishing, 1969.

Commager, Henry S., ed. *Immigration and American History: Essays in Honor of Theodore C. Blegen*. Minneapolis: University of Minnesota Press, 1961.

Curti, Merle. *The Making of an American Community. A Case Study of Democracy in a Frontier County*. Stanford: Stanford University Press, 1959.

Easterlin, Richard A. *Population, Labor Force and Long Swings in Economic Growth. The American Experience*. New York: Columbia University Press, 1968.

Friis, Erik J. *The American-Scandinavian Foundation, 1910–1960. A Brief History*. New York: American Scandinavian Foundation, 1961.

Gjerset, Knut. *Norwegian Sailors on the Great Lakes: A Chapter in the History of American Inland Transportation*. Northfield: NAHA, 1928.

———. *Norwegian Sailors in American Waters: A Study in the History of Maritime Activity on the Eastern Seaboard*. Northfield: NAHA, 1933.

Handlin, Oscar. *Boston's Immigrants, 1790–1880*. Cambridge, Mass.: Harvard University Press, 1969.

Hansen, Carl G. O. *My Minneapolis: A Chronicle of What Has Been Learned and Observed about the Norwegians in Minneapolis through One Hundred Years*. Minneapolis: privately published, 1956.

Hansen, Marcus L. *The Immigrant in American History*, ed. by Arthur M. Schlesinger. Cambridge, Mass.: Harvard University Press, 1942.

Haugen, Einar. *The Norwegian Language in America: A Study in Bilingual Behavior*. 2 vols. Philadelphia: University of Pennsylvania Press, 1953. (2nd ed., Bloomington: Indiana University Press, 1969)

Hutchinson, Edward P. *Immigrants and Their Children, 1850–1950*. Census monograph. New York: Wiley, 1956.

Larson, Laurence M. *The Changing West and Other Essays*. Northfield: NAHA, 1937.

Lindberg, Duane R. Men of the cloth and the social-cultural fabric of the Norwegian ethnic community in North Dakota. PhD thesis, University of Minnesota, 1975.

Lindmark, Sture. *Swedish America, 1914–1932. Studies in Ethnicity with Emphasis on Illinois and Minnesota*. (Stockholm: Läromedelsförlaget, 1971.

Lovoll, Odd S. *A Folk Epic. The Bygdelag in America*. Boston: Twayne Publishers, 1975.
Munch, Peter A. *The Strange American Way*. Carbondale: Southern Illinois Press, 1970.
Nelson, Clifford, and Eugene L. Fevold. *The Lutheran Church among Norwegian-Americans: A History of the Evangelical Lutheran Church*. 2 vols. Minneapolis: Augsburg Publishing, 1960.
Nelson, David T. *Luther College, 1861–1961*. Decorah, Iowa: Luther College Press, 1961.
Nelson, Helge. *The Swedes and Swedish Settlements in North America*. 2 vols. New York: Bonnier, 1943.
Norborg, Sverre. *An American Saga: A History of the Sons of Norway in the United States and Canada*. Minneapolis: Sons of Norway, 1969.
Norwegian-American Studies, vols. 21– , Northfield, Minnesota; vols. 1–5, *Studies and Records* (vol. 1, Minneapolis; 2–5, Northfield); vols. 6–20, *Norwegian-American Studies and Records*, Northfield.
Qualey, Carlton C. *Norwegian Settlement in the United States*. Northfield: NAHA, 1938.
Rice, John G. Patterns of ethnicity in a Minnesota county, 1880–1903, *Geographical Reports*, No. 4, Department of Geography, University of Umeå, 1973.
Rygg, Andrew N. *Norwegians in New York, 1825–1925*. Brooklyn: Arneson, 1941.
Shaw, Joseph M. *History of St. Olaf College, 1874–1974*. Northfield: St. Olaf College Press, 1974.
Skårdal, Dorothy B. *The Divided Heart. Scandinavian Immigrant Experience through Literary Sources*. Lincoln: University of Nebraska Press, 1974.
Stephenson, George M. *The Religious Aspects of Swedish Immigration. A Study of Immigrant Churches*. Minneapolis: University of Minnesota Press, 1932.
Thernstrom, Stephan. *Poverty and Progress: Social Mobility in a Nineteenth Century City*. New York: Atheneum, 1969.
———. *The Other Bostonians: Poverty and Progress in the American Metropolis, 1880–1970*. Cambridge, Mass.: Harvard University Press, 1973.
———, and Sennett, Richard, eds. *Nineteenth-Century Cities: Essays in the New Urban History*. New Haven, Conn.: Yale University Press, 1969.
Thomas, William I., and Florian Znaniecki. *The Polish Peasant in Europe and America*. New York: Knopf, 1958.
Vecoli, Rudolph J. European Americans: From immigrants to ethnics, *International Migration Review*, 1972, 6, 34–49.
Wefald, Jon. *A Voice of Protest: Norwegians in American Politics, 1890–1917*. Northfield: NAHA, 1971.
Wist, Johannes, B., ed. *Norsk-amerikanernes Festskrift, 1914*. Decorah, Iowa: The Symra Company, 1914.
Wittke, Carl. *We Who Built America*. Englewood Cliffs, N.J.: Prentice-Hall, 1939.

Biographies and Reminiscences

Bergmann, Leola N. *Music Master of the Middle West: The Story of F. Melius Christiansen and the St. Olaf College Choir*. Minneapolis: University of Minnesota Press, 1944. (Reprint, New York: Da Capo, 1968)
Curti, Merle, ed. *Paul Knaplund*. Madison: University of Wisconsin Press, 1967.
Dorfman, Joseph. *Thorstein Veblen and His America*. New York: Viking Press, 1945.
Draxten, Nina. *Kristofer Janson in America*. Published for the NAHA. Boston: Twayne Publishers, 1976.
Hustvedt, Lloyd. *Rasmus Bjørn Anderson, Pioneer Scholar*. Northfield: NAHA, 1966.
Jorgenson, Theodore, and Nora O. Solum. *Ole Edvart Rølvaag. A Biography*. New York: Harper, 1939.
Knaplund, Paul. *Moorings Old and New. Entries in an Immigrant's Log*. Madison: State Historical Society of Wisconsin, 1963.

Koren, Elisabeth. *The Diary of Elisabeth Koren, 1853–1855,* ed. by David T. Nelson. Northfield: NAHA, 1955.

Larsen, Karen. *Laur. Larsen: Pioneer College President.* Northfield: NAHA, 1936.

Larson, Laurence M. *The Log Book of a Young Immigrant.* Northfield: NAHA, 1939.

Lucas, Richard. *Charles August Lindbergh Sr. A Case Study of Congressional Insurgence, 1906–1912.* Uppsala: University of Uppsala, 1974.

Mayer, George H. *The Political Career of Floyd B. Olson.* Minneapolis: University of Minnesota Press, 1951.

Michelet, Maren. *Glimpses from Agnes Mathilde Wergeland's Life.* Minneapolis: Free Book Concern, 1916.

Naess, Harald S. *Knut Hamsun og Amerika.* Oslo: Gyldendal, 1969.

Odland, Martin W. *The Life of Knute Nelson.* Minneapolis: Lund Press, 1926.

Osland, Birger. *A Long Pull from Stavanger: The Reminiscences of a Norwegian Immigrant.* Northfield: NAHA, 1945.

Qualey, Carlton C., ed. *Thorstein Veblen: The Carleton College Veblen Seminar Essays.* New York: Columbia University Press, 1968.

Raaen, Aagot. *Grass of the Earth: Immigrant Life in the Dakota Country.* Northfield: NAHA, 1950.

Stephenson, George M. *John Lind of Minnesota.* Minneapolis: University of Minnesota Press, 1935.

Ueland, Andreas. *Recollections of an Immigrant.* New York: Minton Balch, 1929.

Weintraub, Hyman. *Andrew Furuseth, Emancipator of the Seamen.* Berkeley: University of California Press, 1959.

Histories

Derry, T. K. *A History of Modern Norway.* Oxford: The University Press, 1973.

Koht, Halvdan. *The American Spirit in Europe: A Survey of Transatlantic Influences.* Philadelphia: University of Pennsylvania Press, 1949.

Scott, Franklin D. *The United States and Scandinavia.* Cambridge: Harvard University Press, 1952.

———. *Scandinavia.* Cambridge, Mass.: Harvard University Press, 1975.

———. *Sweden: The Nation's History.* Minneapolis: University of Minnesota Press, 1977.

Skard, Sigmund. *The United States in Norwegian History.* Westport, Conn.: Greenwood Press, 1976.

INDEX

INDEX

Aall, Jacob, 28, 29
Aasland, Birger. *See* Osland
Adams, John Quincy, 15: meets Americans in Norway, 8
Adeler, Curt Sivertsen, 7
Ægir, leaves Bergen, 27
Aftenposten, criticizes Norwegian attitudes toward Norwegian-Americans, 170
Ager, Waldemar, 141: comments on Norwegian-American literature, 142; death of, 158
Agriculture: and yields in Norway in the 1800s, 18, 102; in Washington Prairie, Iowa, 76, 77; in late nineteenth-century Norway, 107-8, 109; technological changes in, 108-9; and Norwegians in America, 122. *See also* Farmers
Aid to Norway, organized by Norwegian-Americans, 165
Akershus Fort, Norway, 164
Alaska, gold discovered in, 128
Alexander the Great, 4
Allan Line, steamship company, 129
Allen, William, 13
"America fever," 33, 38-39
America letters, 165-68
America Not Discovered by Columbus, 137
American Lutheran Church. *See* Lutheranism, in America

American Norwegian language, 87-89
American Saloon, The, 141
Americanization, 79, 133-34, 153, 158-59: and Norwegian pastors, 92-95; in Norwegian-American literature, 141; through politics, 151
Amerikabreve ("America Letters"), 88, 142
Anderson, Peder, industrialist, 31
Anderson, Peter, register of deeds in Wisconsin, 91
Anderson, Rasmus B., 25, 137
Anundsen, B. B., 138
Arbeiderforeningernes Blad ("The Workmen's Societies' Paper") supports Ole Bull, 46
Arbeidsfolk ("Working People"), 114
Arne Garborg Club, 145
Asbjørnsen, Peder Christen, 84
Aslakson, Ole, school superintendent in Wisconsin, 91
Assimilation. *See* Americanization
Augsburg College, 135, 159
Augustana Synod, 137
Authors' Society, 152

Bache, Søren: diary of, 66; comments on malaria at Muskego, Wisconsin, 67; provides money for *Nordlyset*, 83; opens store in Muskego, Wisconsin, 87
Bache, Tollef, 81: gives economic support

Hauge, Dean, pastor, 51
Hauge, Hans Nielsen, 65: followers of, 9;
letter writing of, 166
Haugeanism, 8–9, 41, 82: and Quakers,
13; as national religious movement, 34;
and emigration, 34–36; and breakdown
of old customs, 35; and opposition of
rural representatives in *Storting*, 35, 36;
compared with Thranite movement,
48; and opposition to funeral customs
in settlements, 78; influence of on religious leaders, 80; and Christian antiauthoritarianism, 94; and associations
movement, 144
Haugen, Einar, sociolinguistic study of
American Norwegian language, 88
Health, in immigrant ports, 68. *See also*
specific diseases
Heg, Even: in Muskego, Wisconsin, 65;
establishes *Nordlyset*, 83
Heg, Hans Christian, 90: elected prison
director in Wisconsin, 85; opens store
in Muskego, Wisconsin, 87; role of in
Civil War, 96
Helland, Lars Olsen, *Restauration* skip-
per, 15
Hemmestveit brothers, 145
Heritage of Per Smevik, The, 88, 142
Herred, compared to township, 89–90
Herring: and resistance to disease, 101;
disappears from Norwegian coast, 104
Hervin, O. S., 139
Hesthammer, Klein Pedersen. *See* Peer-
son, Cleng
Hoff, Olaf, 128
Holberg, Ludvig, 7
Holden, Minnesota, 70
Holidays, and preservation of rural cus-
toms in settlements, 78
Holmboe, I. A., study tour of, 72–73
Homestead Act, 87, 121
Housing: in Wisconsin settlements,
66–67; in Washington Prairie, Iowa,
74–75, 76
Hovland, Gjert, letters of, 17, 18, 37
Husmandsgutten ("The Cotter's Son"),
141: B. B. Anundsen buys, 138

Ibsen, Henrik, 30: and Thranite move-

ment, 44; attitude of toward America,
126; *A Doll's House* discussed in *Norden*, 140
Iceland, 5, 6, 172: and emigration, 54
Icelanders, farming of in America, 122
Immigration: restricted by United States,
98, 157; state offices for, 105
Indians, American, deprived of land, 73,
121
Indo-Europeans, invade Scandinavia, 3
Industrialization: in Norway, 102, 106,
110–11; midwestern populists alarmed
by, 150
Intellectuals, Norwegian-American, concern of for Norwegian culture, 142
International Order of Good Templars,
147
Ireland, 98: emigration from, 99; potato
diet in, 102

Jaabæk, Søren, 168: comments on
America in *Folketidende*, 126
Jackson, Andrew, 23
Jæger, Luth, 139
Janson, Kristofer, 89
Jansson, Erik, founds Bishop Hill colony,
41
Jensen, Michael, county surveyor in Wis-
consin, 91
Jevne, Christian, 128
Johnson, Martin B., sheriff in Wisconsin,
91
Jørgensen, Knud, 28
Journalists, Norwegian-American,
139–40
Julebukk (Christmas fooling), 78

Kendall, New York, settlement, 15, 16,
21: migration west from, 17
Kielland, Alexander, 30, 114: comments
on America letters, 168
Kleiven, Ivar, 110
Knudsen, Knud, 28
Koht, Halvdan, 34
Koren, Elisabeth, diary of, 74–77
Koshkonong, Wisconsin, settlement, 63,
65, 72: congregational activity at, 82;
religious school at, 93
Kringen, Olav, 139

Kristianiafjord, 129
Krog, Gina, 30
Krohg, Christian, and Quakers, 12
Kvelve, Bjørn, 31, 108, 116: biographical
  sketch of, 25

La Follette, Robert: supported by
  Norwegian-Americans, 150; votes
  against entering World War I, 157
Labor, organized: in Norway, 111–12;
  Norwegian-American, 148
Labor Party, 139
LaCrosse, Wisconsin, medical clinic in,
  138
Land: reclamation of demanded by
  Thranites, 44; obtaining in America,
  70–71, 121–22; low-interest loans for,
  131
Langeland, Knud, favors English for
  children, 94
Language. *See* American Norwegian lan-
  guage, English language, Landsmaal,
  Loanwords, Norwegian language
Larsen, Jacob, district attorney in Wis-
  consin, 91
Lawson, Victor, 128
Le Havre, France, as emigration port, 55
League of Farm Youth, 152
League of Norsemen (*Nordmanns-
  Forbundet*), 171
Lefse, 78, 143, 154
Leprosy, 69
Liberal Party, of Norway, 139, 168
"Liberty Bonds," 156
Lie, Jonas, 30
Lincoln, Abraham, 84: Civil War appeal
  of for enlistees, 96
Literary societies, in America, 140
Literature, Norwegian, 140–42
Loanwords, American, adopted by
  Norwegians, 87–89
Lofoten, Norway, 6
Lutefisk, 128, 143
Luther College, 95, 134, 137, 140, 159
Luther Seminary, 134
Lutheranism, in America, 47, 92, 144,
  154, 171: and sloopers, 14; and obtain-
  ing pastors, 80–81; and clash of high
  and low church, 83; and Missouri

Synod, 93, 94; and schools, 93–94,
  136–37; and debate on slavery, 134;
  and Norwegian Synod's differences
  with low-church groups, 134–35; and
  ecclesiastical change over time, 134–37;
  and Augustana Synod, 137; and congregational splits, 137; and language
  problem of Norwegian-American
  Church, 155
Lutheranism, in Norway, 12, 34: and
  clash of high and low church, 83
Luther's Minor Catechism, translated
  into English, 81

Madison, Wisconsin, literary society at,
  140
Malaria, 67–68, 77
Marriage: of Scandinavian-Americans,
  132, 133; of Norwegian-Americans, 154
Maud, Queen of Norway, 170
Mayflower, 10
Measles, 68
Meidell, Fridtjof, comments on America,
  127
Mejdell, Ditmar, ridicules Oleana, 47
Mental illness, of Norwegian-born in
  Minnesota, 115
Midelfart, Dr., founder of clinic in Wisconsin, 138
Midwest, 16, 21, 40, 45, 68, 84, 120:
  Norwegians' contacts with, 51; immigration offices in, 63; founding of
  synods in, 83; social barriers in, 87;
  local governments of, 89–90; settlement encouraged in, 105, 129; Norwegians in, 122, 159, 163; wages in, 123;
  marriage of Scandinavian-Americans
  in, 132, 133, 154; attitudes toward immigrants in, 133; Bjørnstjerne Bjørnson
  lectures in, 136; formation of People's
  Party in, 150; progressive Republicans
  in, 156–57
Migrations: folk, 4; work, 6; in Norway,
  33–34. *See also* Emigrants, Emigration
Milwaukee, Wisconsin, 65: Moravian
  congregation at, 43
Minneapolis, Minnesota, 146, 152:
  Norwegians seek work in, 123; public
  schools of, 136; Norwegian-language